COERCION AND AGGRESSIVE COMMUNITY TREATMENT

A NEW FRONTIER IN MENTAL HEALTH LAW

THE PLENUM SERIES IN SOCIAL/CLINICAL PSYCHOLOGY

Series Editor: C. R. Snyder
University of Kansas
Lawrence, Kansas

COERCION AND AGGRESSIVE COMMUNITY TREATMENT
A NEW FRONTIER IN MENTAL HEALTH LAW

EDITED BY

DEBORAH L. DENNIS
Policy Research Associates, Inc.
Delmar, New York

AND

JOHN MONAHAN
University of Virginia
Charlottesville, Virginia

PLENUM PRESS • NEW YORK AND LONDON

Library of Congress Cataloging-in-Publication Data

Coercion and aggressive community treatment : a new frontier in mental
  health law / edited by Deborah L. Dennis and John Monahan.
      p.   cm. -- (The plenum series in social/clinical psychology)
    ISBN 0-306-45167-0
    1. Community mental health services.   I. Dennis, Deborah L.
  II. Monahan, John, 1946-   . III. Series.
  RA790.C666 1996
  362.2'2--dc20   95-51527
                                                                   CIP

ISBN 0-306-45167-0

©1996 Plenum Press, New York
A Division of Plenum Publishing Corporation
233 Spring Street, New York, N.Y. 10013

Printed in the United States of America

CONTRIBUTORS

NANCY S. BENNETT, Bronx, New York 10463

JESSICA WILEN BERG, Department of Psychiatry, University of Massachusetts Medical Center, Worcester, Massachusetts 01655

RICHARD J. BONNIE, School of Law, University of Virginia, Charlottesville, Virginia 22903

SUZAN HURLEY COGSWELL, Legislative Office of Education Oversight, Columbus, Ohio 43266

DEBORAH L. DENNIS, Policy Research Associates, Inc., Delmar, New York 12054

RONALD J. DIAMOND, Department of Psychiatry, University of Wisconsin Hospital, Madison, Wisconsin 53792-2475

MARLENE M. EISENBERG, Institute of Law, Psychiatry, and Public Policy, University of Virginia, Charlottesville, Virginia 22902

DIANE ENGSTER, 3825 Gibbs Street, Alexandria, Virginia 22309

WILLIAM P. GARDNER, Western Psychiatric Institute and Clinic, Pittsburgh, Pennsylvania 15213

VIRGINIA ALDIGÉ HIDAY, Department of Sociology, North Carolina State University, Raleigh, North Carolina 27695

STEVEN K. HOGE, Institute of Law, Psychiatry, and Public Policy, University of Virginia, Charlottesville, Virginia 22902

KIM HOPPER, Nathan Kline Institute for Psychiatric Research, Orangeburg, New York 10962

HENRY KORMAN, Cambridge and Somerville Legal Services, Cambridge, Massachusetts 02141

CHARLES W. LIDZ, Western Psychiatric Institute and Clinic, Pittsburgh, Pennsylvania 15213

MARGARITA LOPEZ, 606 East 11th Street, New York, New York 10009

ANNE M. LOVELL, Department of Sociology, University of Toulouse, Le Mirail, 31058 Toulouse, Cedex, France

BONNIE M. MILSTEIN, David L. Bazelon Center for Mental Health Law, Washington, D.C. 20005

JOHN MONAHAN, School of Law, University of Virginia, Charlottesville, Virginia 22903

EDWARD P. MULVEY, Western Psychiatric Institute and Clinic, Pittsburgh, Pennsylvania 15213

BRENDA ROCHE, Division of Epidemiology and Community Psychiatry, New York State Psychiatric Institute, Columbia Presbyterian Medical Center, New York, New York 10032

LOREN H. ROTH, Western Psychiatric Institute and Clinic, Pittsburgh, Pennsylvania 15213

PHYLLIS SOLOMON, School of Social Work, University of Pennsylvania, Philadelphia, Pennsylvania 19104

EZRA SUSSER, Division of Epidemiology and Community Psychiatry, New York State Psychiatric Institute, Columbia Presbyterian Medical Center, New York, New York 10032

PREFACE

Although it is a relatively new field, mental health law has undergone major developments in the past decade, including landmark judicial decisions, dramatic legislative initiatives, and the publication of professional standards and guidelines in both criminal and civil law. All of these developments, however, have been predicated on plausible but untested assumptions about persons with mental disorders, the service delivery system, and the law—and about how these elements affect one another.

In 1988, the John D. and Catherine T. MacArthur Foundation created a Research Network on Mental Health and the Law with the goal of building the empirical foundation for the next generation of mental health laws. The Network has two overriding mandates: to develop new knowledge about the relationship between mental health and the law and to turn that understanding into improved tools and criteria for evaluating individuals and making decisions that affect their lives.

The Network's research portfolio focuses on three pivotal issues facing the field of mental health law: the competence of people with mental disorders to make autonomous decisions, the risk of violence that sometimes accompanies mental disorder, and the coercion that often characterizes interventions to redress incompetence or reduce risk. It is with the last of these that this book deals.

The coercive imposition of mental health services has always been the most controversial issue in mental health law. Debates on the involuntary inpatient hospitalization of persons with mental disorders are several centuries old. Debates on whether people so hospitalized have a right to refuse mental health treatment are now several decades old. While these controversies over involutary institutional-ization and inpatient treatment have by no means been resolved, they have to a considerable extent been overtaken by events in recent years. As the locus for the provision of mental health services has moved from the hospital to the community, so has the venue for de-bates about coercion. Once, the legal and ethical issues to be resolved included whether and for how long a person could be hospitalized before a formal judicial hearing took place. Now, the legally and ethi-cally perplexing questions are more likely to concern whether a per-son with a mental disorder but without a home in the community can be made dependent on an outreach worker's food and friendship as a method of inducing compliance with outpatient treatment.

Little is known about how mental health services are actually provided on the street level. Even less is known about how coercion is used to engage and maintain in community treatment people with se-vere mental disorders who have rejected—or been rejected by—more traditional interventions. It is to address this sea-change in the con-text in which mental health services are coercively administered that this volume was developed.

The Network invited leaders in the field of community treat-ment, including consumers of that treatment, to describe and discuss the issues that arose when treatment was "aggressively" pursued. We were struck with how often treatment providers told us that "we never talk about coercion, but we do it all the time," and with the depth of ambivalence that community coercion generated in both providers and recipients. It was to widen and deepen the conversa-tion about coercion in the community that the Network decided to commission these original chapters.

We hope that this book will interest mental health professionals providing front line services in communities throughout the coun-try, those in legal and policy-making positions who are influencing the content of service provision, and health service researchers who can document the costs and the consequences of coercion in the com-munity.

We are grateful to the members of the Network—in particular to Henry Steadman, who encouraged us to commit this fascinating in-terdisciplinary dialogue to print—to the participants at our meetings, and to the authors of these timely chapters, for sharing their experi-ences and their insights.

ACKNOWLEDGMENT

This volume was conceived and supported by the Research Network on Mental Health and the Law of the John D. and Catherine T. MacArthur Foundation.

CONTENTS

PART I. COERCION: FROM THE HOSPITAL TO THE COMMUNITY

Chapter 1

Coercion to Inpatient Treatment: Initial Results and Implications for
    Assertive Treatment in the Community

John Monahan, Steven K. Hoge, Charles W. Lidz,
    Marlene M. Eisenberg, Nancy S. Bennett, William P. Gardner,
    Edward P. Mulvey, and Loren H. Roth

Chapter 2

Outpatient Commitment: Official Coercion in the Community

Virginia Aldigé Hiday

PART II. COERCION AND TREATMENT:
THE COMMUNITY PROVIDER'S PERSPECTIVE

Chapter 3

Coercion and Tenacious Treatment in the Community: Applications
    to the Real World

Ronald J. Diamond

Chapter 4

"Coercion" and Leverage in Clinical Outreach

Ezra Susser and Brenda Roche

Chapter 5

The Perils of Outreach Work: Overreaching the Limits of
     Persuasive Tactics

Margarita Lopez

PART III. THE SOCIAL CONTEXT OF AGGRESSIVE
COMMUNITY TREATMENT

Chapter 6

Housing as a Tool of Coercion

Henry Korman, Diane Engster, and Bonnie M. Milstein

INTRODUCTION

Deborah L. Dennis and John Monahan

The coercive imposition of mental health services has always been a flashpoint in mental health law. Debates on the involuntary inpatient hospitalization of persons with mental disorder date back centuries. Debates on whether people so hospitalized have a right to refuse mental health treatment are now several decades old.

While these controversies over involuntary institutionalization and inpatient treatment have by no means been resolved, they have to a considerable extent been overtaken by events in recent years. As the locus for the provision of mental health services has moved from the hospital to the community, so has the venue for debates about coercion. Once, the legal and ethical issues to be resolved included whether and for how long a person could be hospitalized before a formal judicial hearing took place. Now, the legally and ethically perplexing questions are more likely to concern whether a person with mental disorder but without a home in the community can be made

DEBORAH L. DENNIS • Policy Research Associates, Inc., Delmar, New York 12054. JOHN MONAHAN • School of Law, University of Virginia, Charlottesville, Virginia 22903.

Coercion and Aggressive Community Treatment: A New Frontier in Mental Health Law, edited by Deborah L. Dennis and John Monahan. Plenum Press, New York, 1996.

dependent on an outreach worker's food and friendship as a method of inducing compliance with outpatient treatment.

Little is known about how mental health services are actually provided on the street level. Even less is known about how coercion is used to engage and maintain in community treatment people with severe mental disorder who have rejected—or been rejected by—more traditional interventions. It is to address this sea change in the context in which mental health services are coercively administered that this volume was created.

AGGRESSIVE COMMUNITY TREATMENT DEFINED

Coercion in community care was not an issue until the assertive community treatment (ACT) model was developed in the 1970s. Before that, it was relatively easy for patients and clinicians to avoid each other if they so chose—and many of them did. Even though aggressive community treatment has been around for roughly 20 years, there simply are no discussions of coercion in this context in either the research or the policy literature.

Defined broadly, aggressive community treatment includes ACT teams, intensive case management, mobile crisis teams, and outreach to difficult-to-reach populations. The "active ingredients" of aggressive community treatment include in vivo service delivery, low client/staff ratios (usually 10 : 1), and receipt of services "as long as their need for help persists, subject only to their own continuing willingness to be served" (McGrew & Bond, 1995; Witheridge, 1991).

First developed and tested in Madison, Wisconsin (Stein & Test, 1985), aggressive community treatment has been adapted, studied, and adopted throughout the United States as arguably one of the most effective mechanisms for providing comprehensive community care for persons with serious mental illnesses (Drake & Burns, 1995; Thompson, Griffith, & Leaf, 1990).

Variations of aggressive community treatment (including intensive case management programs) and mobile crisis teams are the foundation of community mental health in some of the most progressive mental health systems in the country (Bond, McGrew, & Fekete, 1995; Deci, Santos, Hiott, Schoenwald, & Dias, 1995). They are also the intervention of choice for many demonstration programs funded by the National Institute of Mental Health and the Center for Mental Health Services.

In many ways, ACT and mobile crisis teams are the precursor to what has become accepted practice in reaching and treating homeless persons with serious mental illnesses. However, there is little or no discussion in the literature on aggressive community treatment of how members are initially engaged and how they are retained.

As "clinicians of last resort," programs for homeless people with serious mental illnesses face the issue of coercion in community care directly (Dixon, Krauss, Kernan, Lehman, & De Forge, 1995; Susser, Goldfinger, & White, 1990). Their clients have rejected, or been rejected by, innumerable mental health and other service providers. A decade ago, there were a handful of outreach teams operating only in the largest metropolitan areas. Today, nearly every midsize city has one or more homeless outreach teams riding in vans, making their rounds on foot or staffing drop-in centers, and offering warm drinks and sandwiches in an effort to identify people in need, engage them in a trusting relationship, and assess their needs (National Resource Center on Homelessness and Mental Illness, 1991).

SETTING THE STAGE: FROM HOSPITAL TO COMMUNITY

This volume is organized into five parts. Part I examines the implications of court-ordered treatment in inpatient and outpatient settings for less formal mechanisms of negotiating mental health treatment in the community. In Chapter 1, Monahan and his colleagues look at perceived coercion during the process of hospital admission for psychiatric treatment. They find that (1) it is possible to reliably measure people's perceptions of coercion; (2) coercion is more likely to be perceived when threats and force are used, less likely when persuasion and inducement are used; and (3) the *process* of providing treatment matters (i.e., when people perceive that others are acting out of concern, treating them fairly and with respect, they are less likely to feel coerced).

In Chapter 2, Hiday reviews studies of outpatient commitment. She emphasizes the limits of legal coercion when the community-based services necessary to enforce treatment do not exist. She found that negative response to outpatient commitment was related to perceptions that the services required did not meet their needs. Better services not only would have reduced dissatisfaction but also may have reduced the need for legal coercion in the first place. The few studies of outpatient commitment that have been done point to the potential of such commitment for maintaining people in the community. It is unclear, however, what it is that is working. Hiday suggests that providing more intensive services (e.g., outreach, case management, transportation, and skills training) may account for more success than legal coercion.

DEFINING COERCION IN COMMUNITY CARE

Part II includes three chapters on coercion and community care from the perspectives of community-based mental health service providers. As a psychiatrist who worked with one of the first ACT teams, Diamond suggests in Chapter 3 that coercion exists on a continuum that ranges from friendly persuasion to interpersonal pressure to control of resources to use of force. He discusses five limitations of coercion in the community. First, coercion will not lead to more effective treatment if the treatment itself is inadequate. Second, what can be coerced in the community is extremely limited (usually injectable medication). Third, there are major interpersonal costs in moving from less coercive to more coercive approaches (e.g., from collaboration to control). Fourth, coercion is often a short-term solution to a long-term problem, and it may ultimately compromise the resolution of the long-term problem. Finally, coercion is often used when other options are not available.

To decrease the need for coercion, Diamond suggests that mental health service providers (1) develop a continuous range of service options; (2) be clear about goals; (3) ensure that persons with psychiatric disability have a chance for a decent quality of life; (4) develop treatment systems that support respectful relationships developed over time; and (5) be aware of the values of the treatment system and how decisions about paternalism or coercion support or interfere with these values.

In Chapter 4, Susser and Roche point out that coercive tactics and "tolerant" approaches are discussed openly in clinical practice, but the use of leverage and its potential for coercion is not. Outreach is defined by gentle, flexible, persistent development of trust and emotional dependency on the clinician/worker, followed by setting limits or withholding incentives to further engage clients. Providing blankets, food, showers, or clothing as necessary until an individual is ready to accept treatment, an outreach worker (any of a wide variety of professional or paraprofessional staff) tries to "engage" the homeless person in a relationship of trust and familiarity. This is the beginning of an often long process of which the ultimate purpose "is to recruit patients into treatment and other services without resorting to strong-arm tactics" (Susser et al., 1990).

The use of persuasion and leverage is discussed directly and honestly by Lopez in Chapter 5, which provides an account of deception as a key mechanism for engaging people in treatment. She describes the techniques of persuasion used in outreach and engagement of homeless people who have serious mental illnesses: assessment, initial contact, deception, and enticement of someone to accept services to create a level of need that is then used as a means to extract concessions from the client.

As an outreach worker, Lopez has as her primary goal helping people understand their illness, the necessity for treatment, and the consequences of refusal in order to move them to where they can choose a path to recovery without coercion. Persuasive tactics (withdrawal of services or benefits) are most often used during the education process. She argues that a service provider's failure to educate clients involves the greatest degree of coercion and deception, since it leaves clients open to increasingly more coercive tactics and does not empower them to make informed choices.

THE SOCIAL CONTEXT OF AGGRESSIVE COMMUNITY TREATMENT

Coercion in the community can be involved in all aspects of care, beginning with the identification of the need for treatment and going on to treatment planning without client participation and to linking housing and entitlements to compliance with other aspects of treatment. The chapters in Part III examine how housing and money may be used as tools to leverage treatment compliance—more or less coercively.

As one of the scarcest basic resources needed by people with serious mental illnesses in the community, housing is an especially powerful tool for leveraging compliance with treatment. But because finding a decent, affordable place to live often requires the assistance of program staff, it is also a potential area for abuse. In Chapter 6, Korman, Engster, and Milstein discuss the coercive nature of serviced-based housing for people with disabilities. In housing operated by service providers, consumers live with others not of their own choosing and are subject to rules that do not exist in typical housing, under which compliance with treatment is a condition of continued occupancy, rights of tenancy are often in question, and behavior is scrutinized from a clinical perspective in which disagreements over treatment can become cause for loss of housing or involuntary commitment.

Korman and his colleagues argue that coercion cannot be eliminated from housing for persons with disabilities unless services are separate from housing. However, the coercive nature of service-based housing can be mitigated by (1) developing a process of dispute resolution that is attentive to the needs of the participant, the owners, the managers, other residents of the housing, and the program; and (2) offering reasonable accommodations to make it possible for people with disabilities to participate. Principles of equal treatment, equal access, and the individual right to control medical decision-making demand that people with mental disabilities have the same rights of occupancy as any other tenant. At the same time, they also have the same obligations—rent payment, behavior that is nondestructive and does not harm or disturb others.

Coercion is also potentially problematic when finances are at issue. Decisions about what clients' limited funds are to be spent on—rent, food, clothing, recreation, alcohol or drugs—are frequent battlegrounds with treatment and other basic survival implications. Is it coercive for a program to ensure that a client's living expenses are paid before giving him spending money? Can a client decide to live under a bridge and spend her money as she chooses? Clearly, the recent change in the Social Security rules regarding substance abuse indicates that those who wish to continue receiving benefits will be coerced into treatment and with limited lifetime benefit period regardless of the efficacy of treatment or relapse (National Resource Center on Homelessness and Mental Illness, 1995).

In Chapter 7, Cogswell examines the potentially coercive nature of representative payees and other money-management techniques. Suggestions for mitigating coercion include clear expectations for professional conduct, developing processes for monitoring and regulating payees, and having an administrative process for grievances. As with housing, she suggests that treatment and financial decision-making be separated—perhaps allowing clients to choose whether their case manager/provider agency or someone else will be their payee should they need one.

THE NEED FOR MORE RESEARCH

In Part IV, Solomon argues in Chapter 8 that we know too little to be making broad policy shifts toward more coercive community treatment. She urges researchers to help shed light on how to balance the competing values of individual autonomy and the need to protect vulnerable people. She suggests three areas for researchers to examine: formal coercion (e.g., outpatient commitment, probation/parole, conditional release), informal coercion (such as that practiced by families and service providers), and mechanisms for reducing the need for coercion (e.g., client control and choice). Since objectively coercive behaviors may not be perceived as coercive, Solomon also recommends that both subjective and objective perceptions of coercion be studied.

Viewing coercion as a moral construct in Chapter 9, Lovell sets the context for examining coercion and its alternatives (consumer choice, self-help, and consumer-run programs) in the community. From this perspective, ideas of person-centered care, individual rights, and the centrality of agency and personhood are expanding public debate on coercion from inpatient to community care. She introduces the notion of utilitarian compliance where scarcity of necessities—such as housing—is used to enforce compliance.

Lovell recommends two areas for research: the contextual determinants of coercion and the determinants and effectiveness of noncoercive alternatives. The first concerns the impact of organizational constraints (including reimbursement mechanisms and the scarcity of resources) on the relationships among the consumer, the provider, and the provider's constituencies (e.g., police, businesses, families). The second area includes comparisons of consumer-driven approaches with professional approaches.

LEGAL AND ETHICAL IMPLICATIONS OF COMMUNITY-BASED COERCION

In Part V, we turn to the unanswered questions raised by these important issues. In Chapter 10, Berg and Bonnie find that as mental health treatment has moved from inpatient to community care, the legal and ethical implications of aggressive community treatment have been largely ignored. They examine the implications of coercion in the community for the right to make decisions about one's own care and to refuse treatment. Specifically, they address reaching out to assess and monitor clients in the community (privacy) and getting people to accept or comply with community-based treatment (liberty and autonomy).

They concede that the legal mandates to coerce community care are few, and clinicians frequently rely on not fully informing individuals of the legal limits of outpatient commitment or of their right to refuse treatment and their right to privacy. Berg and Bonnie pay particular attention to the withholding of scarce resources such as housing and entitlements. They conclude that law in this area is far from established, and community treatment providers should be aware of this ambiguity and shape their own guidelines in order to minimize abuses.

In his commentary on the chapters in this book, Hopper (Chapter 11) is concerned that increasingly coercive tactics may be on the rise due to the narrowing of the margins ("those endangered spaces on the civic landscape that supplied forgiving accommodations to misfits of all sorts") and the increasing ascendency of managed care, which may be "replacing a muddle that can be made to work for some with a machine that will strenuously resist being plied outside a narrow range of tolerances."

Hopper sees a tendency to assert the moral rightness of whatever we define as appropriate coercion, and he urges that multiple perspectives (including those of consumers) be considered in determining "rightness" and "appropriateness." He asks that attention be paid to the process of negotiation or conflict resolution in order to avoid forced choice. In decreasing the need for obvious coercion, he emphasizes the importance of alternatives to coercion. Finally, he suggests the need for consensus around core values and orienting ideals—"an ethic of public health grounded in values such as equality and solidarity."

CONCLUSION

Four themes are wound through the chapters in this volume. One is the need perceived by mental health service providers to sometimes resort to coercive tactics to sustain people with mental disorders in the community. A second theme is the angst and ambivalence engendered in these providers when they see no viable alternatives to this use of coercion, which they recognize has the potential for great abuse. The importance of the process by which interventions are coercively imposed in the community constitutes a third theme. Finally, almost all the authors of these chapters echo Diamond's contention that "coercion is often used when other resources are unavailable, and could be avoided if other resources were available."

Coercion in the community has been whispered about before, but has never been the subject of sustained descriptive and analytical attention. Our hope is that this airing of issues will help to create a sustained conversation on the clinical, empirical, and legal aspects of the assertive provision of mental health services at the close of the 20th century.

REFERENCES

Bond, G. R., McGrew, J. H., & Fekete, D. M. (1995). Assertive outreach for frequent users of psychiatric hospitals: A meta-analysis. *Journal of Mental Health Administration, 22,* 2–14.

Deci, P. A., Santos, A. B., Hiott, W., Schoenwald, S., & Dias, J. K. (1995). Dissemination of assertive community treatment programs. *Psychiatric Services, 46,* 676–687.

Dixon, L. B., Krauss, N., Kernan, E., Lehman, A. F., & DeForge, B. R. (1995). Modifying the PACT model to serve homeless persons with severe mental illness. *Psychiatric Services, 46,* 684–688.

Drake, R. E., & Burns, B. J. (1995). Special section on assertive community treatment: An introduction. *Psychiatric Services, 46,* 667–668.

McGrew, J. H., & Bond, G. R. (1995). Critical ingredients of assertive community treatment—Judgements of the experts. *Journal of Mental Health Administration, 22,* 113–125.

National Resource Center on Homelessness and Mental Illness (1991). *Reaching out: A guide for service providers.* Washington, DC: Interagency Council on the Homeless.

National Resource Center on Homelessness and Mental Illness (1995). New SSA regulations restrict benefits for substance abuse. *Access, 7,* 10.

Stein, L. I., & Test, M. A. (1985). The evolution of the training in community living model. In L. I. Stein & M. A. Test (Eds.), *The training in community living model: A decade of experience. New Directions for Mental Health Services,* No. 26. San Francisco: Jossey-Bass.

Susser, E., Goldfinger, S. M., & White, A. (1990). Some clinical approaches to the homeless mentally ill. *Community Mental Health Journal, 26,* 463–479.

Thompson, K. S., Griffith, E. E. H., & Leaf, P. J. (1990). A historical review of the Madison model of community care. *Hospital and Community Psychiatry, 41,* 625–634.

Witheridge, T. F. (1991). The "active ingredients" of assertive outreach. *New Directions for Mental Health Services,* No. 52.

PART I

COERCION
FROM THE HOSPITAL TO THE COMMUNITY

CHAPTER 1

COERCION TO INPATIENT TREATMENT
INITIAL RESULTS AND IMPLICATIONS FOR ASSERTIVE TREATMENT IN THE COMMUNITY

JOHN MONAHAN, STEVEN K. HOGE,
CHARLES W. LIDZ, MARLENE M. EISENBERG,
NANCY S. BENNETT, WILLIAM P. GARDNER,
EDWARD P. MULVEY, AND LOREN H. ROTH

Debate over the role of coercion in mental hospital admission frequently invokes the prospective patient's moral right to decision-making autonomy and individual dignity (e.g., Blanch & Parrish,

JOHN MONAHAN • School of Law, University of Virginia, Charlottesville, Virginia 22903.   STEVEN K. HOGE and MARLENE M. EISENBERG • Institute of Law, Psychiatry, and Public Policy, University of Virginia, Charlottesville, Virginia 22902.   CHARLES W. LIDZ, WILLIAM P. GARDNER, EDWARD P. MULVEY, and LOREN H. ROTH • Western Psychiatric Institute and Clinic, Pittsburgh, Pennsylvania 15213.   NANCY S. BENNETT • Bronx, New York 10463.

Coercion and Aggressive Community Treatment: A New Frontier in Mental Health Law, edited by Deborah L. Dennis and John Monahan. Plenum Press, New York, 1996.

1993; Wertheimer, 1993). But empirical arguments for or against coercion are often pressed as well. The empirical issue most often raised is whether coerced treatment "works." On one side, some patient advocates argue that the alleged benefits of treatment to the patient or others can be negated by patients' feelings of alienation and dissatisfaction, as a result of which patients become unlikely to comply with treatment as soon as the coercion is lifted (cf. National Center for State Courts, 1986). Even if coerced treatment benefits those on whom it is imposed, other prospective patients may be deterred from seeking treatment voluntarily for fear that they too will be committed (Campbell & Schraiber, 1989). On the other side, a recent report by the Group for the Advancement of Psychiatry (1994), though it grants that "there seems to be a kind of embarrassment about situations in which the patient did not enter treatment entirely on his or her own initiative" (p. x), concludes that "sometimes involuntary psychiatric treatment is necessary, can be effective, and can lead to freedom from the constraints of illness. Conversely, tight restrictions against coercive treatment can have disastrous consequences" (p. 43).

These empirical issues are extraordinarily difficult to study. A true experiment that would employ a randomly assigned control group of persons thought to be in need of coerced treatment, but deny it for the purposes of the research, seems clearly unfeasible. In this regard, Zwerling, Conte, Plutchik, and Karaser (1978) persuaded the staff at a mental health center to agree to abstain from involuntarily committing anyone for a 1-week experimental period. Only one exception was allowed: If a prospective patient was believed to be one of the rare cases in clear danger of immediate suicide or other violence, a staff member could ask for approval from his or her superior, and if they both agreed, commitment would be permitted. Results showed that there were no differences between the number of persons committed during "no commitment week" and the weeks prior and subsequent to it. *Every* prospective patient was found to be the "rare" exception that clearly demanded commitment.

Not only is it difficult to research the question of whether coerced treatment "works," it may be premature to even try. There is a prior and more basic empirical issue in the study of mental hospital admission: coercion as a "dependent" variable. While not often the subject of systematic inquiry, understanding the determinants and correlates of perceived coercion in mental hospital admission—what makes people feel coerced—is a prerequisite to understanding coercion as an independent variable (i.e., whether and how coerced hospitalization is effective in producing therapeutic outcomes).

This issue of how people come to feel coerced into inpatient mental health care has been the subject of sporadic empirical attention in the past (for a review, see Monahan et al., 1995) and is now the subject of a multisite study supported by the MacArthur Research Network on Mental Health and the Law. In this chapter, we summarize and integrate the findings to date from the MacArthur Coercion Study, and we speculate on the implications of these findings for mental health care delivered assertively in the community.

PERCEIVED COERCION AND FORMAL LEGAL STATUS

The most recent United States data (Rosenstein, Steadman, MacAskill, & Manderscheid, 1986) derive from admission surveys of state and county public mental hospitals, private mental hospitals, and general hospitals during 1980. These data reveal that of the 1,144,785 civil inpatient admissions in 1980, 73% were broadly construed as "voluntary" and 27% as "involuntary." But this ratio varies drastically by state. In Connecticut and Alaska, for example, involuntary admissions outnumber voluntary admissions 3 to 1 (Brakel, Parry, & Weiner, 1985). A recent review of rates of involuntary admission among European countries revealed similar findings: A mean of 15–20% of all mental patients were admitted involuntarily, ranging from 1% in Spain to 93% in parts of Switzerland (Riecher-Rossler & Rossler, 1993).

Gathering data on the prevalence or correlates of legal coercion is complicated by the diversity of commitment systems in existence. Many states have separate procedures for brief "emergency" commitment, somewhat longer "observational" commitment, and long-term "extended" commitment. More problematic is the convention adopted in many statutes of characterizing as "voluntary" what are transparently involuntary admissions: a parent or legal guardian "volunteering" a protesting child or an incompetent adult for admission. The usefulness of formal legal categories as markers of coercion is further undermined by practices whereby "involuntary" commitments are invoked for considerations other than patients' lack of willingness to enter the hospital (e.g., to effect public payment for the transport of indigent patients to the hospital). As a final complication, legal status may, and often does, change over the course of a single hospitalization (Cuffel, 1992).

Because of the many confounds described above, legal admission status conveys only the crudest information regarding patients' experience of coercion. As Brakel et al. (1985) note, "the voluntary–

involuntary distinction is in application quite blurred. Compulsion varies . . . on a spectrum where most commitment decisions fall into a middle grey area while the more distinct extremes of either fully voluntary admission or unwilled, formally resisted commitment are rarely seen" (p. 50).

If formal legal status is at best a crude proxy for patients' experience of being coerced, the best strategy for studying the role of coercion in mental hospital admission may be to seek the views of patients themselves on their experience of their hospital admission (Rogers, Pilgram, & Lacey, 1993; Lucksted & Coursey, 1995). This is the strategy we have taken in the MacArthur research.

THE MACARTHUR COERCION STUDY

After much exploratory research, including separate "focus groups" with patients, staff, and family members (Hoge et al., 1993), we began a preliminary study of patients' experience of mental hospital admission (Lidz et al., in press; Hoge et al., 1994). In this research, we interviewed 157 newly admitted patients within the first day after they were admitted to a mental hospital. Most (102, or 65%) of these patients entered a community-based general psychiatric facility in Pennsylvania, 55 (35%) entered a rural state hospital in Virginia. Both facilities served as the primary inpatient facility for the geographic area in which they were located. Two interviewers at the Pennsylvania site and one in Virginia were trained together and periodically reviewed each other's interviews.

The patients had to be at least 17 years old to be in the sample; their average age was 33 years. As for gender, 59% of the patients were male. Ethnically, 40% of the patients were African-American. Both the modal and the median education was 12 years. Only 13% of the patients were currently married. Patients had a mixture of chart diagnoses, with 19% diagnosed with an affective disorder, 13% with schizophrenia or schizoaffective disorder, 43% having a substance abuse disorder or mixture of an Axis I disorder and a substance abuse disorder, and the remaining 25% having personality disorders, anxiety disorders, or other problems. Pennsylvania patients were more likely to be African-American and less likely to be diagnosed with schizophrenia.

There were other differences between the two sites in the ways in which the patients were treated. Although 42% of the patients in the overall sample were involuntarily committed, 87% of the Virginia state hospital patients were involuntarily committed compared with only 18% of the Pennsylvania community hospital patients.

Each patient was administered the MacArthur Admission Experience Interview, a semi-structured interview that focused on the patients' perceptions of (1) the ways they were treated by others during the process of coming to the hospital and being admitted, (2) the nature of any pressures brought to bear on them to be hospitalized, and (3) the amount of coercion they perceived in the decision to be admitted.

The initial part of the interview was open-ended. In it, patients were encouraged to describe their experiences of coming into the hospital. The second part of the interview was composed of structured questions in which the patient chose from predetermined answer sets.

In order to measure the process issue, we needed to use variables that were at fundamentally different levels. We have two different types of questions: those that concerned the patient's perceptions of particular people who were involved with the decision that the patient would be admitted and those that reflected the patient's global perceptions of the series of events that were involved in the admission. First, for every person whom the patient named as being involved in any way with the decision, we asked four process questions concerning his or her involvement. These questions were: *motivation* ("To what extent did he or she do what he or she did out of concern for you?"), *respect* ("How much respect did he or she treat you with?"), *validation* ("How seriously did he or she consider what you had to say?"), and *fairness* ("How fairly did he or she treat you?"). Of course, for most purposes, these raw questions were difficult to use, since there were different numbers of participants in different cases. After several exploratory analyses, we decided to compute the average values for each question across the different identified participants to generate case-level values for each question.

Two overall case-level questions reflecting the process aspect of the admission decision were also asked of the subjects: whether the patients felt that they had had an opportunity to say what they wanted to about the admission (*voice*) and whether anyone had tricked them or lied to them in the admission process (*deception*). The six values (the four averaged values and the two general questions) correlated highly with one another.

We also asked all patients about the presence or absence of four different ways in which others might have tried to influence the decision about hospitalization (which we will call "pressures"). The pressures asked about were *persuasion* ("Did anyone try to talk you into going to the hospital or being admitted?"), *inducement* ("Did anyone offer or promise you something?"), *threats* ("Did anyone threaten you?"), and *force* ("Did anyone try to force you?").

In a previous paper (Gardner et al., 1993), we presented evidence to show that four questions from the interview constitute a psychometrically sound scale of patient perceptions of coercion that we have called the MacArthur Perceived Coercion Scale. These questions focus on *influence* ("What had more influence on your being admitted: what you wanted or what others wanted?"), *control* ("How much control did you have . . . ?"), *choice* ("You chose" or "someone made you?"), and *freedom* ("How free did you feel to do what you wanted . . . ?"). A perceived coercion score on a 0 to 5 scale (mean = 1.75, SD = 2.07) based on these questions was computed for each subject.

Results

Patient Legal Status

Several findings cloud the distinction between "voluntary" and "involuntary" patient status (Hoge et al., 1994). First, patients' reports belie the idealized view of the voluntary admission process as involving a patient who recognizes his or her illness, seeks professional help, and initiates hospitalization. We found that 34% of voluntary patients did not believe they had a mental illness. In 49% of cases, someone other than the patient initiated coming to the hospital; indeed, in 14% of the cases, patients were in some form of custody at the time of presentation. Moreover, only about half (49%) of the patients expected to be admitted at the time of presentation; after evaluation, 44% attributed the idea to be admitted to someone else; even after the admission decision had been made, 25% felt that there were reasonable alternatives to hospitalization. Furthermore, 39% of the legally voluntary patients believed that they would have been involuntarily committed if they had not "volunteered" to be hospitalized (with a further 36% of this group of subjects believing that they would not have been committed and the remaining 25% not knowing what would have happened). Threats were reported as having been made at some time in the process by 9% of voluntary patients; force, by 3%.

Our findings also belied the characterization of involuntary commitment as inevitably involving patients who deny they are ill and protest the hospitalization process. We found that 34% believed they were mentally ill. Perhaps more surprising, we found that 22% reported that it was their idea to come to the hospital for help, and 20% stated that they initiated the admission. About half (47%) said that there were no reasonable alternatives to hospitalization. While some (18%) were unaware of their legal status, the great majority of those who knew they had been committed (81%) reported that they were not offered the opportunity to voluntarily enter the hospital, and more than half (56%) of these patients indicated that they would have entered voluntarily if they had been given the opportunity. While we did not interview admitting clinicians and therefore do not know for certain what motivated them to commit, some patients' reports suggest that involuntary procedures were invoked in order to arrange transportation to the hospital.

Pressures

About half the patients reported no pressures of any type (46%). However, 38% reported efforts to persuade them, and 19% reported the use of force. Only 9% reported threats and only 4% an inducement. Of course, patients did not report just one type of pressure or one instance of the same pressure. Some cases involved multiple people placing pressures on them, and some people tried different approaches to getting the patient to do what they wanted. Patients reported a mean of 0.99 pressure per case (SD = 1.37). They reported a mean of 0.62 positive pressure per case (SD = 0.95) and a mean of 0.37 negative pressure (SD = 0.83).

Because of the low rates of threats and inducements, we collapsed together, for analytical purposes, persuasion and inducements into "positive" pressures and threats and force into "negative" pressures. We conceptualized positive pressures as those that sought to show that patients would be better off if they were admitted and negative pressures as those that would indicate to patients that they would be worse off if they resisted admission. Table 1 shows the frequencies of these pressures.

TABLE 1 Percentages of Patients Reporting Pressures to Be Hospitalized

None	46%
Positive only	31%
Negative only	12%
Both positive and negative	11%
Total	100%

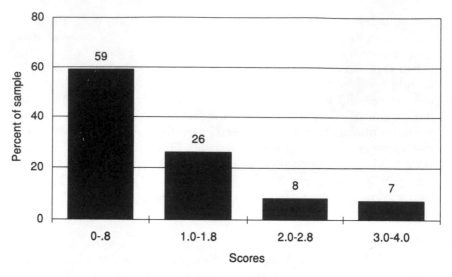

FIGURE 1. Process.

Process

Figure 1 shows the distribution of scores on our measure of "process." Low scores on this 4-point scale indicate "high" process (e.g., much voice). It can be seen that somewhat over half the patients (59%) believed that they were treated very well in the hospitalization process, with the remainder believing to varying degrees that the process was inadequate.

Perceived Coercion

Figure 2 presents the distribution of scores on the 6-point MacArthur Perceived Coercion Scale. The values 0 to 5 identified on the x axis represent intervals of data created by rounding to the nearest integer. The value 0 ranges from −0.1 to 0.2; 1 ranges from 0.5 to 1.4; 2 ranges from 1.7 to 2.3; 3 ranges from 2.6 to 3.5; 4 ranges from 3.8 to 4.4; 5 ranges from 4.7 to 5.3. Almost half the patients (46%) reported that they felt little or no coercion in the decision to be admitted to the hospital. On the other extreme, over one quarter (26%) of the patients reported that very high levels of coercion (scores of 4 or 5) had been

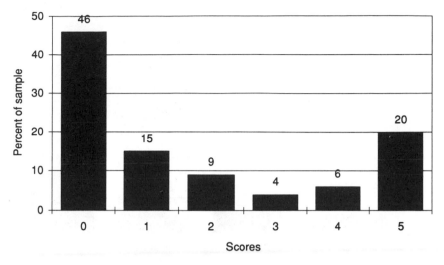

FIGURE 2. Perceived coercion.

applied to them. Perceptions of coercion appear to be unrelated to patient age, race, or gender.

The key findings concern whether perceived coercion was affected by the pressures applied to the patients and by the degree to which they had been involved in the process of deciding whether to be admitted to the hospital. For these two analyses, we used the percentage of patients who scored high (4–5) on the Perceived Coercion Scale as the "dependent" variable.

Perceived Coercion by Pressures. Recall that "persuasion" and "inducement" were combined to form "positive" pressures and "threats" and "force" were combined to form "negative" pressures. Figure 3 presents the findings regarding perceived coercion as a function of whether the patient reported having been subjected to positive pressures only, negative pressures only, both positive and negative pressures, or no pressures. It can be seen that the vast majority (89.5%) of persons reporting that they had been subjected only to negative pressures (threats and force) scored 4 or 5 on the perceived coercion scale. Only a small portion (10.2%) of patients who reported being subjected only to positive pressures (persuasion and inducements) reported feeling similarly coerced, a portion not significantly different from

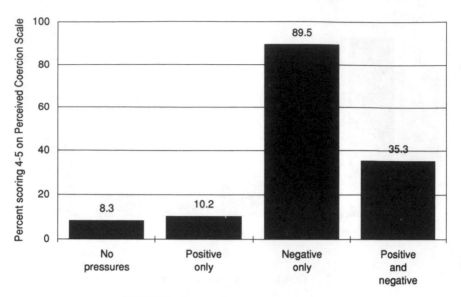

FIGURE 3. Perceived coercion by pressures.

that of people who reported no pressures at all (8.3%). Interestingly, positive pressures not only do not appear to result in an increased level of perceived coercion, but also seem to mitigate the effect of negative pressures. When negative pressures are applied without positive pressures (i.e., negative only), almost all persons (89.5%) report feeling very coerced. But when positive pressures are "added to" negative pressures (positive and negative in Figure 3), only about one third (35.3%) of the patients report feeling very coerced.

Perceived Coercion by Process. Finally, we present the findings regarding the effects of "process" on perceived coercion. Here, we divided the subjects evenly into three groups depending on their scores on the process variable. A "high" process score ranged from -0.95 to -0.628; a "medium" process score from -0.627 to 0.124; and a "low" process score from 0.125 to 2.90. In Figure 4, it can be seen that very few (2%) of the patients who were in the upper third of the process scores ("high process") perceived themselves as being very coerced. The rate of feeling very coerced was somewhat higher (11%) in the middle third of the process scores ("medium process"), and a majority (52%) of the patients in the lowest third ("low process") felt very coerced.

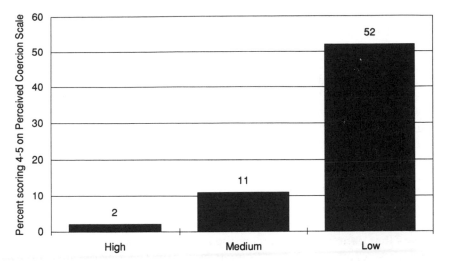

FIGURE 4. Perceived coercion by process.

Conclusions

There are three take-home findings from this preliminary study of co-ercion to mental hospital admission, findings that may have relevance to the study of coercion to treatment in the community as well.

The first finding is methodological. It is possible to reliably mea-sure people's perceptions of coercion independent of their formal le-gal status of "voluntary" or "involuntary." Legal status is at best a crude proxy for people's experience of coercion. Many legally "volun-tary" patients "volunteer" to sign themselves into the hospital in the belief that they will be involuntarily committed if they do not. Simi-larly, many do not believe that they are mentally ill. On the other hand, many legally "involuntary" patients report that they want treatment and would sign themselves into the hospital voluntarily if that option were made available.

The second finding has to do with how others attempt to influ-ence the disposition of a person regarding mental hospitalization. Very high levels of perceived coercion were reported when others' at-tempts at influence were limited to negative strategies of threats and force. The positive approaches of persuasion and inducement, in contrast, were associated with no increase in perceived coercion (compared to cases in which there were no reported pressures at all).

Persons who stated that both positive and negative pressures were applied to them reported an intermediate level of perceived coercion—higher than those subjected only to positive pressures, but much lower than those subjected only to negative pressures.

The third finding concerns the process of being admitted to a mental hospital. Patients who had a "good" admissions process—who reported that others acted out of concern for them, treated them fairly, with respect, and without deception, gave them a chance to tell their side of the story, and considered what was said in making the admission decision—were much less likely to feel coerced, particularly when the decision ultimately made was not the one they preferred.

The strength of the findings on "process" surprised us. We had not gone into the research with process concerns in mind. The statements that patients gave to us in the interviews made the importance of process even more clear (Bennett et al., 1993). Consider just three excerpts from the interviews.

In the following excerpt, the patient complained about his therapist in a manner that illustrates the anger patients felt when they were not included in the admission process:

PATIENT: I talked to him this morning. I said, "You . . . didn't even listen to me. You . . . call yourself a counselor. . . . Why did you decide to do this instead of . . . try to listen to me and understand . . . what I was going through." And he said, "Well, it doesn't matter, you know, you're going anyway. . . ." He didn't listen to what I had to say. . . . He didn't listen to the situation. . . . He had decided before he ever got to the house . . . that I was coming up here. Either I come freely or the officers would have to subdue me and bring me in.

Becoming involved in the process of deciding whether the patient should come into the hospital was one of the most frequently mentioned ways in which others were expected to show their concern for the patient. Patients might have had different reasons for wanting their families' or friends' involvement, such as needing assistance in figuring out how to get help, needing emotional support, or needing approval before being able to ask for help, but whatever form the involvement of these trusted individuals took, it was taken as a sign of caring and was therefore appreciated, as the second excerpt illustrates:

INTERVIEWER: How did you feel about that [a friend becoming involved in the hospitalization decision when the patient threatened to hurt herself]?

PATIENT: I was happy. Because nobody ever cared enough about me to do that. . . . Because he heard what I had to say. He wasn't all right with me attempting to do what I had to do. He told me my life was worth something.

Conversely, when a family member or friend whom a patient thought should become involved in the decision to be hospitalized failed to do so, or did not do so soon enough, patients were often disappointed and angered. Since involvement was taken as a sign of caring, when someone whom the patient expected to care seemed not to, it was interpreted as a breach of a moral duty.

Finally, the simple notion that patients should be treated by others with respect and, as much as possible, as equals received wide endorsement in our interviews. Patients believed in a version of the Golden Rule: They wanted to be treated by their family members and friends, and by the hospital staff, as these people would wish themselves to be treated in similar circumstances. This patient's complaint was about the evaluating staff:

PATIENT: . . . I think it should have been my decision. And I don't think . . . that they have to put an order on me like some kind of animal or something. Forced me to do something that I don't really need. I mean I don't think *they'd* appreciate it if it was forced on *them*. *They* would be a little upset too.

We emphasize that our findings are tentative and preliminary. The primary reason for this caveat is that our data are all drawn from one-time assessments of patients. We did not "triangulate" the accounts given by patients with those given by other sources of information, such as family members and hospital staff. Whether the patients actually were pressured by threats, for example, or whether they were denied an opportunity to have "voice" in the admission process, cannot be determined from these data. There are two reasons we cannot automatically accept the patient's account of the events that transpired: (1) *Any* person's account of an interpersonal transaction—whether the person is mentally disordered or not—is subject to self-serving bias (e.g., one spouse's account of a marital dispute often differs from the other spouse's account of the "same" dispute; juries listen to both litigants' accounts of the "facts" in a legal case before reaching a judgment, not just the "facts" presented by one litigant). (2) Mental disorder may have an additional effect on the perceptions and judgment of the affected person. Note that we make no presumption that the hospitalized person's account is not "factual" or should not be "validated" in the research. Rather, we desire additional sources of information (e.g., clinical status measures) before reaching a final judgment on this issue.

We cannot discount the possibility that the direction of causality is opposite to that portrayed here—that perceiving oneself as coerced leads to the belief that one has been threatened or forced, or that the admission process has been inadequate—or that some third causal factor underlies the relationships reported here (e.g., people who do not have insight into the fact that they are mentally disordered and yet find themselves in a mental hospital may reason that they must have been forced or threatened and that the admission process must have been unfair). Likewise, our distinction between substantive "pressures" and procedural "process" variables may be overstated; "pressures" and "process" are not wholly independent experiences for patients (Lidz et al., 1994). Ongoing research incorporating data from family members and clinicians and following patients over time is attempting to narrow the range of plausible interpretations of the data we have obtained.

But if future research should confirm our now-tentative findings, we would have a clear set of implications for the practice of delivering mental health care in an institutional setting. Whether the same admonitions would apply in the context of treatment delivered in the community is a topic deserving of much research [research on legal commitment to outpatient treatment, using a modified version of the MacArthur Perceived Coercion Scale, is already in progress (see Swartz et al., 1995)]. The admonitions are:

1. Use positive approaches, such as persuasion, as the strategies of choice to get people to accept treatment. A positive approach is unlikely to be seen as coercive in itself, and it is possible that a positive approach may mitigate the effect of any negative strategies that are ultimately used.
2. Use negative approaches, such as threats, only as a last resort to secure needed care. While we do not yet have data on the effect of perceived coercion on compliance with treatment or on the avoidance of seeking treatment in the future, the very high

levels of perceived coercion that are associated with negative pressures should restrict their use to emergencies or occasions when all other options have failed.

3. In all circumstances, but especially when negative pressures have been used, afford patients as much "process" as possible. This means conveying that you are acting out of concern for the patients, treating them fairly, with respect, and without deception, giving them a chance to tell their side of the story, and seriously considering what prospective patients have to say in making treatment decisions.

ACKNOWLEDGMENT. This research was supported by the MacArthur Research Network on Mental Health and the Law.

REFERENCES

Bennett, N., Lidz, C., Monahan, J., Mulvey, E., Hoge, S., Roth, L., & Gardner, W. (1993). Inclusion, motivation, and good faith: The morality of coercion in mental hospital admission. *Behavioral Sciences and the Law, 11,* 295–306.

Blanch, A., & Parrish, J. (1993). Reports of three roundtable discussions on involuntary interventions. *Psychiatric Rehabilitation and Community Support Monograph, 1,* 1–42.

Brakel, J., Parry, J., & Weiner, B. (1985). *The mentally disabled and the law* (3rd ed.). Chicago: American Bar Foundation.

Campbell, J., & Schraiber, R. (1989). *In pursuit of wellness: The well-being project,* Vol. 6. Sacramento: California Department of Mental Health.

Cuffel, B. (1992). Characteristics associated with legal status change among psychiatric patients. *Community Mental Health Journal, 28,* 471–482.

Gardner, W., Hoge, S., Bennett, N., Roth, L., Lidz, C., Monahan, J., & Mulvey, E. (1993). Two scales for measuring patients' perceptions of coercion during mental hospital admission. *Behavioral Sciences and the Law, 11,* 307–321.

Group for the Advancement of Psychiatry (1994). *Forced into treatment: The role of coercion in clinical practice.* Washington, DC: American Psychiatric Press.

Hoge, S., Lidz, C., Eisenberg, M., Gardner, W., Monahan, J., Mulvey, E., Roth, L., & Bennett, N. (1994). Coercion in the admission of voluntary and involuntary psychiatric patients. Unpublished manuscript.

Hoge, S., Lidz, C., Mulvey, E., Roth, L., Bennett, N., Siminoff, A., Arnold, R., & Monahan, J. (1993). Patient, family, and staff perceptions of coercion in mental hospital admission: An exploratory study. *Behavioral Sciences and the Law, 11,* 281–293.

Lidz, C., Hoge, S., Gardner, W., Bennett, N., Monahan, J., Mulvey, E., & Roth, L. (in press). Perceived coercion in mental hospital admission: Pressures and process. *Archives of General Psychiatry.*

Luckstead, A., & Coursey, R. (1995). Consumer perceptions of pressure and force in psychiatric treatments. *Psychiatric Services, 46,* 146–152.

Monahan, J., Hoge, S., Lidz, C., Roth, L., Bennett, N., Gardner, W., & Mulvey, E. (1995). Coercion and commitment: Understanding involuntary mental hospital admission. *International Journal of Law and Psychiatry, 18,* 249–263.

National Center for State Courts (1986). Guidelines for involuntary civil commitment. *Mental and Physical Disability Law Reporter, 10,* 409–415.

Riecher-Rossler, A., & Rossler, W. (1993). Compulsory admission of psychiatric patients: An international comparison. *Acta Psychiatrica Scandinavica, 87,* 231–236.

Rogers, A., Pilgram, D., & Lacey, R. (1993). *Experiencing psychiatry: Users' views of services.* London: Macmillan.

Rosenstein, M., Steadman, H., MacAskill, R., & Manderscheid, R. (1986). Legal status of admissions to three inpatient psychiatric settings, United States, 1980. *Mental Health Statistical Note Number 178.* Washington, DC: National Institute of Mental Health.

Swartz, M., Burns, B., Hiday, V., George, L., Swanson, J., & Wagner, H. (1995). New directions in research on involuntary outpatient commitment. *Hospital and Community Psychiatry, 46,* 381–385.

Wertheimer, A. (1993). A philosophical examination of coercion for mental health issues. *Behavioral Sciences and the Law, 11,* 239–258.

Zwerling, I., Conte, H., Plutchik, R., & Karaser, T. (1978). "No commitment week": A feasibility study. *American Journal of Psychiatry, 135,* 1198–1201.

Chapter 2

OUTPATIENT COMMITMENT
OFFICIAL COERCION IN THE COMMUNITY

Virginia Aldigé Hiday

Coerced mental health treatment in the community that is mandated by court order is known as *outpatient commitment.* This official mandatory mental health treatment in the community grew out of the 1960s and 1970s civil rights reform of mental health law when basic principles of due process and protection of individual liberties were applied to mental patients (Chambers, 1972; Hiday & Goodman, 1982; LaFond & Durham, 1992). Interpreting the Constitution as requiring a state to use the least drastic means when basic liberty is at stake (*Shelton v. Tucker,* 1960), both state statutes and federal appellate courts called for application of the least restrictive alternative in civil commitment cases.[1]

---

[1]Representative cases include (*Covington v. Harris,* 419 F.2d 617 (D.C. Cir. 1969); *Wyatt v. Stickney,* 325 F. Suppl. 781 (M.D. Ala. 1971); *Lessard v. Schmidt,* 379 F. Supp. 1376 (E.D. Wis. 1974); *Dixon v. Wineberger,* 405 F. Supp. 974 (D.D.C. 1975)).

Virginia Aldigé Hiday • Department of Sociology, North Carolina State University, Raleigh, North Carolina 27695.

Coercion and Aggressive Community Treatment: A New Frontier in Mental Health Law, edited by Deborah L. Dennis and John Monahan. Plenum Press, New York, 1996

"Least restrictive alternative" meant that persons who meet the legal criteria for involuntary hospitalization could be able to avoid that hospitalization if their dangerous behavior and mental illness could be controlled by other, less restrictive means. Outpatient commitment was seen as another measure of treatment and control that was less restrictive than the ultimate loss of individual liberty imposed by involuntary confinement in a hospital.

State legislators were motivated not only by concerns with the Constitution but also by concerns with inadequate care in state mental hospitals, institutionalization, and, perhaps more important, finance problems (Benson, 1980; Chambers, 1972; Robitscher, 1976). Outpatient commitment seemingly offered an easy solution, allowing states to treat and control mental patients more cheaply, to reduce institutionalization, overcrowding, and inadequate care, and to satisfy constitutional issues of liberty. Unfortunately, legislators did not consider, much less specify, mechanisms for operation and enforcement, and they gave little or no attention to possible problems in the use of outpatient commitment, such as overextension of state control, professional liability, and lack of community resources (Appelbaum, 1986; Hiday & Scheid-Cook, 1991).

Initially, outpatient commitment was used only for persons who met the criteria for involuntary hospitalization (mental illness and dangerousness in most states) and who could be maintained in the community if they received treatment. These included patients with a wide variety of diagnoses, many of whom had neither a severe nor a persistent mental disorder (Hiday & Goodman, 1982). Later, some states enacted legislation enabling a second form of outpatient commitment for chronically mentally ill patients who revolved in and out of both courts and hospitals. In the hospital, these patients became stabilized on medication and were released after short stays; yet, after release, they stopped taking their medication and decompensated, becoming overtly psychotic and eventually dangerous again. Since the initial criteria for outpatient commitment were identical to the criteria for involuntary hospitalization, families of these patients and their mental health caregivers had to wait until these patients became dangerous enough to be recommitted. In response to pleas of these families and mental health practitioners, some state legislatures enacted a second form of outpatient commitment. This second form applies less stringent criteria than those required for involuntary hospitalization, allowing court intervention during the decompensation stage before dangerous behavior develops (Brooks, 1987; Hiday & Scheid-Cook, 1987). In addition to mental illness but in place of the more restrictive dangerousness standard, some states substituted the psychiatric history standard. This standard required that there be a need for treatment in order to prevent further disability or deterioration that would predictably result in dangerousness based on the civil commitment candidate's own illness pattern.[2]

By 1985, all states except New York either made explicit provisions for some form of outpatient commitment (26 states and the District of Columbia) or did not prohibit its use (23 states) (Keilitz & Hall, 1985; Keilitz, Conn, & Giampetro, 1985). Even so, outpatient commitment was infrequently employed. Court officers and mental health clinicians continued to think in terms of the traditional choices of either release or involuntary hospitalization (Hiday & Goodman, 1982). Outpatient commitment, as a relatively new alternative, suffered from being unknown and unfamiliar. At this time, a national survey of state mental health program directors and attorneys general found widespread ignorance of what outpatient commitment was and what it did. Some respondents to the survey did not even know that outpatient commitment was statutorily authorized in their states when it was (Miller, 1985). Even where mental health professionals were knowledgeable about it, they still tended to resist employing outpatient commitment because of lack of enforcement mechanisms and liability protections (Appelbaum, 1986; Miller & Fiddleman, 1984).

By the late 1980s, outpatient commitment began to receive increasing attention as a less restrictive alternative to involuntary hospitalization and as a means to slow the revolving doors of rehospitalization and recommitment of the severely and persistently mentally ill who are resistant to treatment in the community. Scholarly articles brought outpatient commitment to the attention of professionals and policy makers. The National Center for State Courts (1986), in its "Guidelines for Involuntary Civil Commitment," presented outpatient commitment as an essential dispositional alternative to inpatient civil commitment. Rather than suggest legislation and statutory language, the guidelines proposed practical action, procedures, and structural arrangements for its effective operation. The American Bar Association commended the guidelines to those implementing civil commitment laws. Shortly thereafter, the American Psychiatric Association followed by recommending use of outpatient commitment

[2]For instance, see the prototypical statute of North Carolina [N.C.G.S. §122C–263 (d) (1) (c) (1990)]. North Carolina's statute also attempts to ensure that this lower standard encompasses only those who are capable of surviving safely in the community with available supervision and who are limited in ability to seek voluntarily or comply with treatment because of their mental illness [N.C.G.S. §122C–263 (d) (1) (b and d) (1990)].

and published specific procedural provisions for legislative enactment, which aimed to solve previous problems limiting its use up to
that time (American Psychiatric Association, 1988).

State legislatures subsequently became active, studying and implementing mandatory community treatment legislation (McCafferty
& Dooley, 1990). Among states that previously used outpatient commitment, some passed laws to encourage its use and facilitate its
operation (Arkansas, Georgia, New Hampshire, New Mexico, Ohio,
Utah, Virginia, Washington, and Wisconsin). Among states previously
without explicit provisions authorizing outpatient commitment, some
added authorization to their mental health statutes (Indiana, Kansas,
Minnesota, Oregon, and Wyoming), while others have considered legislation (Alabama, Maine, Mississippi, Missouri, and Pennsylvania).
Some states were studying outpatient commitment for possible revi-
sion of their laws (Colorado, Florida, Nevada, Ohio, and South Carolina) (McCafferty & Dooley, 1990). New York state, which had earlier
prohibited outpatient commitment, has enacted legislation authorizing a 3-year pilot project of outpatient commitment in New York City
beginning in 1995 (New York Mental Hygiene Law §9.61).

Some analysts have included conditional release as a third form
of outpatient commitment (Gould, 1995; McCafferty & Dooley, 1990;
Miller, 1994). It is the oldest and may be the most common form of
mandatory community treatment today, and it is official by being enforceable by law (Brakel, Parry, & Weiner, 1985), but conditional release from civil commitment traditionally did not involve court or administrative review or a direct court order, as did the other two types
of official coerced community treatment (Hinds, 1990; Keilitz & Hall,
1985). Although a court may have ordered the involuntary hospitalization, it was a psychiatrist or hospital administrator who granted
the conditional release to a patient civilly committed to the hospital
and who set the conditions of release. This traditional form of conditional release is still permitted by statute in many states (Brakel et al.,
1985), but since the civil rights reforms of mental health law requiring
due process in civil commitment, judicial orders of conditional release
also occur. Some judges have adopted the parole model from criminal
law and have released patients to the community conditionally rather
than discharging them outright (Miller, 1994).

The release conditions of both judges and psychiatrists tend to be
only admonitions to a patient of taking medicine, visiting the mental
health center, doing well, and not becoming dangerous, rather than
specific orders for community treatment. Where granted by a psy-

chiatrist, conditional release may be revoked by that psychiatrist if release conditions are not met. But except in those places where inpatient facility staff also serves as the outpatient staff, a hospital psychiatrist is unlikely to know whether the release conditions are met. Revocation most often occurs when family or friends return a conditionally released patient to the hospital or report that the patient's behavior has become too symptomatic or dangerous to continue without intervention. Revocation also frequently occurs when new commitment procedures bring the patient to the hospital and the conditional release is used to override the new commitment procedures so as to simplify the readmission process. Since the mid-1970s, several state and federal courts have required hearings at which patients can contest evidence upon which revocation is sought before they may be returned to inpatient status. Exceptions for emergency situations permit immediate involuntary hospitalization, but hearings must be held within a specified limited time (Brakel et al., 1985; Hinds, 1990).

APPLICATION OF OUTPATIENT COMMITMENT

The extent to which official mandatory treatment in the community is used has not been well documented. We do not know how often conditional release or either of the two types of outpatient commitment occurs in the United States or the extent to which any treatment is required or followed. Coercion may not even be made use of if, as frequently happens, no official in the community assumes responsibility for ensuring treatment (Bursten, 1986; Hiday & Scheid-Cook, 1987, 1989, 1991; Miller & Fiddleman, 1984). On the other hand, when mental health practitioners reach out to committed patients with a range of desired services and engage them in treatment plans, patients may respond positively enough so that coercion may not occur beyond the written orders in court records.

There are no published studies in this country on the frequency of conditional release among persons civilly committed to mental hospitals and relatively few studies on the frequency of outpatient commitment in specific localities or states. The studies we have report only limited use of either type of outpatient commitment, varying from no cases to 14% of total civil commitment cases or to 27% of total committed persons (Hiday & Scheid-Cook, 1987; Miller, 1988; Wood & Swanson, 1985). As mental health statutes, administrative policies, and resources vary by state, we can expect variation in use of outpatient commitment, and evidence exists that variation in outpatient commitment use occurs within states across judicial and mental health authorities (Hiday & Scheid-Cook, 1987).

With either type of outpatient commitment, the amount of coercion that occurs varies greatly with the policies and organization of community mental health centers where patients are committed, with the philosophy and values of individual clinicians, and with patient needs. In dealing with noncompliant patients who are severely and persistently mentally ill, centers tend to focus on maintenance of psychotropic medication, often requiring biweekly prolixin shots for those seen as least likely to follow a medication regimen (Hiday & Scheid-Cook, 1991; Scheid-Cook, 1993; Schmidt & Geller, 1989; Wood & Swanson, 1985). Treatment plans may also include any or any combination of daily attendance at day programs, weekly group therapy, and monthly counseling sessions, but often treatment includes no more than a short med check. Some patients ordered to outpatient commitment may have no treatment plans, and thus no requirements to follow, because mental health centers or individual clinicians do not enforce the mandatory court orders (Hiday, 1992; Hiday & Scheid-Cook, 1991; Miller & Fiddleman, 1984).

Despite the establishment of outpatient commitment as a mechanism to ensure treatment outside the hospital for mentally ill persons who resist or are unable to comply voluntarily, many mental health professionals have a distaste for coercion, believing that treatment will have better results if patients participate willingly (American Psychiatric Association, 1993; Miller, 1987). Additionally, mental health professionals have a distaste for the required paperwork and court appearances that formal legal coercion entails (Decker, 1980, 1981, 1987; Gilboy & Schmidt, 1971; Reed & Lewis, 1990). Thus, they resist using formal legal coercion. Instead, they often attempt to persuade reluctant patients to accept voluntary treatment, but their methods of persuasion may be viewed as coercive by both observers and patients (Gilboy & Schmidt, 1971; Hiday, 1992; Lucksted & Coursey, 1995).

Several studies have shown that such persuasion or informal coercion occurs frequently in hospital admission and in preparation for court review (Decker, 1987; Gilboy & Schmidt, 1971; Lewis, Goetz, Schoenfield, Gordon, & Griffin, 1984; Reed & Lewis, 1990; Rogers, 1993), but less is known about its use in the community. A recent survey of severely mentally ill outpatients in rehabilitation centers reported that 26% had felt "pressured or forced" to attend outpatient treatment in the previous year, and 42% of them had felt so pressured or forced as frequently as once or twice a week (Lucksted & Coursey, 1995). Respondents named mental health practitioners most frequently (76%) as the source of the informal coercion. Half of the respondents described the pressure or force as attempts to persuade them that it was in their best interests to go for treatment, and just over half said that some time in the past, the pressure or force involved threats of hospitalization or deprivation of a resource such as housing or disability checks. None described physical force being used to get them to go for community treatment (Lucksted & Coursey, 1995).

PATIENT RESPONSES TO COERCION

Patient attitudes toward coercion in hospitalization tend to change from admission to discharge or later in the community, becoming more positive with a decrease in symptoms and the passage of time (Beck & Golowka, 1988; Edelsohn & Hiday, 1990; Gove & Fain, 1977; Kane, Quitkin, & Rifkin, 1983; Killian & Bloomberg, 1975; Toews, el-Guebaly, & Leckie, 1981; Toews, el-Guebaly, Leckie, & Harper, 1984). Where anger and resentment dominate at the time coercion is applied, these negative feelings tend to subside afterward and be replaced with appreciation of the earlier need for coercion. Likewise, attitudes toward coercion in the community can be expected to change over time. In the study of severely mentally ill outpatients discussed above, 43% of those who said they had experienced pressure or force to go for treatment some time in the past stated that at those times they felt angry. Another 43% of them stated that they had felt afraid (of involuntary hospitalization if they did not attend outpatient treatment). But looking back later, a majority of these respondents felt that it was in their best interests to have been pressured or forced into community treatment (Lucksted & Coursey, 1995).

Only one research project has studied patient attitudes toward official coercion in the community. Its results showed that the great majority of patients who were placed on outpatient commitment had positive attitudes toward mandatory treatment in the community. They found it helpful in talking about their problems, giving them a place to go, and often providing services they otherwise would not

have received: transportation, vocational rehabilitation, and free medication (Hiday, 1992; Scheid-Cook, 1993). Most basically, they liked
it because it enabled them to stay in their home communities outside the hospital; thus, they appreciated it as what the law intended
it to be, a less restrictive alternative to hospitalization (Scheid-Cook,
1991).

In this study, the minority who were negative toward outpatient
commitment focused on its compulsory components. They disliked
being "forced" to attend the mental health center and to take medicine. The negative minority also reported dissatisfaction with the services offered because the services did not meet their needs (Hiday,
1992; Scheid-Cook, 1993). It may be that better services that addressed
their problems would have ameliorated both criticisms. Better services may even be able to ameliorate much of the apparent need for
formal legal coercion.

Since some patients fail to follow their treatment plan not because of recalcitrance, but because of problems beyond their control,
outreach and planning may solve the problems and remove the need
for coercion. The first outpatient commitment evaluation found that
respondents often missed scheduled appointments because of situations with which they could not deal, such as sickness or lack of transportation (Hiday & Goodman, 1982). Our research on outpatient commitment over the past 15 years has reinforced that early observation.
Patients commonly become noncompliant with treatment plans because of their lack of transportation or child care; their inability to afford the cost of medication; their social and mental disorganization,
which limits their ability to follow a routine of medication or visits to
a center; or their dependence on persons who are unreliable. A mental
health center could overcome these causes of patient noncompliance
with assertive outreach to identify the causes of noncompliance and
to plan and offer individualized solutions such as van pick-up, day
treatment, and home or "hang-out" visits. Reaching out to patients in
these ways requires that a mental health center command the resources necessary to have small enough case loads and to provide diverse services—requirements that often are not met.

We have observed that some patients with severe and persistent
mental disorder vary in their willingness to comply with treatment
as their illnesses ebb and flow. When symptoms escalate, they discontinue treatment either because of mental disorganization or because they believe they are not sick. In either case, a predictable pro-

gression ensues: deterioration, dangerousness, and rehospitalization. When these patients' illnesses intensify and they become treatment-resistant, outpatient commitment can avoid the progression to dangerousness and rehospitalization by ensuring continued treatment in the community. When official legal coercion is necessary, these patients are negative toward it, but as their symptoms ebb and court orders are no longer needed to get them treatment, their attitudes toward the earlier coercion change to being more positive. Advance directives, described in Chapter 8, may be a viable alternative to state intervention with these patients.

We have also observed that some patients are recalcitrant. They do not want to go to a mental health center, see a representative of the center, or take medication regardless of the services offered. These patients resist treatment because they do not want to admit to being sick or do not recognize that they are sick. Since complying would be an admission of being sick, they willfully neither take medication nor keep mental health appointments. In such cases, official legal coercion, in addition to assertive outreach and better services, is necessary to assure treatment. Although they do not recognize their illnesses, these patients can recognize the authority of the law and tend not to resist outpatient commitment orders. With some of these patients who have severe and persistent mental disorders, the need for formal coercion will dissipate over time as they experience the benefits of treatment and develop an understanding of their illness (Geller, 1986).

While we yet have no published quantitative studies on patient perceptions of how they are treated during official legal coercion in the community, studies on the hospital admission process suggest that the manner in which the official coercion is carried out makes an important difference; that is, patient responses to coercion vary with how they are treated while being legally coerced. Patients feel invalidated and coerced into the hospital, regardless of legal status or objective indicators of coercion, when admission staff and accompanying others do not seem to be concerned about their well-being, do not seem to act in good faith, and do not include them in treatment decisions. But when treated with concern, respect, and fairness, patients tend not to feel coerced (Bennett et al., 1993; Gardner, Hoge, Roth, & Gardner, 1993; Lidz et al., 1994) (see also Chapter 1).

In summary, patient responses to official coercion in the community can be expected to vary with their reasons for noncompliance, with the nature and course of their illnesses, with the type and amount of services offered, and with how they are treated while being coerced.

EFFECTS OF OUTPATIENT COMMITMENT

Although scholarly articles helped bring outpatient commitment to the attention of professional associations and policymakers, relatively few of them were empirical studies that evaluated the success of this formal legal coercion. The few empirical studies we have present difficulties in knowing whether it is the legal mandate—that is, the court order to obtain treatment—or other factors that account for the outcomes examined. Patient characteristics, illness characteristics, mental health treatment, and social services provided are inadequately described and seldom statistically controlled. Lack of random assignment and natural field experiments has also hampered interpretation of results. Nonetheless, this first generation of outpatient commitment evaluation studies points to the potential to reduce hospitalization for those who would otherwise be committed to an inpatient facility and the potential to maintain in the community those who would otherwise repeatedly be involuntarily hospitalized.

The first study reporting effects of outpatient commitment found that most patients so committed were successful in the community in that only one in eight of them became dangerous enough to require involuntary hospitalization during the 90-day commitment period (Hiday & Goodman, 1982). Although all these patients met the restrictive criteria for involuntary hospitalization, they were selected on the basis of characteristics expected to produce success, such as employment and family support; thus, one does not know whether these characteristics or the coerced treatment caused success. Nonetheless, to the extent that all these patients would have been involuntarily hospitalized if outpatient commitment were not an option, its success can be measured by reduction in costs to patients and taxpayers. On the other hand, if their characteristics were the basis for success, these patients could have been released with no legal coercion and even lower costs.

Another study in the same state but in a different region reported a lower rate of effectiveness as measured by opinions of mental health center clinicians about outpatient commitment cases seen in two 6-month periods (Miller & Fiddleman, 1984). These workers believed that mandatory community treatment helped just less than half (46%) of the cases. Although not a majority of outpatient commitment patients, this percentage constitutes a rather high success rate in light of the proportions who remained in treatment for the full 90 days of commitment (i.e., 77% in the first period and only 50% in the second). Still, it is difficult to determine the effects of outpatient commitment in this study, since clinicians often did nothing to enforce the order when patients failed to comply, thus removing the element of coercion after the initial court order.

Greeman and McClellan (1985) reported on outcomes of mandatory treatment in the community for patients whose involuntary hospitalization was judicially stayed (not technically outpatient commitment, but essentially identical) by comparing their adjustment with patients released after 72-hour emergency holds and patients involuntarily hospitalized. Using compliance with medication and scheduled appointments, and absence of disruptive symptoms, to measure adjustment, they found relatively few of any group doing well. But a larger proportion of patients on court-ordered community treatment did well compared to the other two groups (24% vs. 14% and 4%, respectively). Again because of possible selection bias, one cannot know whether differences were caused by the coercive community treatment.

Zanni and deVeau (1986) avoided the selection bias problem by comparing the hospital experience of committed outpatients 1 year after their court orders with that experience 1 year prior to their court orders. Among a small sample (N = 42) of patients receiving both in- and outpatient treatment at the same hospital, they found significantly fewer hospitalizations per patient after patients were placed on outpatient commitment (0.95 vs. 1.81), and a tendency to shorter stays (38 vs. 55 days). We do not know, however, whether hospital admissions and length of stays declined for other patients during the same time period.

Van Putten, Santiago, and Berren (1988) evaluated outpatient commitment by comparing three groups of patients: (1) all patients committed at an Arizona county hospital in the last 6 months before statutory change permitted outpatient commitment, (2) all patients committed at that same hospital in the first 6 months under the new outpatient commitment law, and (3) all patients committed there in the second 6 months of the new law. They reported three positive outcomes: (1) Although all committed outpatients were initially ordered to inpatient treatment, hospital stay was significantly less after the statutory change (11 and 8 days for the first and second 6 months under the new law vs. 21 days earlier). (2) No patient on outpatient commitment caused serious harm or was a victim of it while under court order. (3) The proportion of patients who voluntarily used community mental health services after their court orders ended or expired increased significantly from before to after the statutory change. Only 6% of those committed prior to statutory change sought community treatment; after the change, 21% of those involuntarily hospitalized and then released without being placed on outpatient commitment, and 71% of those involuntarily hospitalized and then ordered to outpatient treatment, sought services at a mental health center. Since both types of patients in the postchange periods had significant increases in voluntary community aftercare, one must look to changes at mental health centers (e.g., improved programs and services or increased outreach toward committed patients) for a partial explanation of the increases.

Evaluating outpatient commitment that included a new, less restrictive standard and new facilitating procedures, Hiday and Scheid-Cook (1987) compared civil commitment respondents ordered to mandatory community treatment with two other groups of civil commitment respondents: (1) those ordered to involuntary hospitalization and later released without mandatory treatment in the community and (2) those initially released by the court with no treatment order. They found that persons committed to outpatient treatment who actually began treatment were no different 6 months after their court hearings from others on numerous outcomes: living situation, rehospitalization rate, days rehospitalized, social interaction outside the home, employment, dangerousness, and arrest. Outpatient commitment, however, did make a difference in treatment response. Patients ordered to community treatment who began it were significantly different in being less likely to refuse medication even once and less likely to be noncompliant with other treatment even once. These patients were also more likely to visit the community mental health center and to remain in treatment 6 months after their hearings, even when their court orders had expired. The same analysis conducted on severe and persistently mentally ill persons who revolve through the doors of both mental hospitals and courts produced the same outcomes except that differences in noncompliance with medication and other treatment did not reach statistical significance (Hiday & Scheid-Cook, 1989).

A more recent study of the same state reported that outpatient commitment dramatically reduced institutionalization rates (Fernandez & Nygard, 1990). It sampled all patients in the state who had a first outpatient commitment in the 3-year period beginning 1 year after a less restrictive standard and new procedures for outpatient commitment became effective. To compensate for patient differences in lengths of time before and after each of their outpatient commitment orders, researchers standardized their two outcome measures: number of involuntary hospitalizations and length of stay. They found that these patients had fewer involuntary hospitalizations after than before their outpatient commitments, declining from 3.7 to 0.7 mean involuntary hospital admissions; the patients also had shorter lengths of stay, declining from 57.6 to 38.4 mean days. Because the researchers did not control for changes in involuntary hospital admissions and length of stays during this time period among other patients, we do not know whether the decreases were due to outpatient commitment or to changing hospital policies that reduced admissions and lengths of stay for all.

Only one study reported no positive outcome of mandatory treatment in the community (Bursten, 1986). Although there was a decline in the readmission rate of patients ordered to mandatory treatment following involuntary hospitalization, it was not significantly different from a decline in the rate among a control group. Bursten concluded that mandatory outpatient treatment was ineffective in reducing readmissions, but this conclusion is questionable since there was strong evidence that the outpatient commitment law was not enforced. One cannot fairly evaluate mandatory community treatment if no treatment occurs.

In summary, all first-generation evaluation studies of mandatory outpatient treatment but Bursten's point to positive outcomes for a substantial number of civil commitment patients, including those with severe and persistent mental disorders.

ISSUES NEEDING INVESTIGATION

Since something seems to be working when mental patients are officially coerced to receive treatment in the community, the next generation of studies needs to investigate the specific mechanisms that cause patients to comply with treatment and remain out of the hospital.

Studies should explore patient, family, provider, and mental health center characteristics associated with success. Previous studies, having incorporated unspecified selection bias of those recommending and ordering outpatient commitment, left unknown the level of patient symptomatology, functioning, social support, and often, even diagnosis and chronicity. Since these patient characteristics, rather than the legal coercion, could have made a difference in success, they need to be measured and controlled in future analyses.

Treatment type, frequency, and intensity, which most previous studies left unspecified, could also have made a difference in success. The few studies that described treatment given under court order showed great variation in "dosage"; indeed, many mentally ill ordered to outpatient commitment did not receive even one "dose" in that they never had a clinic visit. If treatment consists of only biweekly shots or monthly medication checks with no psychosocial therapy or programs, it is understandable why mental patients would be resistant to treatment; however, if necessary medication is accompanied by appropriate psychosocial programs and more frequent contact based on comprehensive planning for each patient's needs, mental health centers are more likely to overcome patients' treatment resistance (Swartz et al., 1995). Since previous research described many centers responding to court orders by aggressive outreach with services to capture treatment-resistant chronic patients, and since these centers were the ones that appeared to have more success with patients on outpatient commitment (Hiday & Scheid-Cook, 1987), it could have been intensive case management and psychosocial services such as group counseling, skills training, and transportation, rather than the legal coercion, that accounted for positive outcomes.

If outpatient commitment itself makes a difference in patient outcomes, we need to know the mechanism by which it works. Does a general respect for (or fear of) the law compel compliance, or are more specific enforcement measures necessary? We know very little about how often court orders are enforced. Only one previous study described steps taken to enforce outpatient commitment (Hiday & Scheid-Cook, 1991). Future studies should describe what legal coercion beyond a court order is used and how it is applied. Although some states authorize sheriff and police departments to pick up a noncompliant patient and take the patient to a mental health center for treatment, little is known about whether and how this process operates, that is, how police and sheriffs are engaged, how they cooperate, and how they deal with a noncompliant patient, especially whether they apply handcuffs or other physical force during pick-ups. Little is known about how often mental health crisis workers are deputized for pick-ups and how they work. In those states that permit involuntary medication or rehospitalization or both without hearings for noncompliance, we also know little about the extent and effects of their use.

As discussed earlier, some persons with severe and persistent mental disorders remain noncompliant or cycle into noncompliance even with mental health center outreach and a strong program of services. If treatment resistance cannot be overcome with good services and if advance directives are not engaged, these patients could possibly be regularly reordered to outpatient commitment to keep them in treatment for their active lives. No data exist on how often outpatient commitment orders are renewed for chronic patients and how long they are kept on these orders, and very little is known of the court review process for renewal beyond statutory provisions. We need to know how review for renewal operates: Do mental health centers and courts cooperate in scheduling continuation hearings, in issuing notification orders, in facilitating procedures: Are patients' rights protected? And what are patients' understandings of these legal proceedings? We have noticed that some patients react to certain due process protections such as notification by the sheriff and hearings at the courthouse as though these protections were punitive. This reaction seems to be related to lower class status or drug abuse that would have influenced previous encounters with police and courts. Patients whose only experience with the law involves prosecution for criminal violations are likely to view civil outpatient commitment procedures as steps in criminal prosecution, and such perceptions are likely to affect their treatment adherence over time. Do other persons who have mental disorders but have not been respondents in civil commitment proceedings share these perceptions, and are they driven way from treatment because of fear of such official coercion?

Since we know that informal coercion plays an important role in getting patients into treatment in the community as well as in the hospital, future studies should examine the nature and extent of its influence on compliance and outpatient commitment success. How much do family, friends, and mental health professionals remind patients of their commitment orders or of possible police pick-up and return to the hospital when trying to get patients to take their medicine and

keep their mental health appointments? How much do these significant others tell patients that loss of valued resources, such as income,
a car, and a residence, will follow failure to comply? And what effect
do these threats or attempts at persuasion have on patients? Such informal coercion may act to reinforce court orders such that no other
formal coercive measures need be taken.

Whether patients perceive informal coercion measures as threats
or persuasion attempts is likely to be affected by the concern and respect shown them by those trying to obtain their compliance (Bennett
et al., 1993; Hoge et al., 1993; Lidz, Mulvey, Arnold, Bennett, & Kirsch,
1993; Lucksted & Coursey, 1995; Rogers, 1993). Despite being under a
court order for outpatient treatment and being presented with unat-
tractive alternatives to compliance, patients may not perceive coercion and may not hold negative feelings if mental health professionals
and others engage them in planning treatment, give them choices
where possible, solicit their opinions, listen to their concerns, address
their needs, and attempt to accommodate their wishes. Although it is
plausible that such measures could be effective, we do not know
whether these manifestations of concern and respect can remove negative feelings from the treatment environment so that official legal coercion can be avoided, and whether it can be avoided with all types of
patients including those with the seemingly most intractable treatment resistance.

Clearly, there are many lacunae in our empirical base of knowledge. We still do not have much rudimentary information on the operation of outpatient commitment laws. Without it and without more
complex information on the interaction between official legal coercion and informal coercion, patient characteristics, and mental health
center and provider characteristics, we will not be able to understand
the causal mechanisms that underlie patient success with outpatient
commitment. These empirical data and causal understandings are essential to addressing basic civil liberty concerns about enlarging the
state's net of control without justification (Mulvey, Geller, & Roth,
1987; Stefan, 1987).

REFERENCES

American Psychiatric Association (1988). *Involuntary commitment to outpatient treatment.*
    Washington, DC: American Psychiatric Press.

American Psychiatric Association (1993). *Consent to voluntary hospitalization.* Washington, DC: American Psychiatric Press.

Appelbaum, P. S. (1986). Outpatient commitment: The problems and the promise. *American Journal of Psychiatry, 143,* 1270–1272.

Beck, J., & Golowka, E. (1988). A study of enforced treatment in relation to Stone's "thank you" theory. *Behavioral Sciences and the Law, 6,* 559–566.

Bennett, N. S., Lidz, C. W., Monahan, J., Mulvey, E. P., Hoge, S. K., Roth, L. H., & Gardner, W. (1993). Inclusion, motivation and good faith: The morality of coercion in mental hospital admission. *Behavioral Sciences and the Law, 11,* 295–306.

Benson, P. R. (1980). Labeling theory and community care of the mentally ill in California: The relationship of social theory and ideology to public policy. *Human Organization, 39,* 134–141.

Brakel, S. J., Parry, J., & Weiner, B. A. (1985). *The mentally disabled and the law,* 3rd ed. Chicago: American Bar Foundation.

Brooks, A. D. (1987, Winter). Outpatient commitment for the chronically mentally ill: Law and policy. In D. Mechanic (Ed.), *Improving mental health services: What the social sciences can tell us* (No. 36, pp. 117–128). San Francisco: Jossey-Bass.

Bursten, B. (1986). Posthospital mandatory outpatient treatment. *American Journal of Psychiatry, 43,* 1255–1258.

Chambers, D. L. (1972). Alternatives to civil commitment of the mentally ill: Practical guides and constitutional imperatives. *Michigan Law Review, 70,* 1107–1200.

Covington v. Harris, 419 F.2d 617 (D.C. Cir. 1969).

Decker, F. H. (1980). Changes in the legal status of mental patients as waivers of a constitutional right: The problem of consent. *Journal of Psychiatry and Law, 8,* 31–58.

Decker, F. H. (1981). Changes in the legal status of mental patients and hospital management. *Journal of Applied Behavioral Science, 17,* 153–171.

Decker, F. H. (1987). Psychiatric management of legal defense in periodic commitment hearings. *Social Problems, 34,* 156–171.

Dixon v. Wineberger, 405 F. Supp. 974 (D.D.C. 1975).

Edelsohn, G., & Hiday, V. A. (1990). Civil commitment: A range of patient attitudes. *Bulletin of the American Academy of Psychiatry and the Law, 18,* 65–77.

Fernandez, G., & Nygard, S. (1990). Impact of involuntary outpatient commitment on the revolving-door syndrome in North Carolina. *Hospital and Community Psychiatry, 41,* 1001–1004.

Gardner, W., Hoge, S. K., Roth, L. H., & Gardner, W. (1993). Two scales for measuring patients' perceptions of coercion during mental hospital admission. *Behavioral Sciences and the Law, 11,* 307–322.

Geller, J. L. (1986). Rights, wrongs, and the dilemma of coerced community treatment. *American Journal of Psychiatry, 143,* 1259–1264.

Gilboy, J., & Schmidt, J. (1971). "Voluntary" hospitalization of the mentally ill. *Northwestern University Law Review, 66,* 429–453.

Gould, K. K. (1995). New approach to outpatient commitment launched in New York. *Report on Mental Disability Law, 1,* 9–10 & 14.

Gove, W. R., & Fain, T. (1977). A comparison of voluntary and committed psychiatric patients. *Archives of General Psychiatry, 34,* 669–676.

Greeman, M., & McClellan, T. A. (1985). The impact of a more stringent commitment code in Minnesota. *Hospital and Community Psychiatry, 36,* 990–992.

Hiday, V. A. (1992). Coercion in civil commitment: Process, preferences and outcome. *International Journal of Law and Psychiatry, 15*, 359–377.

Hiday, V. A., & Goodman, R. R. (1982). The least restrictive alternative to involuntary hospitalization, outpatient commitment: Its use and effectiveness. *Journal of Psychiatry and Law, 10*, 81–96.

Hiday, V. A., & Scheid-Cook, T. L. (1987). The North Carolina experience with outpatient commitment: A critical appraisal. *International Journal of Law and Psychiatry, 10*, 215–232.

Hiday, V. A., & Scheid-Cook, T. L. (1989). A follow-up of chronic patients committed to outpatient treatment. *Hospital and Community Psychiatry, 40*, 52–58.

Hiday, V. A., & Scheid-Cook, T. L. (1991). Outpatient commitment for revolving door patients: Compliance and treatment. *Journal of Nervous and Mental Disease, 179*, 85–90.

Hinds, J. T. (1990). Involuntary outpatient commitment for the chronically mentally ill. *Nebraska Law Review, 69*, 346–412.

Hoge, S. K., Lidz, C. W., Mulvey, E. P., Roth, L. H., Bennett, N. S., Siminoff, L., Arnold, R., & Monahan, J. (1993). Patient, family and staff perceptions of coercion in mental hospital admission: An exploratory study. *Behavioral Sciences and the Law, 11*, 281–294.

Kane, J. M., Quitkin, F., & Rifkin, A. (1983). Attitudinal changes of involuntarily committed patients following treatment. *Archives of General Psychiatry, 40*, 374–377.

Keilitz, I., Conn, D., & Giampetro, A. (1985). Least restrictive treatment of involuntary patients: Translating concepts into practice. *St. Louis University Law Journal, 29*, 691–745.

Keilitz, I., & Hall, T. (1985). State statutes governing involuntary outpatient civil commitment. *Mental and Physical Disability Law Reporter, 9*, 378–397.

Killian, L. M., & Bloomberg, S. (1975). Rebirth in a therapeutic community: A case study. *Psychiatry, 38*, 39–54.

LaFond, J. Q., & Durham, M. (1992). *Back to asylum*. New York: Oxford University Press.

Lessard v. Schmidt, 379 F. Supp. 1376 (E. D. Wis. 1974).

Lewis, D. A., Goetz, E., Schoenfield, M., Gordon, A. C., & Griffin, E. (1984). The negotiation of involuntary civil commitment. *Law and Society Review, 18*, 630–649.

Lidz, C. W., Hoge, S. K., Gardner, W. P., Bennett, N. S., Monahan, J., Mulvey, E. P., & Roth, L. H. (1994). Perceived coercion in mental hospital admission: Pressures and process. Unpublished manuscript.

Lidz, C. W., Mulvey, E. P., Arnold, R. P., Bennett, N. S., & Kirsch, B. L. (1993). Coercive interactions in a psychiatric emergency room. *Behavioral Sciences and the Law, 11*, 269–280.

Lucksted, A., & Coursey, R. D. (1995). Consumer perceptions of pressure and force in psychiatric treatments. *Psychiatric Services, 46*, 146–152.

McCafferty, G., & Dooley, J. (1990). Involuntary outpatient commitment: An update. *Mental and Physical Disability Law Reporter, 14*, 276–287.

Miller, R. D. (1985). Commitment to outpatient treatment: A national survey. *Hospital and Community Psychiatry, 36*, 265–267.

Miller, R. D. (1987). *Involuntary commitment of the mentally ill in the post-reform era*. Springfield, IL: Charles C. Thomas.

Miller, R. D. (1988). Outpatient civil commitment of the mentally ill: An overview and an update. *Behavioral Sciences and the Law, 6*, 99–118.

Miller, R. D. (1994). Involuntary civil commitment to outpatient treatment. In R. Rosner (Ed.), *Principles and practice of forensic psychiatry* (pp. 118–121). New York: Chapman & Hall.

Miller, R. D., & Fiddleman, P. (1984). Outpatient commitment: Treatment in the least restrictive environment? *Hospital and Community Psychiatry, 35,* 147–151.

Mulvey, E. P., Geller, J. L., & Roth, L. H. (1987). The promise and peril of involuntary outpatient commitment. *American Psychologist, 42,* 571–584.

National Center for State Courts' Institute on Mental Disability and the Law (1986). Guidelines for involuntary civil commitment. *Mental and Physical Disability Law Reporter, 10,* 409–514.

Reed, S. C., & Lewis, D. A. (1990). The negotiation of voluntary admission in Chicago's state mental hospitals. *Journal of Psychiatry and Law, 18,* 137–163.

Robitscher, J. (1976). Moving patients out of hospitals—In those interest? In P. I. Ahmed & S. C. Plog (Eds.), *State mental hospitals: What happens when they close?* (pp. 141–175). New York: Plenum Press.

Rogers, A. (1993). Coercion and "voluntary" admission: An examination of psychiatric patient views. *Behavioral Sciences and the Law, 11,* 259–268.

Scheid-Cook, T. L. (1991). Outpatient commitment as both social control and least restrictive alternative. *Sociological Quarterly, 32,* 43–60.

Scheid-Cook, T. L. (1993). Controllers and controlled: An analysis of participant constructions of outpatient commitment. *Sociology of Health and Illness, 15,* 179–198.

Schmidt, M. J., & Geller, J. L. (1989). Involuntary administration of medication in the community: The judicial opportunity. *Bulletin of the American Academy of Psychiatry and Law, 17,* 283–292.

Shelton v. Tucker, 364 U.S. 479 (1960).

Stefan, S. (1987). Preventive commitment: The concept and its pitfalls. *Mental and Physical Disability Law Reporter, 11,* 288–302.

Swartz, M. S., Burns, B. J., Hiday, V. A., George, L. K., Swanson, J., & Wagner, H. R. (1995). New directions in research on involuntary outpatient commitment. *Psychiatric Services, 46,* 381–385.

Toews, J., el-Guebaly, N., & Leckie, A. (1981). Patients' reactions to their commitment. *Canadian Journal of Psychiatry, 26,* 251–254.

Toews, J., el-Guebaly, N., Leckie, A., & Harper, D. (1984). Patients' attitudes at the time of their commitment. *Canadian Journal of Psychiatry, 29,* 590–595.

Van Putten, R. A. Santiago, J. M., & Berren, M. R. (1988). Involuntary outpatient commitment in Arizona: A retrospective study. *Hospital and Community Psychiatry, 39,* 953–958.

Wood, W. D., & Swanson, D. A. L. (1985). Use of outpatient treatment during civil commitment: Law and practice in Nebraska. *Journal of Clinical Psychology, 41,* 723–728.

Wyatt v. Stickney, 325 F. Suppl. 781 (M.D. Ala. 1971).

Zanni, G., & deVeau, L. (1986). Inpatient stays before and after outpatient commitment. *Hospital and Community Psychiatry, 37,* 941–942.

PART II

COERCION AND TREATMENT
THE COMMUNITY
PROVIDER'S PERSPECTIVE

CHAPTER 3

COERCION AND TENACIOUS TREATMENT IN THE COMMUNITY
APPLICATIONS TO THE REAL WORLD

RONALD J. DIAMOND

Coercion in community-based programs has become an increasing concern (Parrish, 1992). Much of this concern has coincided with the development of assertive (or aggressive) community treatment programs. Prior to active community outreach teams, attempts to coerce the behavior of clients living in the community were limited by practical realities. Clients in traditional mental health systems always had the option of just not showing up. It is true that clients could be threatened with rehospitalization under court order, but enforcing such orders required cooperation from police, who typically had little interest in searching for a mentally ill client who had not committed any crime (Cesnik & Puls, 1977).

RONALD J. DIAMOND • Department of Psychiatry, University of Wisconsin Hospital, Madison, Wisconsin 53792–2475.

Coercion and Aggressive Community Treatment: A New Frontier in Mental Health Law, edited by Deborah L. Dennis and John Monahan. Plenum Press, New York, 1996.

The development of Program for Assertive Community Treatment (PACT), assertive community treatment (ACT) teams, and a variety of similar mobile, continuous treatment programs has made it
possible to coerce a wide range of behaviors in the community (Test &
Stein, 1972). The staff on these ACT teams can visit clients who miss
appointments or, if needed, go to a client's apartment on a daily basis
to ensure that medication is being taken. Staff often have regular communication with landlords, families, and employers. The ACT teams
can apply to the Social Security Administration to get a financial
payee assigned to control the client's Supplemental Security Income
(SSI) money, or apply for a guardianship to control other aspects of
the client's life. The involvement of the treatment team in all aspects
of the client's life and with all elements of the client's support system
is responsible both for the effectiveness of these teams and for their
potential coerciveness.

These mobile treatment teams are, in essence, a new technology
that raises many ethical issues not previously perceived as a problem
in the community (Diamond & Wikler, 1985; Curtis & Hodge, 1995).
What should be the appropriate goals of community-based treatment
for persons with serious and persistent mental illness? Is stability
enough, or is something more than stability needed to help our clients
make life worth living? Whose goals should be considered—how
much say should clients have in setting goals for their own life? How
much say should the client's family, or the rest of society, have in setting goals? What kind of role relationships do we want to be in with
our clients? These issues concerning the appropriate place of paternalism are closely connected to decisions on the appropriate use of
coercion in community settings.

It is easy to argue in the abstract that we should always place
our clients' goals first. Unfortunately, when working with real people, these issues become very confused. For a client with a history of
many relapses and rehospitalizations, the family's demands for maintained supervision or no medication reduction often seem legitimate—even when the client strongly disagrees. Alan Rosen, a well-
known Australian community psychiatrist, outlines the differences
between working on the high ground and working in the swamp. On
the high ground, questions are carefully asked so that research can
provide clear answers. Ethical principles are well defined. Decisions
are clear and pristine. Everything is easy because you can see into the
distance. Down in the swamp, everything is dirty and mucky. Lines
do not stay straight, questions are complex, and research gives ambiguous answers. Unfortunately, almost everyone lives in the swamp,

and the swamp is where all of the important questions are to be found. One can believe that it is important to support the consumer/client's own goals, important to be a client advocate, and important to avoid being an agent of social control. When working with real people in the real world, however, it is frequently hard to be clear how to make decisions based on these values. Clinicians are often confronted with the need to make decisions in the face of competing goals and concerns.

This chapter will discuss (1) paternalism as the basis of coercion in most clinical situations, (2) coercion and the range of coercive interventions available in the community, (3) court-ordered treatment as the most extreme end of the continuum of coercive interventions, and (4) how the need for coercion can be decreased.

PATERNALISM IN ASSERTIVE COMMUNITY TREATMENT PROGRAMS

Paternalism has been a part of assertive community treatment from its very beginning. In the original PACT research project that began more than 20 years ago in Madison, Wisconsin, staff from a nearby state hospital provided community-based treatment for clients who would otherwise have been committed to that same state hospital (Stein & Test, 1980). Paternalism was to a large extent accepted with little question. All the clients would have been coerced had they been hospitalized, and whatever the community-based team did was considered less coercive than the alternative.

In the early stages of PACT, consumer empowerment was not a serious consideration (Chamberlin, Rogers, & Sneed, 1989). Although the original model attempted to build on the client's strengths, it was designed to "do" for the client what the client could not do for himself or herself. Staff were assumed to know what the client "needed." Even the goal of getting clients paid employment was a staff-driven value that was at times at odds with the client's own preferences (Russert & Frey, 1991). Current assertive treatment programs continue to be influenced by traditions that arose from this early history. Paternalism continues to be reinforced by mandates from the community to "control" the behavior of otherwise disruptive clients or at the least to decrease need for psychiatric hospitalization by keeping these clients stable in the community.

Twenty years ago, paternalism was not a significant concern and was rarely discussed if a program was successful in keeping clients out of the hospital, if it improved client's quality of life as the staff understood it, or if staff were "doing good things." Our current concern about the limits and justification of paternalism is based on a deeper examination of values and an attempt to inject a sense of humility into what we are doing as clinicians (Kalinowski, 1992; Freund, 1993; Everett & Nelson, 1992). It is an acknowledgment that what we think is best for a client may not give us the entire answer to what we should be doing. There is recognition that paternalism, even well intentioned, can interfere with the client's own sense of personal effectiveness and rehabilitation.

This is not to argue that paternalism can be entirely dismissed. Many ACT teams are willing or even targeted to work with clients who may initially not want any services, yet have dramatically demonstrated through multiple hospitalizations or arrests that they cannot maintain themselves in the community without help. It is not unusual for an ACT team to continue to visit a client and attempt to establish a relationship despite initial protests from the potential client to "stay away." The relationship thus often starts off from a paternalistic premise of involving client in treatment for their own good. To stop the "revolving door" of repeated psychiatric hospitalizations, staff may initially feel the need to make sure that rent is paid from the client's SSI check or that food money is budgeted to last throughout the month.

Despite the paternalism inherent in these programs, many community-based programs have been working to redefine the basic relationship between staff and client from one that is paternalistic to one that is more collaborative. Assertive community treatment is changing to tenacious community treatment. This is not just a question of semantics, but an attempt to refocus on the nature of the relationship between staff and client and increasing interest in making treatment programs and staff behavior more client-centered. Staff may need to continue to establish and maintain a relationship over a client's objection, but as much as possible treatment focuses on the client's own goals and involves the consumer in all aspects of treatment planning. These "new-generation" ACT teams are typically more willing to take risks to support client decisions and to demonstrate more concern over issues such as autonomy. Increasingly, staff in ACT teams struggle between being "too paternalistic" and abandoning clients to live with the consequences of their own decisions when their lives have been devastated by an illness that at times makes it extremely difficult for them to make appropriate decisions.

COERCION IN THE COMMUNITY

There are a number of different justifications for coercion (Wertheimer, 1993). Police commonly use maintenance of safety and public order as legitimate justifications for coercion. Treatment programs, on the other hand, typically use paternalism to justify coercion. Mental health staff have a clear obligation to do what they can to prevent violence toward others, but their primary concern is to do what they feel is best for their client.

Coercion is much more than just court-ordered treatment. A National Institute of Mental Health (NIHM) roundtable that included consumers, families, and mental health professionals considered coercion to be "a wide range of actions taken without consent of the individual involved" (Blanch & Parrish, 1939). Coercion exists on a continuum—from friendly persuasion to interpersonal pressure to control of resources to use of force (Lucksted & Coursey, 1995). Mental health commitment and other court-ordered treatment is thus just the extreme end of the spectrum of pressures or restrictions that makes up coercion. Coercion based on a court order is relatively rare, while coercion of the type included in the NIMH roundtable definition is extremely common.

In Madison, Wisconsin, only a minority of people that the police bring into the emergency services unit of the mental health center end up being hospitalized under a commitment order. Most of the people either go back to their own home, go to a crisis home, are given shelter in a nearby hotel, stay temporarily with family or friends, or agree to a "voluntary" hospitalization. All the outpatient options include follow-up mental health services. Considerable persuasion or coercion may have been applied to some of these clients, either under the threat of an emergency commitment or through other kinds of pressures such as use of resources (see Chapter 1).

For example, the client may be allowed to go back to his apartment rather than being hospitalized if he agrees to start taking medication, or allows his family to be contacted, or agrees to a follow-up visit the next day. A client who does not want to return home may be allowed access to a resource such as a crisis home if she takes medication, or the crisis team may pay for a motel room if the client agrees to let the treatment team temporarily control how he spends his next SSI check.

Controlling a client's behavior by controlling resources is commonly used in community-based treatment programs. When clients are told that they can leave the hospital only if they agree to live in a group home, the coercion is fairly blatant. The coercion is more subtle if a client is told that he can live anywhere he wants, but the only available place for him to live is a group home. Often, what is meant is that there is no other "appropriate" place for the person to live and that the only place that staff feel is an appropriate discharge residence is the group home.

The situation becomes more complicated when the treatment staff support the client's own choice of where to live, but because of low income and lack of housing subsidies the only affordable option is a bed in a group home. A lack of resources may be unfortunate but is not necessarily coercion—many of us lack the resources to live where we want and do what we want. The issue in many cases, however, is more than just a limitation of resources. Policy decisions that make beds available in group homes rather than making subsidies available to support people in their own apartments reflect decisions about where and in what kind of settings people with a mental illness should live. Group homes are funded because that is where people "should" live; that is where they will "do best." Use of resources in this way is clearly paternalistic and can be considered coercive in that resources are allocated so as to force people to live in particular places.

Housing for persons with psychiatric disabilities often comes with special rules (Segal & Aviram, 1978). Group homes and other congregant living arrangements often specify that residents must be out of the house during the afternoon or that they are not allowed to entertain overnight guests even if they have a room of their own. Often, a client living in housing controlled by the mental health system does not even have a key to his or her own home, and mental health staff regularly enter the client's home and bedroom without permission. Even when clients do have their own apartments, housing is often contingent on continuing in a particular treatment program or continuing to take medication. Clients can be evicted from housing with little due process protection for reasons that would never lead to eviction for someone without a mental illness. This can all be considered coercion—control of a person's behavior without the person's consent.

The other resource, besides housing, that is commonly used to coerce behavior is money. A significant number of the clients in the community support programs in Dane County, Wisconsin, where I work have been assigned a financial payee who controls their SSI or Social Security Disability Insurance (SSDI) income. If a client is on either SSI or SSDI and has repeatedly had serious crises related to poor financial decisions, staff can apply to the Social Security Administration to have a financial payee assigned who then controls the person's entitlement money (Brotman & Muller, 1990) (see also Chapter 7). It is to be hoped that a number of noncoercive steps will have been taken first, including voluntary assistance with budgeting and other kinds of collaborative problem solving, but both client and staff know that a financial payee is an option that can be imposed with little due process protection.

This kind of coercion can be extremely effective in helping to stabilize someone in the community. The use of a payee can ensure that rent and utilities are paid. At times, money can be used to provide the client a degree of structure in the community. For example, the payee can forward money to the treatment program that staff will use to go grocery shopping with the client or arrange for vouchers that the client can use at specific restaurants or a laundromat. Obtaining spending money can be made to some degree dependent on participating in other parts of treatment. A client can be required to come in daily to pick up spending money, and can then be pressured by staff to take prescribed medication. Legally, the client can demand the money and refuse the medication, but the pressure to take the required medication in this kind of situation can be enormous.

Control, if it is needed in a community setting, can be kept very focused. While money from SSI or SSDI is controlled with some frequency, money from other sources is rarely controlled. Legally, ethically, and clinically, SSI or SSDI money is commonly treated as different from earned income. Legally, it is extremely easy to have a financial payee assigned to control SSI money, but extremely difficult to have a guardian assigned to control other money. Ethically, staff makes distinctions between money from SSI and money that is "really the client's money." SSI or SSDI can be considered an entitlement given to the recipient to be used however he or she wants. Alternatively, one can consider SSI or SSDI to be provided as part of an implicit social contract to provide for basic necessities of living. Staff who feel that SSI or SSDI is part of this implicit contract will feel more comfortable in taking control of the money to make sure it is used as intended. The same staff that is involved in controlling a client's SSI money may also help the client find a job with the clear understanding that the client can keep and control all money received from work. Clinically, money from SSI or SSDI is also somewhat different from money earned by the client. SSI or SSDI money continues to come, even if it is used to buy drugs or alcohol that increases the client's behavioral difficulty. Money earned by work can also be used to buy drugs or alcohol, but this kind of problem rapidly takes care of itself without any need for staff intervention. If a client is too "stoned" or intoxicated to go to work, he will earn less money and subsequently have less money to buy drugs. Clients either learn to control their drug and alcohol use or lose their jobs and stop having money available to buy the drugs and alcohol anyway.

While control of housing and control of money are the most common and obvious forms of coercion in the community, other kinds of control are also possible. An important part of the effectiveness of modern community support programs lies in their ability to coordinate all parts of the client's treatment and support system. This process may include communication with other treaters, friends, family, landlords, employers, family physician, or minister. This communication, even when done with the client's permission, allows enormous pressure to be applied for the client to take medication, stay in treatment, live in a particular place, or "follow the plan" in any number of ways. This pressure can be almost as coercive as the hospital in controlling behavior, but with fewer safeguards.

Staff often justify a given intrusion into a client's life by asking themselves whether the proposed restriction on the client is likely to prevent more severe restrictions in the future. For example, if taking control of money will keep the person out of the hospital and in the community where he has more choices, taking control of money may be justified. Similarly, forcing a client to take medication may be justified if doing so will allow the client to have more control over many other spheres of his life. Staff may justify limiting a client's autonomy in a particular way if they feel this will increase the client's autonomy in other ways or in the future. This paternalism must be balanced by clients' own views on how to maximize their autonomy and their desire to stay in control of their own lives. There is also the problem of agreeing about the severity of a restriction (Hoffman & Foust, 1977; Gardner et al., 1993; Byalin, 1993). For example, some clients may feel that forced medication is more restrictive than prolonged hospitalization.

COURT-ORDERED TREATMENT—THE EXTREME END OF THE CONTINUUM

Court-ordered treatment, be it hospital- or community-based commitment, is the most extreme use of coercion and thus attracts the most attention. In most jurisdictions, the finding of dangerousness either to self or others is required whether the commitment is to a hospital or to the community. Mental health commitment and other court-ordered treatments are commonly used even in treatment systems that are trying to be more client-centered and less coercive. In Dane County, there has been a continuing decrease in mental health commitments over the past ten years.* There is surprisingly little data about the frequency of court-ordered coercion in different jurisdictions.

In Wisconsin, mental health commitment is to a county human services board rather than to a hospital. This procedure means that a client might initially require a brief hospitalization, but may continue on a commitment order in the community for several months. While there are problems and limitations with any commitment, either to a hospital or in the community, extending commitment into the community may help get some clients out of the "revolving door" (Appelbaum, 1986; Hiday & Scheid-Cook, 1991; Schwartz, Vingiano, & Bezirganian, 1988; Tavolaro, 1992). Community commitment, within the context of a good community-based treatment system, can allow a period of community stability to develop so that the client can make more appropriate decisions, as the following two case illustrations demonstrate.

> Susan was a 28-year-old woman with a history of many psychiatric hospitalizations. She responded well to medication in the hospital, but always discontinued it immediately upon discharge. She would then rapidly become very disorganized and paranoid, raving at people on the street, threatening her parents, and stopping up her toilet to keep out the voices. When she initially began working with one of the tenacious treatment teams, she was on a mental health commitment that extended for several months after hospital discharge. She initially threatened to discontinue medication and drop out of treatment the day her commitment expired. By the time that date arrived, however, she had an apartment that she liked, a volunteer job that she felt good about, and friends with whom she got together weekly to play cards, and had reestablished a relationship with her parents. As the date for the expiration of her commitment passed, she stopped talking

---

*In 1993, there were 128 involuntary hospitalizations in Dane County, Wisconsin (360,000 population). This number included 12 involuntary hospitalizations from the jail and 11 patients who came into a psychiatric hospital voluntarily but were not allowed to leave because they were felt to be dangerous. Of the involuntary hospitalizations, 33 led to a mental health commitment, 52 led to a settlement agreement, and 8 were converted to a guardianship. With the other 35 patients, the commitment was either dropped by consent of both parties or discontinued by the hearing examiner.

about dropping out of treatment, and staff elected to just avoid talking about the change in her legal status.

The ability to force medication can, at times, make it safer to use less medication. Marge was a 58-year-old woman who would do well for long periods of time, then discontinue her medication and continue to do well for a year or more, but would then inevitably become more reclusive, stop her very active social life, drop out of her many volunteer jobs, stop eating, and eventually be rehospitalized after her condition became medically dangerous. Normally, she was willing to continue taking medication, but in the past had been unwilling to restart medication once this process of decompensation had begun. She was initially placed on a limited guardianship during one of these dysfunctional periods, but it became very evident that she was fully competent when she was functioning at her baseline. She elected to stay on the guardianship because it made it much safer for her to go off the medication, knowing that it might be a year or more before she would really need it, but that it could then be restarted before she had completely decompensated.

Just as there can be positive effects from coercion, coercion can also lead to significant problems (Durham & LaFond, 1985). Commitment laws are typically introduced with the explanation that they will be used only for those few individuals who absolutely need to be coerced for the good of themselves or the community. The data suggest that if commitment laws are available they will be used (Durham, 1985; Hasbe & McRae, 1987). There are a great number of people who are potentially dangerous, and it is difficult if not impossible to predict who in this large group will actually engage in dangerous behavior. There would be legal liability as well as a sense of personal responsibility if a mental health commitment might stop a person from engaging in dangerous behavior and a commitment were not sought. As a result of mental health workers' desire to avoid "false negatives," many people end up with a mental health commitment under a dangerousness standard who would not actually have done anything dangerous if they had not been committed.

In addition to the problem of overuse, five observations can be made about the operation of court-ordered treatment.

1. *Coercion will not lead to more effective treatment if the treatment system itself is inadequate.* In many parts of the United States, there is pressure to change the law to make it easier to commit someone with

a mental illness. It is often argued that easier commitment, and particularly easier community-based commitment, will improve the treatment and outcome for persons who are now dropping out of treatment (Mulvey, Geller, & Roth, 1987). Changing the commitment laws is often seen as a way to keep clients in treatment after they leave the hospital. It is very unclear, however, how coercion will help increase a client's connection with treatment in the community if there is no effective community-based follow-up (Zusman, 1985).

The problem of people with serious mental illness refusing treatment is due more often to failures in the treatment system than to failures in commitment laws (Stein, Diamond, & Factor, 1990; Diamond & Factor, 1994). In most treatment systems, there is little response to clients who fail to follow through. There may be a letter or phone call, but rarely will staff try to find the client in the community or try to establish a treatment program that seriously considers what the client wants for his or her own life. When effective community-based treatment teams are available, the effectiveness of community-based coercion increases, but the need for such coercion is less. This is not to say that community commitment laws are completely ineffective, but they are unlikely to be a panacea when the treatment system is the problem.

2. *What can be coerced in the community is extremely limited.* Most often, attempts are made to coerce medication. In order to force someone to take medication, courts must be willing to order it, clinicians must be comfortable working with a coerced client, and police must be willing to implement the treatment plan. With few exceptions, medication can be forced only by threatening the client with further hospitalization. The only medications that can be truly forced in the community are long-acting injections, and even then the police must be willing to find the client, bring him to the mental health center or hospital, and hold him down for the injection if necessary (Geller, 1987).

3. *There are major interpersonal costs in coercion—in moving from a collaborative to a controlling relationship.* The need for court-ordered treatment is indicative of a failure of the relationship between the client and the treatment staff, at least for that moment in time. It indicates a major discrepancy between what the client feels he or she needs and what clinical staff feel is needed. It can have a major influence on the treatment relationship, an influence that can last for years after the actual event (Blanch & Parrish, 1993). Much of what we try to

do in mental health requires a collaborative relationship—a sense that the clinician and the client are working together toward a commonly defined goal.

If the treatment goal is stability, a controlling relationship through the use of a commitment order may be effective. Increasingly, we are concerned with more than stability. Issues of working with the client to increase his or her quality of life require the development of personal goals, hope, a sense of growth and accomplishment, and a sense of personal autonomy. Control of our own life is important for most of us, and persons with mental illness are no exception. Stability is an important component of quality of life, but not the only component. There is an inherent conflict between encouraging the client to take control of his or her life and instituting a coercive relationship that constantly reinforces the sense that the client really has little control.

4. *Coercion is often a short-term solution to a long-term problem.* Coercion is typically used as part of a response once a crisis has developed. Once police have brought a client into an emergency room in handcuffs, there are often few options available other than an emergency detention. Too often, the client is much too upset to consider other options, the staff in the emergency room is too busy with too many other clients to have the time to develop a noncoercive option, and too often no other options are really available other than hospitalizing the client or letting him or her return to the street. The frequent use of emergency commitment and other coercion is often the result of a crisis-oriented system of care, rather than one based on providing ongoing supports and treatment.

Most episodes involving coercion involve clients with a chronic illness. These clients require an ongoing rather than an episodic approach to treatment. The current treatment system in most of the United States (and indeed most of the world) provides enormous resources to hospitalize mentally ill individuals who are in crisis. When a client is brought in by police, emergency staff are mobilized to respond, hospitalization at many hundreds of dollars a day is made available, and tremendous pressure is brought to stabilize a client's behavior rapidly. This approach often means doing whatever is necessary to get the client to take medication as soon as possible.

Most serious mental illness is persistent. The problem is not just to manage the crisis over the next few days or weeks, but to help the client manage his or her illness over the next few years. The issue is not whether the medication-responsive client is taking medication a week later, but whether the client is taking medication a year later. Coercion tends to be a relatively short-term solution to this long-term problem. Hospitalizing a client under a commitment order and forcibly starting medication may in a particular situation help that person stabilize and agree to continue taking the medication after discharge. In many other situations, however, the process of committing a client to a hospital and forcing medication may make it less likely that the client will be willing to stay connected with the treatment system or continue to take medication after discharge from the hospital. A commitment may get the client back on medication rapidly, but a more collaborative approach in the community over weeks or months may increase the likelihood that the client will use medication appropriately over the long haul (Diamond, 1983).

5. *Coercion is often used only because other options are not available.* The corollary to this is that coercion could often be avoided if other resources were available. In the emergency room of many hospitals, the only options available for persons in psychiatric crisis are hospitalization or release with little follow-up. Where clients can be offered a range of options, both the frequency of use of coercion and the degree of coercion can be decreased. For example, a client coming into the crisis service in Madison, Wisconsin, can be offered follow-up the next day, overnight accommodations in a nearby hotel, the short-term use of a crisis home (a bedroom in a private home rented by the crisis team), or a variety of other options. Often, a plan can be worked out that feels acceptable to all parties with little sense of coercion. At other times, some degree of coercion is present. A client may agree to stay overnight at a hotel and come back to see the crisis team in the morning rather than go back to his apartment, where he has been arguing with his roommate. The degree of coercion in such cases is less than what would have been imposed if fewer alternatives were available.

The development of these less coercive options takes considerably more staff time than just committing someone to a hospital and requires that alternative resources be available. It may take some hours to establish a relationship with an angry client, bring in the client's family or friends, call around to see what alternatives are available, and work with the client to come up with a collaborative solution. Many clinical situations that initially seem as though commitment will be inevitable can end with a less coercive solution if the staff have the time, resources, training, and attitude to look for alternatives (Factor & Diamond, in press).

A Natural Experiment on the Effect of
Court-Ordered Coercion in the Community

A recent Wisconsin Supreme Court decision led to a natural experiment that allowed data to be collected on the effects of changing from a coercive to a noncoercive approach to treatment. Wisconsin statutes allow several ways of legally coercing treatment in the community. Mental health commitment is not to a hospital, but to the county mental health board. While the first few days or weeks of this commitment may be in a hospital, it is not unusual for a client to be discharged from the hospital and continued under commitment in the community for several additional months.

Alternatively, clients who are adjudicated to be incompetent can have a guardianship assigned. A limited guardianship can be assigned for purposes of making medication-related decisions for persons who are adjudicated as incompetent only in this one area. As of October 1992, 129 people were on guardianships for mental illness in Dane County, of whom 87 were on limited guardianship for medications. Most of the individuals on limited guardianships had schizophrenia and were living in the community in their own apartments or homes. In October 1992, the Wisconsin Supreme Court ruled that limited guardianships could not be used to coerce the use of psychotropic medications. (The law governing limited guardianships has since been rewritten, and guardians can again coerce the use of medication by court order.) Ten months after the court ruling, follow-up data were collected on clients who had previously been on a limited guardianship.

Of the total group of 87 who had been on limited guardianship, 16 clients were reported to have had difficulty following the termination of coerced medication. When initially questioned, staff felt that most of the problems incurred by these clients could have been avoided if the coercive force of the guardianship had still been in place. Often, clients went through transient difficulties before restarting their medication voluntarily. For example, staff would say things like, "John went off medication and got really crazy for a while before he finally decided to take medication voluntarily, and now he's doing fine. He didn't lose his job." Or, "Susan stopped coming in and we had to go after her—it was hard to work with her for a while. Thank God she stabilized and she didn't have to go back to the hospital." It seemed, in retrospect, that many of the problems identified by staff were part of the conversion process from a more coercive to a more collaborative treatment relationship. Few of these difficult periods led to longer-term problems.

On reassessment, it appeared that 6 of these clients, approximately 7% of the entire group of people on limited guardianships, had more significant relapses, either hospitalization or other major life disruptions, that seemed connected to medication noncompliance that was in turn related to the change in guardianship. This natural experiment can simultaneously be used to justify the need for coercion and to justify that coercion is probably unnecessary for the vast majority of clients to whom it is applied. Over the 10-month follow-up, most clients had few problems after coercion was discontinued. It also appears, however, that a small but significant number of clients who had been doing well with coercion got into difficulty once it was discontinued.

There are significant limitations to this "experiment." The survey may have missed some clients who got into difficulty, the outcomes were anecdotal, and the follow-up was only 10 months. It is unclear to what extent all the clients in this group really knew their rights and knew that they could now refuse medication. It is also important to remember that these clients were in a comprehensive community-based system of care and had a significant, ongoing relationship with staff. This study was about what happened when coercion was discontinued, not what would happen if coercion had not initially been used. The initial period of coercion may have been important in initially stabilizing the person in the community, even if it was no longer needed to maintain that stability. It is also clear that terminating a court order does not stop a whole range of persuasion and pressure that staff use to encourage clients to take prescribed medication.

DECREASING THE NEED FOR COERCION

Given the problems inherent in coercion, it would seem important to do everything possible to decrease the need for court-ordered treatment. Many states are discussing changes that would make it easier to commit people, under the assumption that doing so will get more people with serious illness into the treatment system earlier. Much of the pressure to change the commitment laws seems to come from areas where the current mental health treatment system is inadequate. As already discussed, commitment laws and other kinds of coercion will not work if the treatment system is not both effective and available. If treatment designed to meet the real needs of persons with mental illness is available, many previously "treatment-refusing" individuals will accept help. There are at least five ways that a treatment system can minimize the need for coercion (Blanch & Parrish, 1993).

1. *Develop a continuous range of service options.* Too often, we offer a person in crisis one kind of treatment and consider him or her a "treatment refuser" if he or she rejects that one option. We call clients "treatment-resistant" if they refuse hospitalization or refuse to take prescribed medication. Many of us would refuse hospitalization on a locked ward of a state hospital, no matter how much distress we are in. Many clients will instead accept hospitalization on an open, unlocked hospital unit, especially if it is physically nice and staff seem friendly. Other clients who refuse a hospitalization will gladly accept a place to stay for a few days during a crisis, especially if it is decent and comes with supportive people. People who initially refuse medication might be willing to talk to someone or have a cup of coffee with a staff person, and in doing so perhaps establish enough of a trusting relationship to eventually accept medication. The more different options and approaches that we can offer, the more likely will a person in crisis, even if psychotic, paranoid, and afraid, be willing to accept one of them.

2. *Be clear about the goals of coercion.* It is important to be clear about the goals of any clinical intervention, but particularly an intervention that involves coercion. Too often, mental health workers commit a client in reaction to a problem or crisis, without thinking through how the commitment will help. A decision to commit a person to a hospital is merely a decision about where the person will live. It is important to also be clear about what treatment interventions are necessary and whether there are any alternative interventions that might be effective in meeting the same goals (Diamond, 1979). It is also important to consider from the beginning how long the commitment is likely to continue and what will happen after that. The following case illustrates a number of these issues:

> At a recent case conference, staff discussed whether a petition should be filed to initiate the process for forcing Sam to stay in treatment and stay on his medication. Sam was an angry, often threatening man who firmly believed that a large amount of money had been stolen from him by the police. Staff from a mo-

bile community program had begun to establish a relationship with him over the past several months, but he had recently stopped taking his prescribed antipsychotic medication.

On further discussion, staff agreed that there was little evidence that the medication had helped very much, and Sam's behavior had not changed since he stopped taking it. He was generally threatening toward the world, but did not make any specific threats toward any specific person. If anything, when staff tried to pressure Sam to take medication, he became more angry and threatening. It became apparent to staff during the ensuing discussion that medication was not effective enough to justify coercion and that there was little else that coercion would accomplish. He was not so acutely dangerous as to require social control, and there was a large risk that being coercive would interfere with his slowly developing relationship with staff.

3. *Ensure that persons with psychiatric disability have a chance for a decent quality of life.* Hope is important for all of us. It is especially important that people with serious mental illness can have a realistic hope that their life will get better. People with a biologically caused illness can fight to stay in control or can give up. For example, one of my clients used to spend several months every year in a psychotic state on a locked psychiatric unit. She now has her own apartment and a job and is fighting to regain custody of her child. She still hears voices that tell her to "do things," but as she now says, she "has to stay in control"—she now has too much to lose to let herself get that crazy and out of control. She still needs to go to the hospital, but it is typically for a few days or a few weeks and is voluntary. She still takes medication, but she has become skilled in telling staff when she needs more and when she can get by with less. Other clients find that they are much more able to control their behavior when they have something worth keeping—an apartment, a job, friends, or other elements that make their life worth living.

4. *Develop treatment systems that support respectful relationships developed over time.* Most treatment systems are designed to respond to a crisis, but are not designed to support people in ways to avoid a crisis. Resources are available to hospitalize someone who comes into an emergency room saying that the voices are telling him to kill himself. Too often, it is not possible to spend that same money to prevent the next crisis by hiring staff to drop by the same person's apartment to see that he is OK, to help him find decent housing, or to make sure that he knows how to use the bus system. Most important, treatment

systems have traditionally not encouraged the development of long-term, trusting, and respectful relationships (Kanter, 1989). If the focus of most interactions with staff is to pressure a client to take a medication that he does not like, he is likely to feel unheard and distrustful. If staff are willing to take time to develop a relationship and to start that relationship with the client's own goals—be it a better apartment, a better job, a ride to the grocery store, or just someone to talk to—the client is more likely to listen to the staff person's suggestions about medication and everything else. We listen best to people who listen best to us. This kind of listening, especially with people with serious mental illness who find it difficult to connect with people, takes time. After staff and client know each other over years, a different kind of relationship develops than one that starts in a busy emergency room.

5. *Be aware of the values of the treatment system and of how decisions about paternalism or coercion support or interfere with these values.* I have already mentioned that coercion is often a short-term solution to a long-term problem. The issue is not how to get the person to take his or her medication now or for the next week; the issue is how to help this person have a better quality of life over the next few years. If we feel that medication is an important part of this improved quality of life, the issue becomes how we can develop the kind of collaborative relationship that will encourage the client to see medication similarly to the way we see it. In this process, we will need to understand the world more from the client's point of view. Paternalism and coercion may be necessary, but it is important to be aware of how they promote or interfere with long-term goals. An important part of these goals is attention to the relationship between staff and client and support for the client's sense of control over his or her own life.

CONCLUSION

Coercion in the community refers to much more than court-ordered treatment. The hallmark of an assertive community treatment (ACT) team is their involvement in all parts of a client's life. ACT teams often control important resources—example being access to housing or help getting a job—and communicate with many of the people who are important to the client—from family members to landlords. This comprehensive engagement in the client's life allows these programs to be effective, but also gives them the ability to exert sufficient pressure to be coercive. Coercion is not necessarily bad. In specific situations, coercion, either through a court order or implemented through a less formal mechanism, may be necessary to help clients maintain both their stability and their quality of life. At the same time, there are major ethical and clinical problems with coercion and the paternalism that underlies it.

Historically, mental health staff have assumed that they know what is best for their clients. This kind of paternalism, by its very nature, limits clients' autonomy and implicitly encourages them to settle for stability rather than growth. It now appears that many clients will achieve a higher quality of life if helped to achieve their own goals, rather than being forced to follow paths laid down by a therapist or case manager. There has been growing interest in taking seriously the ideas that in most cases clients know best what they need and that the job of the mental health system is to help clients achieve goals that they themselves have set.

To take this view is not to discard all paternalism. Many of the clients initially referred to ACT teams would refuse all services if the team were not tenacious in continuing to engage until a relationship was established. Other clients may need some limits on their autonomy, be it persuasion to take medication or control over their SSI money, or even more severe restrictions on autonomy would be likely to ensue. Increasingly, however, the assumptions that underlie traditional assertive community treatment have been called into question. Historically, ACT teams made decisions for their clients and slowly gave back control once staff felt is safe to do so. "New-generation" assertive community treatment programs start with the value that it is the client's life and that the client should be in control of his or her own life. The core issue in relationship with the client is collaboration rather than control, and the goals are those of the client rather than those of the staff.

Assertive community treatment will inevitably continue to have some elements of paternalism. Coercion, broadly defined, will continue to be a part of at least some of the therapeutic interventions. Assertive community treatment is neither needed nor best for everyone. Other treatment models are available that seem effective for some clients, without the inherently paternalistic overlay. Some clients, however, will have both a better and a more stable life when given the special supports available only through an ACT team. Some of these clients will need a team that is willing to be tenacious in maintaining a relationship even over the client's objection. At times, the team will need to provide help that the client may not want and may even need to enforce a structure that the client objects to. ACT teams will continue to struggle with the problems raised by paternalism and coercion. These issues will always be more difficult for teams that "go to the client," rather than working with clients willing to come in to treatment. At the same time, many ACT teams now find that they can function effectively while being much less paternalistic and less coercive than in the original model of assertive community treatment. A clear articulation of the underlying ethical and clinical principles of these "new teams" does not yet exist. The underlying ideology of the new teams is likely to develop out of the cauldron of actual clinical work. It is clear that assertive community treatment is no longer a single entity, but rather is an admixture of different ways of working with clients, different degrees of tenaciousness, different uses of coercion, and different approaches to the problem of paternalism.

REFERENCES

Appelbaum, P. S. (1986). Outpatient commitment: The problems and the promise. *American Journal of Psychiatry, 143,* 1270–1272.

Blanch, A. K., & Parrish, J. (1993). Reports of three roundtable discussions on involuntary interventions. *Psychiatric Rehabilitation and Community Support Monograph, 1,* 1–42.

Brotman, A. W., & Muller, J. J. (1990). The therapist as representative payee. *Hospital and Community Psychiatry, 41,* 167–171.

Byalin, K. (1993). In defense of "restrictiveness": A critical concept in consumer-oriented treatment planning. *Journal of Psychosocial Rehabilitation, 16,* 93–100.

Cesnik, B., and Puls, M. (1977). Law enforcement and crisis intervention services: A critical relationship. *Suicide and Life-Threatening Behavior, 7,* 211–215.

Chamberlin, J., Rogers, J. A., & Sneed, C. S. (1989). Consumers, families and community support systems. *Psychosocial Rehabilitation Journal, 12,* 93–106.

Curtis, L. C., & Hodge, M. (1995). Old standards, new dilemmas: Ethics and boundaries in community support services. *Psychosocial Rehabilitation Journal* (in press).

Diamond, R. J. (1979). The role of the hospital in treating chronically disabled. In L. Stein (Ed.), *New directions in mental health services* (pp. 45–55). San Francisco: Jossey-Bass.

Diamond, R. J. (1983). Enhancing medication use in schizophrenic patients. *Journal of Clinical Psychiatry, 44,* 7.

Diamond, R. J., & Factor, R. M. (1994). Treatment resistant patients or a treatment-resistant system? *Hospital and Community Psychiatry, 45,* 197.

Diamond, R. J., & Wikler, D. I. (1985). Ethical problems in the community treatment of the chronically mentally ill. In L. I. Stein & M. A. Test (Eds.), *The training in community living model—A decade of experience* (pp. 85–93). San Francisco: Jossey-Bass, *New Directions in Mental Health Services.*

Durham, M. L. (1985). Implications of need-for-treatment laws: A study of Washington State's involuntary treatment act. *Hospital and Community Psychiatry, 36,* 975–977.

Durham, M. L., & LaFond, J. Q. (1985). The empirical consequences and policy implications for broadening the statutory criteria for civil commitment. *Yale Law and Policy Review, 3*, 395–446.

Everett, B., & Nelson, A. (1992). We're not cases and you're not managers: An account of a client–professional partnership developed in response to the "borderline" diagnosis. *Journal of Psychosocial Rehabilitation, 15*, 77–86.

Factor, R. M., & Diamond, R. J. (in press). Emergency psychiatry and crisis resolution. In J. V. Vaccaro & G. H. Clark (Eds.), *Community psychiatry, a practitioner's manual.* Washington, DC: American Psychiatric Press.

Freund, P. D. (1993). Professional role(s) in the empowerment process: "Working with" mental health consumers. *Journal of Psychosocial Rehabilitation, 16*, 65–73.

Gardner, W., Hoge, S. K., Bennett, N., Roth, L. H., Lidz, C. W., Monahan, J., & Mulvey, E. P. (1993). Two scales for measuring patients' perceptions for coercion during mental hospital admission. *Behavioral Sciences and the Law, 11*, 307–321.

Geller, J. L. (1987). The quandaries of enforced community treatment and unenforceable outpatient commitment statutes. *Journal of Psychiatry and the Law, 17*, 288–302.

Greeman, M., & McClellan, T. A. (1985). The impact of a more stringent commitment code in Minnesota. *Hospital and Community Psychiatry, 36*, 990–992.

Hasbe, T., & McRae, J. (1987). A ten-year study of civil commitments in Washington State. *Hospital and Community Psychiatry, 38*, 983–987.

Hiday, V. A., & Scheid-Cook, T. (1991). Outpatient commitment for "revolving door" patients: Compliance and treatment. *Journal of Nervous and Mental Disease, 179*, 83–88.

Hoffman, P., & Foust, L. (1977). Least restrictive treatment of the mentally ill: A doctrine in search of its senses. *San Diego Law Review, 14*, 1100–1154.

Kalinowski, C. (1992). Beyond compliance: An approach to client-directed prescribing of psychotropic medication. Unpublished manuscript.

Kanter, J. (1989). Clinical case management: Definition, principles, components. *Hospital and Community Psychiatry, 40*, 361–368.

Lucksted, A., & Coursey, R. D. (1995). Consumer perceptions of pressure and force in psychiatric treatments. *Psychiatric Services, 46*, 146–152.

Marx, A. J., Text, M. A., & Stein, L. I. (1973). Extro-hospital management of severe mental illness. *Archives of General Psychiatry, 29*, 505–511.

Morse, S. J. (1982). A preference for liberty: The case against involuntary commitment of the mentally disordered. *California Law Review, 70*, 54–106.

Mulvey, E. P., Geller, J. L., & Roth, L. H. (1987). The promise and peril of involuntary outpatient commitment. *American Psychologist*, 571–584.

Parrish, J. (Ed.). (1992). Proceedings of roundtable discussion on the use of involuntary interventions: Multiple perspectives. Report of a meeting held in Washington, DC, October 1–2, 1992.

Russert, M. G., & Frey, J. L. (1991). The PACT vocational model: A step into the future. *Psychosocial Rehabilitation Journal, 14*, 7–18.

Schwartz, H. I., Vingiano, W., & Bezirganian, C. (1988). Autonomy and the right to refuse treatment: Patients' attitudes after involuntary medication. *Hospital and Community Psychiatry, 39*, 1049–1054.

Segal, S. P., & Aviram, U. (1978). *The mentally ill in community-based sheltered care.* New York: John Wiley.

Stein, L. I., Diamond, R. J., & Factor, R. M. (1990). A system approach to the care of persons with schizophrenia. In M. J. Herz, S. J. Seith, & J. P. Docherty (Eds.), *Handbook of schizophrenia*, Vol. 4, *Psychosocial treatment of schizophrenia.* Amsterdam: Elsevier.

Stein, L. I., & Test, M. A. (1980). An alternative to mental hospital treatment. I. Conceptual model, treatment program and clinical evaluation. *Archives of General Psychiatry, 37*, 392–397.

Tavolaro, K. B. (1992). Preventive outpatient civil commitment and the right to refuse
treatment: Can pragmatic realities and constitutional requirements be reconciled?
Medical Law, 11, 249–267.

Test, M. A., & Stein, L. I. (1972). Practical guidelines for the community treatment of
markedly impaired patients. *Community Mental Health Journal, 12*, 72.

Wertheimer, A. (1993). A philosophic examination of coercion for mental health issues.
Behavioral Sciences and the Law, 11, 239–258.

Zusman, J. (1985). APA's model commitment law and the need for better mental health
services. *Hospital and Community Psychiatry, 36*, 978–980.

CHAPTER 4

"COERCION" AND LEVERAGE IN CLINICAL OUTREACH

EZRA SUSSER AND BRENDA ROCHE

This chapter addresses the issues of coercion and leverage in clinical outreach to persons who are homeless and have a severe mental illness. The terms coercion and leverage refer to a broad array of strategies that are used to pressure patients to adhere to treatments or social acts prescribed by outreach clinicians. Coercion in the more narrow sense of "forced action" is not the primary focus. Therefore, we shall henceforth use the term *leverage* to refer to this broad array of strategies.

In clinical outreach, the use of tolerant approaches is openly discussed, while the use of various forms of leverage is generally not. The reluctance to discuss this aspect of clinical work may be due to the negative connotations that surround coercion. There is a tendency to equate any leverage with coercion and the more extreme examples of involuntary treatment such as forced psychiatric treatments and the abuse of patient rights (Frank, 1986).

EZRA SUSSER and BRENDA ROCHE • Division of Epidemiology and Community Psychiatry, New York State Psychiatric Institute, Columbia Presbyterian Medical Center, New York, New York 10032.

Coercion and Aggressive Community Treatment: A New Frontier in Mental Health Law, edited by Deborah L. Dennis and John Monahan. Plenum Press, New York, 1996.

Yet the use of leverage in clinical treatment has a more extensive and complex history. Almost all clinical work involves some degree of leverage (Bellows-Blakely, 1985; Aviram, 1990; Geller, 1991). For instance, limit-setting and strong persuasion are common practices in both inpatient and outpatient settings. Moreover, it is rarely the case that clinical treatments are purely voluntary or involuntary. The distinction is at best blurred rather than sharp. The reluctance to discuss coercion is understandable, but not useful. Rather, it serves to hinder any critical examination of when its use is legitimate and appropriate and when its use is questionable, raising ethical and legal questions.

We propose that when balanced with gentle and supportive techniques, leverage can play a valuable, and at times critical, role in shaping the treatment plan. It often remains, however, the unspoken part of clinical work. In this chapter, we seek to open a dialogue about the use of coercion as a treatment strategy in clinical outreach and the balance of these techniques with more tolerant approaches.

BACKGROUND

The current research literature on coercion is limited in both scope and conceptual framework. Theoretical discussions tend to be broad, perhaps too broad, debating paternalism vs. patient autonomy (Carroll, 1993; Rubenstein, 1986; Wertheimer, 1993; Mulvey, Geller, & Roth, 1987). Yet, in our impression, neither of these choices is satisfactory when taken to an extreme. Neither is effective in ensuring the patient's right to available treatment.

The empirical literature, on the other hand, remains narrowly defined. Considerable attention is placed on the use of leverage in inpatient settings involving extreme interventions such as involuntary hospitalizations (Abroms, 1968; Frank, 1986). Yet beyond these extreme forms of coercion, there is a lack of openness in discussing coercion.

Very little attention has been paid to the use of coercion in outpatient treatment, even though it is currently the primary locus of treatment for even severely disabled patients (Witheridge, 1991; Aviram, 1990). What little information exists about outpatient treatment and coercion tends to fall along the lines of enforced or mandatory care and involuntary commitment (Diamond & Winkler, 1985; Geller, 1990, 1992; Mulvey et al., 1987; Bursten, 1986).

As an example, Geller (1990) describes a system of monitoring treatment compliance whereby if medication levels drop during the outpatient period, the individual is automatically readmitted. He proposed that this practice would reduce recidivism among chronic psychiatric patients. Such approaches have shown some success in reducing rehospitalization and increasing adherence to outpatient treatments (Geller, 1991, 1992; Hiday, 1989). There remains little information on the more subtle ways in which clinicians can and do apply pressure in outpatient treatment to effect changes in patient behavior (Diamond & Winkler, 1985).

The use of coercion in clinical outreach programs has received even less attention in the research literature. It has been highlighted as an issue, however, within the popular media. This was clearly illustrated in the case of Joyce Brown (also known as Billie Boggs) in New York City (Cournos, 1989; Marcos, 1991). Ms. Brown was involuntarily committed to hospital as a result of a city policy introduced in 1987 to address the increasing numbers of homeless mentally ill in New York.

The policy aimed to address individuals who demonstrated significant personal neglect and were considered to be at risk to themselves or others. This policy enabled mobile outreach teams, following a preliminary evaluation, to order the police to involuntarily transport a patient to a hospital for further psychiatric evaluation (Marcos & Cohen, 1986; Marcos, 1991; Marcos et al., 1990). Prior to actual involuntary commitment, the patient would be evaluated three times within a 48-hour period, by three independent psychiatrists.

Joyce Brown was the first person to experience involuntary hospitalization as a result of this policy. Furthermore, her case received considerable attention in the popular media as a result of a lawsuit she filed against the city with the support of the American Civil Liberties Union, which she won (although she later lost, following an appeal by the city) (Marcos, 1991; Cournos, 1989). This case dramatically highlighted the controversies surrounding the use of coercion to involuntarily treat the homeless mentally ill.

However, this case represents the extreme applications of coercion. Models of assertive community treatments, including clinical outreach, rely on the use of more persuasive strategies (Lamb, 1980).

LEVERAGE IN OUTREACH

Outreach programs, particularly with hard-to-reach populations, must rely on innovative and adaptive clinical strategies. For example, among the homeless mentally ill, there may be a distrust of service providers, possibly exacerbated by their life circumstances placing them beyond the realm of traditional clinical services. Outreach with such a population requires a supportive strategy that is gentle and nonthreatening in nature. To achieve such a strategy, the clinician must meet the patient on his or her own turf and strive to be as unintrusive as possible (Susser, Goldfinger, & White, 1990; Susser, Valencia, & Goldfinger, 1992).

Successful clinical outreach relies on a balance between gentle respect and the application of leverage (Susser, 1990; Susser et al., 1992). Persuasive techniques can span a wide range from offering incentives to engaging the client in conversation to limiting setting and insisting on medication compliance as a condition of services (Chen, 1991; Marcos & Cohen, 1986).

Outreach usually begins very gently. Initially, it may involve befriending the client, perhaps offering tangible assistance such as coffee or a sandwich. Gradually, contact is increased over time. The principles that shape clinical work at this point are flexibility and persistence (Susser et al., 1990; Valencia, Susser, & McQuiston, 1993). As this shift in frequency of contact occurs, we often see a change in clinical style, from gentle and tolerant support to a more persuasive and assertive approach. The timing in implementing these shifts is critical to the success of the intervention.

It should be emphasized that over time, tangible incentives give way to less tangible benefits—someone who cares about a person and who will listen to him or her, which can often have a more dramatic effect than tangible incentives. Inherent in this process is the development of trust and even a certain dependency. These elements are especially critical as catalysts in the treatment process. Furthermore, these elements can serve as leverage in fulfilling treatment goals.

FORMS OF LEVERAGE

There are a variety of types of leverage that are used in clinical outreach. Especially important is the emotional dependency that people develop on clinicians, as mentioned above. The threat of a change in or loss of this relationship can be very powerful. Even the implied threat of loss of this relationship can have a powerful effect. In its initial stages, a great deal of outreach involves the offering of incentives to engage clients. Later, clinicians may set limits on these incentives or withhold them to promote adherence to treatment plans. These seemingly dissonant approaches are often used together, although at different stages one may take precedence over the other. Together, these approaches have a powerful impact on the treatment process.

In the more explicit and concrete uses of leverage, three "tangibles" are most often used: money, housing, and the threat of hospitalization.

MONEY

Most case-management programs offer some form of money management to clients. While there are legal avenues that allow clinicians to assume control of a patient's money, these approaches tend to be cumbersome and somewhat ineffectual. More often, programs develop a spectrum of techniques for controlling people's money that are less formal and are dependent upon an understanding between the clinician and the patient (see Chapter 7). For example, the patient may work out a budgeting system with his or her worker or family members. The system is informally worked out and does not give anyone the legal right to withhold money from the patient. It is a "voluntary" arrangement. However, it does enable the clinician to use access to money as a means of leverage in the treatment process.

For example, in situations in which the patient is dealing with substance abuse, the clinician may limit access to money by subtly imposing delays. Ultimately, the worker cannot refuse a patient his or her own money, but the worker can delay access. The barrier that is created between asking for money and getting it can be a powerful deterrent to using the money for drugs or alcohol.

HOUSING

Housing is a second powerful means of leverage. People who are homeless and in outreach programs with an aim toward housing are threatened with stalling the process of finding housing until they go along with what is being suggested.

For example, individuals who abuse drugs or alcohol may find themselves experiencing delays in housing referrals. Most supportive housing programs require that clients demonstrate a commitment to being drug- and alcohol-free, yet many substance-abusing patients are unreceptive to the option of highly structured treatment programs. The clinician may develop a contingency plan with the patient whereby he or she will be referred for housing following adherence to less structured plans, such as attending support groups like Alcoholics Anonymous, entering a short-term detoxification program, or agreeing to regular urine screening. Without some demonstration of a commitment in this area, the clinician may postpone housing placement. The promise of housing referrals then becomes the leverage to pressure the patient to adhere to some form of treatment.

Even after placement in housing programs, the threat of losing housing can be a powerful way to ensure that residents comply with rules and structure (see Chapter 6). Often in such settings, loss of housing is related to resident violence. Understandably, housing programs have a limited number of ways of dealing with violence, and the threat of eviction can be one effective way.

HOSPITALIZATION

Finally, there is the threat of hospitalization. The patient may be offered a choice between outpatient treatment and being taken to the hospital (where he or she would likely be offered the choice of involuntary or "voluntary" hospitalization). Unlike the situation in an emergency room, outreach programs have an advantage of having likely established some relationship with the patient. This rapport increases the likelihood that the patient will accept the option of outpatient treatment.

The process of implementing such leverage remains the subtle and unspoken part of clinical work. We propose that leverage can be a useful part of an integrated clinical strategy. Using leverage does not always imply a loss of autonomy for the patient even with respect to the patient's short-term interests. For instance, with a drug-abusing client, access to money can not only be counterproductive to the treatment process but also cause irreparable damage to the patient's autonomy in a very short time.

For example, the staff in our program are familiar with the case of a man who received a $10,000 back payment from Supplemental Security Income (SSI). He spent the entire $10,000 on cocaine in two weeks, and it virtually ruined his life. If an informal system of money management had been implemented (including the use of money as leverage and delaying access), it may have been ultimately in his best interests.

As another example, while leverage may be used to hospitalize a patient, the process of hospitalization rather than the fact of hospitalization may be critical in the end for patient autonomy (see Chapter 1). An outreach worker can accompany and offer support to the patient through this difficult process. In this way, the positive aspects of hospitalization are reinforced and the relationship between the worker and the patient may be improved.

It is also important to recognize that coercion and leverage are often used in conjunction with more gentle approaches, at times simultaneously. The balance that is achieved allows for the continuation of a clinical rapport while permitting the introduction of more goal-oriented treatment.

For example, a Cuban patient who believed in Santeria was under treatment in an outpatient program. Santeria is a religious system that blends African and Catholic beliefs (see Garrison, 1977). A key feature of this system is the belief in spirit possession.

In the course of interviews, the clinician engaged him in long discussions about the history of Santeria and his family's experience with healing. He was immensely proud of his knowledge in this area and felt some validation from the comments of the doctor, nurse, and other clinicians. In the course of these discussions, the clinicians insisted that he resume his lithium medication and, in fact, framed the medication within the medicinal remedies with which he was familiar. Thus, at the same moment that he was enjoying a sense of dignity conveyed by these clinicians, he was implicitly being threatened with the loss of that relationship unless he adhered to the treatment they were prescribing.

To our knowledge, the ethics of these practices have never been systematically addressed in clinical outreach. The answers are not clear-cut. We illustrate these issues with two case examples.

ILLUSTRATIVE CASES

CASE 1

The first example is from a large men's shelter in New York City. A patient had been living in this shelter for more than a decade—never leaving the shelter because of his extreme paranoia (except for fire drills that lasted only a few minutes). His paranoia was so intense that he even refused to sleep in his assigned bed on the drill floor. Instead, he slept on the floor outside the clinical program.

Despite the intensity of his symptoms, the patient was likeable. We believe that he fended off trouble in part by giving a portion of his disability check to gang leaders within the shelter. In addition, he was "adopted" by the kitchen staff. Over a period of 5 years, he worked in the kitchen for a few hours a day.

The on-site clinical program had reached out to this man over many years, and a certain trust and dependency had developed. Gradually, he became a regular client. From a clinical standpoint, however, progress was minimal. He remained actively psychotic and unreceptive to clinical treatment. Over time, the program staff grew frustrated, having worked with this patient for many years with little evidence of clinical progress. Finally, the clinical staff thought his position as a kitchen helper could be used as leverage in treatment.

The program psychiatrist approached the kitchen staff, conveying his belief to them that they were the most important thing in the man's life and that they were the only thing that could help to convince him to begin treatment. On the psychiatrist's advice, the kitchen staff agreed to make the following condition: If the patient would not be willing to take medication, then he would not be able to work in the kitchen. Clearly, this approach involved strong leverage, may have been traumatic, and was very powerful. The patient agreed to take his medication as a result.

What is important to highlight in this case is that it was not the threat alone that had an impact on the patient, it was also the caring and trusting relationship he had developed with the clinical staff. This is illustrated by the sequence of events that took place when the patient agreed to take medication for the first time. He asked for his two favorite outreach program staff to be with him at the time. One held his hand and the other gave him a gentle bear hug because he was so terrified. But he trusted these people, and he was given an injection.

Subsequently, this man's life was entirely transformed. He turned out to be medication-responsive, and the results were dramatic. He reestablished contact with his family, whom he had not seen for ten years. Within three months, he moved out to one of the best community residences in New York City.

Perhaps what is most interesting in this case is that this patient remains very positive about the circumstances that led to his taking medications. Even though he was clearly pressured into accepting treatment, he regards it as a positive decision.

Similar patient perceptions have been documented among psychiatric patients admitted to a hospital setting (Bennett et al., 1993; Hoge et al., 1993; Rogers, 1993). In such situations, a balance has been achieved between the gentle and caring relationship on one hand, and leverage, on the other—a balance whereby the patient may simultaneously recognize the experience as somewhat coercive, yet a confirmation that people care about him or her.

CASE 2

The second case was a woman who lived in one of the most down-and-out single room occupancies in midtown Manhattan. The woman was middle-aged and schizophrenic. She was very paranoid and delusional and dressed in a manner that could best be described as bizarre. Despite this, she was also a very gentle person and was well known in the Times Square area. She spent a lot of time in neighborhood coffee shops, and over time, people got to know and like her.

However, her ability to care for herself was seriously impaired. Her room was absolutely filthy, filled with garbage and rotten meat. While she possessed the necessary skills to clean her room, the garbage was part of her delusional system. Over time, the accumulation resulted in a serious health problem at the hotel. Her room became a haven for rats and mice, and it would have been dangerous for her in the event that she ate any of the rotten food. The hotel finally got to the point where they were ready to evict her if something was not done about the garbage.

An outreach psychiatrist who visited the hotel had gradually developed a relationship with the woman. She had developed a certain dependency on and fondness for the psychiatrist. However, she had never agreed to take medications or have any formal treatment, in part because she was delusional about medications. Eventually, the outreach team offered her a choice between involuntary hospitalization and on-site treatment. Under the threat of hospitalization, which she feared more than anything, she agreed to take a dose of medication and have her room cleaned up.

Over the ensuing months, this woman improved significantly. Her tie to the doctor was, if anything, strengthened, because she understood it was part of caring.

In contrast to the previous case, however, this patient never entirely forgave the outreach team for having forced treatment on her. For her, it was an unwelcome intrusion. Because she had feared hospitalization, but for no other reason, she continued to take medication over the next several months. If the threat was ever withdrawn, she probably would have stopped taking the medication.

These two cases illustrate the subtleties that can be involved in the use of leverage. The programs that are the most caring can also be the most intrusive. Surprisingly, these same programs may be those most oriented to patient autonomy, that is, to patients' having as much choice and freedom as possible in determining their treatment goals. The patients' perceptions of these methods are equally complex. They will depend in part on the amount of choice and control the patient has over the process. At least as important, however, will be the individual's personality, belief system, and personal experience, including those with treatment systems. Moreover, like any other individual's, a patient's views about past experience and possible future experience will change over time.

CONCLUSIONS

In this chapter, we have sought to examine some issues related to the use of coercion and leverage within clinical outreach. What becomes clear from this discussion is the absence of a systematic evaluation of the uses of leverage in such settings. Yet almost all clinical programs rely on the use of leverage as a clinical strategy.

Outreach clinicians should not be encouraged to use coercion indiscriminately. There is a need, however, to recognize the unspoken use of coercion in clinical outreach and to examine whether at times it can be a useful approach in treatment. In this context, coercion does not always translate into the loss of patient autonomy. Rather, it may enable the clinician to use persuasive and assertive interventions in situations in which other approaches are not productive. The results of these interventions may in fact enhance patient autonomy.

REFERENCES

Abroms, G. M. (1968). Setting limits. *Archives of General Psychiatry, 19,* 113–119.
Aviram, U. (1990). Community care of the seriously mentally ill: Continuing problems and current issues. *Community Mental Health Journal, 26* (1), 69–88.
Bellows-Blakely, D. S. (1985). Coercion and countertransference. *Psychiatric Hospital, 16,* 177–181.
Bennett, N. S., Lidz, C. W., Monahan, J., Mulvey, E. P., Hoge, S. K., Roth, L. H., & Gardner, W. (1993). Inclusion, motivation and good faith: The morality of coercion in mental hospital admissions. *Behavioral Sciences and the Law, 11,* 295–306.

Bursten, B. (1986). Posthospital mandatory outpatient treatment. *American Journal of Psychiatry, 143,* 1255–1258.

Carroll, J. S. (1993). Consent to mental health treatment: A theoretical analysis of coercion, freedom, and control. *Behavioral Sciences and the Law, 9,* 129–142.

Chen, A. (1991). Noncompliance in community psychiatry: A review of clinical interventions. *Hospital and Community Psychiatry, 42,* 282–287.

Cournos, F. (1989). Involuntary medication and the case of Joyce Brown. *Hospital and Community Psychiatry, 40,* 736–740.

Diamond, R. J., & Winkler, D. I. (1985). Ethical problems in community treatment of the chronically mentally ill. In L. I. Stein and M. A. Test (Eds.), *The training in community living model: A decade of experience* (pp. 85–93). *New Directions in Mental Health Services,* No. 26. San Francisco: Jossey-Bass.

Frank, L. R. (1986). The policies and practices of American psychiatry are oppressive. *Hospital and Community Psychiatry, 37,* 497–501.

Garrison, V. (1977). Doctor, espiritista, or psychiatrist? Mental health seeking behavior in a Puerto Rican neighborhood of New York City. *Medical Anthropology, 1,* 65–180.

Geller, J. L. (1990). Clinical guidelines for the use of involuntary outpatient treatment. *Hospital and Community Psychiatry, 41,* 749–755.

Geller, J. L. (1991). Rx: A tincture of concern in outpatient treatment? *Hospital and Community Psychiatry, 42,* 1068–1069.

Geller, J. L. (1992). Clinical encounters with outpatient coercion at the CMHC: Questions of implementation and efficacy. *Community Mental Health Journal, 28,* 81–94.

Hiday, V. A. (1989). A follow-up of chronic patients committed to outpatient treatment. *Hospital and Community Psychiatry, 40,* 52–59.

Hoge, S. K., Lidz, C., Mulvey, E., Roth, L., Bennett, N., Siminoff, L., Arnold, R., & Monahan, J. (1993). Patient, family and staff perceptions of coercion in mental hospital admission: An exploratory study. *Behavioral Sciences and the Law, 11,* 281–293.

Lamb, H. R. (1980). Structure: The neglected ingredient of community treatment. *Archives of General Psychiatry, 37,* 1224–1228.

Marcos, L. R. (1991). Taking the mentally ill off the streets: The case of Joyce Brown. *International Journal of Mental Health, 20,* 7–16.

Marcos, L. R., & Cohen, N. L. (1986). Taking the suspected mentally ill off the streets to public general hospitals. *New England Journal of Medicine, 315,* 1158–1161.

Marcos, L. R., Cohen, N. L., Nardacci, D., & Brittain, J. (1990). Psychiatry takes to the streets: The New York City initiative for the homeless mentally ill. *American Journal of Psychiatry, 147*(11), 1557–1561.

Mulvey, E. P., Geller, J. L., & Roth, L. H. (1987). The promise and peril of involuntary outpatient commitment. *American Psychologist, 42,* 571–584.

Rogers, A. (1993). Coercion and "voluntary" admission: An examination of psychiatric patients' views. *Behavioral Sciences and the Law, 11,* 259–267.

Rubenstein, L. S. (1986). Treatment of the mentally ill: Legal advocacy enters the second generation. *American Journal of Psychiatry, 143,* 1264–1269.

Susser, E. (1990). Working with people who are homeless and mentally ill: The role of a psychiatrist. In R. Jahiel (Ed.), *Homelessness: A preventive approach* (pp. 207–217). Baltimore: Johns Hopkins Press.

Susser, E., Goldfinger, S., & White, A. (1990). Some clinical approaches to the homeless mentally ill. *Community Mental Health Journal, 26,* 459–476.

Susser, E., Valencia, E., & Goldfinger, S. (1992). Clinical care of the homeless mentally ill: Strategies and adaptations. In H. R. Lamb, L. Bachrach, & F. Kass (Eds.), *Treating the homeless mentally ill* (pp. 127–140). Washington, DC: American Psychiatric Press.

Valencia, E., Susser, E., & McQuiston, H. L. (in press). Critical time points in the clinical care of homeless mentally ill individuals. In J. Vaccaro & G. Clurke (Eds.), *Community psychiatry: A practitioner's manual*. Washington, DC: American Psychiatric Press.

Wertheimer, A. (1993). A philosophical examination of coercion for mental health issues. *Behavioral Sciences and the Law, 11*, 239–258.

Witheridge, T. F. (1991). The active ingredients of assertive outreach. *New Directions For Mental Health Services, 52*, 47–65.

CHAPTER 5

THE PERILS OF OUTREACH WORK
OVERREACHING THE LIMITS OF PERSUASIVE TACTICS

MARGARITA LOPEZ

Outreach

In this hollow sphere of never-ending night
We work our way through paths into their homes;
Quietly we sneak, most coercive in our sight
To heal the sick, to damn their sorrows some.
Who gives Us leave? Who grants us ministry
To mark the air with words of hope and faith?
What stranger, wrangling in his artistry,
Should take us to his home on rocks of slate?
We cannot but deceive with truths so sweet
They touch as lies; We fool them all.
We pray that at our end we one day meet
That stranger lying hollow to our call.

And yet in all the fooling, fool and fair,
We may grow closer, willing that we dare.

—JULIAN BALL

MARGARITA LOPEZ • 606 East 11th Street, New York, New York 10009.

Coercion and Aggressive Community Treatment: A New Frontier in Mental Health Law, edited by Deborah L. Dennis and John Monahan. Plenum Press, New York, 1996.

As the doors of mental institutions closed behind the thousands of patients who once roamed their corridors, the streets of urban centers around the country became open-air wards for unmedicated and untreated mentally ill people who numbered among the many homeless and destitute in the city streets. This product of failed social and political policies required the development and implementation of new intervention strategies for workers who provided the population of homeless mentally ill clients with sorely needed treatment and support services. This worker became known as the "outreach worker."

The primary mission of this provider was to canvass the streets/wards to identify mentally ill clients in need of medication, treatment, and homes. No longer was the provider's venue a sterile, therapeutic hospital environment; the worker now had to view city streets and parks as the client's home.

The outreach worker necessarily had to invent strategies that would facilitate establishing contact with a prospective client who eschewed any contact with the "outside world" and, for whatever reason, had fled from mental health workers.

To determine whether the tactics or ploys that were designed to reach out to these clients are coercive, one must acknowledge that the outreach worker is in a position of power when she or he relates to a client. This presentation is based on the assumption that power is inherently coercive.

If the forceful and involuntary committal of a mentally ill person into a psychiatric facility is unquestionably a true measure of what constitutes coercive treatment, how are the tactics and ploys used by outreach workers to induce homeless mentally ill clients to accept psychiatric and other treatment to be weighed in the scale of coercive and noncoercive strategies? Are the prolonged and often aggressive outreach efforts of workers who seek to remove the admittedly psychotic and homeless prospective client from the streets, to place them in shelters and provide psychiatric treatment, tantamount to an involuntary committal?

The complexity of the issues posited by these questions cannot be readily understood unless the relationship between the homeless mentally ill client and his or her outreach worker is defined. The manner in which, as well as the circumstances under which, this relationship evolves must also be discussed so that the interaction between the parties can be understood.

Perhaps the ultimate determinant of whether outreach efforts are coercive is whether the client voluntarily, without the use of deceptive and intrusive tactics, agrees to take medication and follow a treatment plan that is mutually conceived by him or her and his or her out-reach-worker-turned-case manager. The expectation is that a client who accepts treatment because he or she deems it necessary and beneficial will achieve psychiatric stability.

THE STREET IS A HOME WHEN
YOUR CLIENT LIVES THERE

The absence of a traditional home or environment for the homeless mentally ill client forced the outreach worker to lose sight of what defined the boundaries of a client's space and circle of privacy. Without such clearly defined boundaries, workers were likely to invade park benches, street corners, or makeshift carton houses without regard to whether the intrusion was welcome. Thus, a need arose to understand that although the homeless mentally ill client was incapable of shutting a door to an unwanted, uninvited "visitor," such a client did not lose the right to be left alone in the privacy of any home of his or her making when that client called the city street his or her place of residence.

The challenge for the outreach worker, then, was to define the homeless mentally ill client's environment so that the level of intrusion into the client's privacy would be minimized. This challenge was predicated on the simple precept that mentally ill clients, as is true for all United States citizens, have a fundamental right to privacy and other privileges and, to a certain degree, to choose whether to accept or reject treatment. This basic tenet of human rights helped the United States Postal Service recognize that a person was entitled to receive his mail at a park bench and a federal court to grant homeless persons the right to register and vote with the use of an address at an empty lot.

MEETING THE STRANGER WHO COULD BE A CLIENT

Like the involuntarily committed client who is interned at a facility for "his own or someone else's safety," the homeless mentally ill person is often relegated to the status of "client" without his acquiescence. While the committed client is afforded certain protections that ensure that he is not wrongfully identified as a person in need of psychiatric treatment, or that he will not remain confined without judicial or administrative review, the homeless mentally ill client is open to intrusive strategies, but has no means of denouncing his identification as a mentally ill person or the deprivation of his privacy or freedom of movement. This reality necessarily means that outreach workers must devise strategies and approaches that will mitigate erroneous identifications and acknowledge clients' right to privacy and refusal of treatment when their lives are not at risk. How, then, does an outreach worker identify the prospective client?

The outreach worker must canvass and comb the streets, parks, and other places where homeless people converge or secrete themselves, to identify those among the many who might be both homeless and mentally ill. The factors that are weighed in deciding whether the prospective client is a member of this class of individual are as follows:

1. The frequency of sightings in areas known to be inhabited by homeless people.
2. The individual's relative hygienic state.
3. The frequency of clothing changes throughout the period of observation.
4. The nature and volume of belongings carried by the individual.
5. The positive and negative symptoms of mental illness.
6. Whether the person is under the influence of alcohol or drugs.

Of course, these factors must be weighed and evaluated within the context of the individual's ethnic and cultural background. A client who is sighted in a park speaking in a tongue not recognized by a worker, for example, may be identified as speaking "gibberish" when in fact he may be speaking a foreign language! Once someone is identified as being homeless and mentally ill, it then becomes necessary to design a strategy to reach out to the individual in a manner that is neither intrusive nor coercive.

KNOCKING ON A CLIENT'S DOOR

The approach used by an outreach worker to "enter the home" of a client is determined by his or her understanding of what constitutes a client's home. An outreach worker who case-manages a client residing in his own home or at his parents' home, for example, would not presume to enter the home without first announcing himself or herself. If the worker acknowledges the park bench or the large rock as the client's home, then his or her approach into the client's space will recognize this boundary.

The methodology of approach or contact employed in a park or street, for example, does not deviate too much from what is daily used in our dealings with people who are fortunate enough to have a home or similar place of residence. It differs only in that the homeless mentally ill client is usually "persuaded or enticed" to grant entry to the uninvited guest by means of deceptive and invasive tactics.

Typically, the outreach worker who approaches a prospective client announces his or her presence before entering the client's "space," very much like the visitor who rings the doorbell or makes a telephone call to announce his or her immediate or imminent presence as a visitor. This announcement serves to acknowledge the client's right to claim an area of his own and avoids frightening the client. The announcement is conveyed when the worker speaks to the client as he or she approaches the area.

Once the distance between the client and the worker is narrowed, the worker requests permission to approach, get close, and speak with the client. If the client agrees to give the worker an audience, the worker then lets the client know that the visit is not random, that the worker is associated with an outreach organization or agency that serves the homeless population, and that the organization has a vehicle to transport him to a facility. It is at this point in the encounter that the worker deceives the client. The worker's representation that the outreach organization is dedicated to the homeless population without mention of their mentally ill status is a deceptive omission.

The deception is continued further when the worker offers a paper bag to the prospective client. The client is told that the bag contains both a sandwich and a written message. This message contains the organization's name, address, and telephone number. The client is also told that the message describes the benefits and services available in the agency, namely, food, shelter, housing, clothing, showers, and a lounge area in which to congregate during the day; no mention is made of the availability of psychiatric care and administration of medication.

The initial encounter or contact with the prospective client represents the first and least coercive approach. The aggressive demand that the prospective client listen to the worker is made less coercive by the manner in which the demand is conveyed. The client is approached in a sensitive and respectful manner and made to feel that he or she has some say in subsequent events. This approach often has positive results. As more contacts are made, the approach becomes increasingly aggressive.

The truly recalcitrant candidate for services is not engaged in any discussion but simply greeted on a daily basis or left a bagged sandwich while he is asleep. He is also surreptitiously observed so that the worker can glean the interests or needs that are of the most concern to the client. If he is a smoker, he is offered cigarettes. If he is a writer or sketch artist, he is provided paper or charcoal pencils. These tactics are employed until the client relents and agrees to engage in conversation, during which the same perceived necessities, such as showers or clothing, that were extended to his more cooperative colleagues are offered to him.

Throughout the course of these interactions, the worker's use of tactics meant to entice the client to agree to accept services such as food, clothing, and shelter creates a level of need in the client that is then used as a means to extract concessions from the client, the most important of which is that he accept medication and psychiatric treatment. The use of these benefits as bargaining "chips" establishes a dynamic interaction between worker and client that may or may not develop coercive attributes. The worker's power over the client will increase proportionately with the level of services that the client accepts. The more benefits the client accepts, the greater will be the worker's ability to exact concessions in return for the continuation of the service. This interactive dynamic presents the greatest risk of coercive tactics to the client. The worker, who concededly must use deception to engage the client, must minimize the level of coercion employed during interaction with the client.

WHAT IS COERCION?

If a client's voluntary intake of medication and participation in a treatment program is the definitive proof of noncoercion, how do we determine whether the client's conduct is indeed an expression of free will and not a response predicated on long-term subjection to coercive and deceptive practices?

While this question is best answered by the client, it raises serious concerns for the worker, who must ensure that whatever accord is reached with the client, it is not simply a passing response to coercive tactics, but a clear understanding about the merits of treatment and medication. A client armed with such understanding will be more likely to freely agree to accept medication and treatment.

Thus, coercion, usually defined as the act of compelling someone to do something by the use of power, intimidation, or threats, should be defined in terms of the level of understanding that a client has about his illness, the necessity and consequences of treatment, and the perils of refusal of treatment.

Under this definition, the prospective psychotic client who is incapable of exercising any sound judgment about his need for care and treatment cannot be deemed to be a victim of coercion when he is forcefully removed from a park in subfreezing temperatures. He has not been *compelled* to do anything; it has been done for him. This definition also presents to health care professionals—who all too often decide what treatment their clients will be submitted to without discussing the issues with them—a challenge to fully engage their clients in the treatment process.

The client's understanding about the nature of mental illness and all the attendant consequences is gained through education. The client must be taught about the origin of the illness, the different ways in which it manifests itself among the affected population, the available medication and its side effects, and how to manage the illness. To the extent that the client understands these issues, he will not have to be coerced into accepting treatment options presented to him.

This educational process will necessarily propel the client into a state of mourning. The worker must confront the client about his feelings that he has "lost his life to an illness" and show him that this stage of mourning will lead to his recovery. The client's feelings of societal rejection and discrimination must also be validated, as must the feeling that the illness is undesirable. The client must learn and understand that the illness may be controlled. Education about these matters will allow the client to understand that he can *elect* to take medication and accept psychiatric treatment.

It is during this critical educational process that a worker is most tempted and compelled to employ coercive tactics. During discussions about the client's need to accept his illness and understand all its facets, the worker *must* threaten to withdraw benefits so that the client will remain engaged. That is why it is essential that the tally of benefits afforded the client reach its highest point before the educational process is commenced. The coercion levels will be minimized if during the initial stages of this process the worker withdraws the least significant services or benefits. So, for example, a client will be denied clothing or the use of a shower, but not shelter, if he refuses to participate in the process in a winter month. Shelter may be denied in a summer month, but under no circumstances will the client be denied any benefit or service that would put his life at risk.

The clearest definition of coercion is the denial of, or failure to provide, education. This denial is the ultimate coercive tactic. Education obviates the need to employ deception. If a client is simply directed to see a psychiatrist when he denies that he is mentally ill or has a substance abuse problem, he will never understand how such treatment will help him. Similarly, deceiving a client about why he has to consent to prescribed treatment only engenders mistrust against the mental health system and will deter him from seeking or accepting treatment. If you educate the client about why he experiences certain symptoms and how they can be controlled, he will understand that he should want to accept treatment.

CONCLUSION

While the homeless mentally ill population must be treated with respect and allowed to maintain their dignity, workers must employ whatever tactics are necessary to both acknowledge their right of privacy and dignity and ensure that they are not left to succumb to disease and neglect and die alone. Whatever the manner of tactics employed to induce them to accept the opportunity to obtain and maintain psychiatric stability and a home, the tactics must educate the clients about their disease and their ability to control their lives. To do anything less is to coerce the clients and deny them their basic human rights.

Without education, our clients simply will move beyond our grasp and fall into despair and madness.

PART III

THE SOCIAL CONTEXT
OF AGGRESSIVE
COMMUNITY TREATMENT

CHAPTER 6

HOUSING AS A TOOL OF COERCION

HENRY KORMAN, DIANE ENGSTER, AND BONNIE M. MILSTEIN

Brian S. lived in a privately owned and operated group home funded by the state department of mental health. The home suffered from a series of physical conditions that violated local health and safety law. Brian complained to program staff about the bad conditions. He was ignored. He then called the local board of health, which inspected the facility and confirmed the existence of the unsanitary situation. Following the inspection, the program staff told Brian that his complaint to the board of health indicated that he was uncooperative and not ready for community living. He was offered a choice: voluntary commitment in a local state hospital or an immediate eviction from the group home. He declined to be hospitalized and was put out of the home that afternoon. He remained homeless for several days.

Few people doubt the fundamental importance of housing. It is, after all, where we live. It gives us shelter from the elements; thus, we want

HENRY KORMAN • Cambridge and Somerville Legal Services, Cambridge, Massachusetts 02141.   DIANE ENGSTER • 3825 Gibbs Street, Alexandria, Virginia 22309.   BONNIE M. MILSTEIN • David L. Bazelon Center for Mental Health Law, Washington, D.C. 20005.

Coercion and Aggressive Community Treatment: A New Frontier in Mental Health Law, edited by Deborah L. Dennis and John Monahan. Plenum Press, New York, 1996.

it to be decent, safe, and sanitary. We also want our housing to be affordable, giving us security against eviction and displacement. More fundamentally, housing gives us respite from the congress of social life. It is where we want to be nurtured and where we nurture our families. Without a home, we have no center, no stability.[1]

Most of us, regardless of status or disability, believe that obtaining stable housing is an ideal that is achievable for most of our lives. With advances in treatment, assistive technology, and community attitudes, those of us with disabilities are able to live in stable housing of our choice. Nonetheless, for many people with mental disabilities and little income, home can be something far from this ideal because often the only option is to live in housing designed as a community-based residential treatment program.

For residents of this type of housing, home is where they live with others not of their own choosing, under rules of conduct that do not exist in typical housing. Continued occupancy is often conditioned on compliance with a treatment plan that may or may not have been designed with the resident's participation. Program staff may be assigned tremendous power to determine sanctions for noncompliance with treatment. Behavior is scrutinized from a clinical perspective in which disagreements over treatment, living conditions, and even the small details of daily life can be interpreted as symptoms of illness or decompensation. Anything but total acquiescence to program and staff mandates can result in involuntary commitment, in summary discharge, or in homelessness. In such settings, the human need for shelter can turn into a tool of coercion, interfering with an assortment of individual rights.

CIVIL RIGHTS FOR PEOPLE WITH DISABILITIES: LIVING IN THE LEAST RESTRICTIVE ENVIRONMENT, THE RIGHT TO CHOOSE TREATMENT, AND THE PROMISE OF INTEGRATION

The decades of the 1970s and 1980s offered people with mental disabilities significant advances in their civil rights. While these advances most often involved the rights of institutionalized people with

---

[1]See Stone (1993), pp. 14–31 , who recognizes the sharp contrast between the reality of many people's housing situation and this ideal. He notes that much housing is in fact substandard, deteriorated, and unaffordable. He also understands that the reality of domestic violence and discrimination undermines our ability to consider our homes true havens.

mental disabilities, they are nonetheless critical in understanding the high premium people with disabilities place on affordable, non-service-based housing. These rights include the right to live in the least restrictive living environment, the right to direct and participate in medical treatment decisions, and the right to full, equal participation in all social and economic aspects of society.

The right to the least restrictive mode of treatment has been repeatedly recognized by federal courts as part of the rights of institutionalized people with mental illness. It is rooted in the Constitution's protection of individual liberty. The congressional recognition of this right led to the 1980 enactment of the federal Bill of Rights for people with mental disabilities (Mental Health Systems Act, 1980). Among the many rights recognized in that law is:

(A) The right to appropriate treatment and related services in a setting and under conditions that
  (i) are the most supportive of such person's personal liberty; and
  (ii) restrict such liberty only to the extent necessary [and] consistent with such person's treatment needs, applicable requirements of law, and judicial orders [Mental Health Systems Act, 1980, §9501(1)(A)].[2]

Constitutional notions of individual liberty also protect people from unwanted intrusion in medical decision-making. Thus, the Bill of Rights for Mental Health Patients guards the right to participate in and direct individual treatment, and the right to refuse treatment.[3]

Finally, one of the most profound advances in civil rights for people with disabilities stems from the recognition that they have histori-

---

[2]Congress restated the Bill of Rights for Mental Health Patients when it created the protection and advocacy system for people with mental disabilities in 1986 (see Protection and Advocacy for Mentally Ill Individuals Act of 1991, Bill of Rights, §10841). The Bill of Rights protects both people who are confined to institutions and those who reside in "community facilities for individuals with mental illness, board and care homes, [and] homeless shelters" [see Protection and Advocacy for Mentally Ill Individuals Act of 1991, 42 U.S.C. §10802(3) (definition of "facilities")]. Its application to service-based housing is unclear, if only because the courts have so far refused to permit people with mental disabilities to enforce the law in individual cases (see *Monahan v. Dorchester Counseling Center, Inc.*, 1991). Indeed, some courts examining comparable state law standards view the promise of patient rights as words of mere "aspiration and encouragement" (*Woodbridge v. Worcester State Hospital*, 1981).

[3]See Protection and Advocacy for Mentally Ill Individuals Act of 1991, 42 U.S.C. §10841(1)(B), (C) and (D). See also *Cruzan v. Dir., Missouri Dept. of Health* (1990, p. 2851) (Constitution protects individual right to direct medical treatment).

cally been excluded from the mainstream of society. On the federal level, three laws were enacted in the span of 17 years to redress such discriminatory treatment. First, in 1973, Congress passed the Rehabilitation Act, which, among its many provisions, specifically prohibited discrimination against people with disabilities in any program receiving federal financial assistance and specifically required that federal grantees administer their programs "in the most integrated setting appropriate to the needs of qualified individuals with handicaps" [HUD Rehabilitation Act Rule, §8.4(d)] (see also Rehabilitation Act of 1973).

Then, in 1988, Congress amended the Fair Housing Act to include new provisions that protect people with disabilities from discrimination in the sale and rental of housing (Fair Housing Act Amendments of 1988). Last, in 1990, Congress passed the Americans with Disabilities Act (ADA). The ADA reaches into every aspect of social life, protecting against discrimination in employment, government services, public accommodations, and transportation (Americans With Disabilities Act of 1990).

These laws created a "clear and comprehensive national mandate to end discrimination against individuals with disabilities and to bring those individuals into the economic and social mainstream of American life" [H. R. Rep. No. 485(III), 1990, p. 23].[4] These rights have a fundamental importance for those of us who have disabilities. The exercise of liberty associated with choice and equal participation in society must also be realized "at home," where personal security, personal identity, and a zone of privacy are respected and preserved. When a person's home is a residential treatment facility, choice, equal participation, personal security, identity, and privacy are all at risk. Residents of treatment facilities seek an additional ideal: that housing be not only safe and affordable but also free from restrictions based solely on one's status as a person with a mental disability (Hitov, 1992, p. 604).

OBTAINING THE IDEAL: THE DIMINISHING SUPPLY OF AFFORDABLE HOUSING

Since 1959, it had been national policy to offer decent, safe, affordable housing opportunities to people with disabilities in federally assisted

---

[4]See also H. R. Rep. No. 711 (1988), p. 18 (Fair Housing Act "is a clear pronouncement of a national commitment to end the unnecessary exclusion of persons with handicaps from the American mainstream"). For a more complete description of the legal workings of the ADA and the Fair Housing Act, see Milstein, Pepper, and Rubenstein (1989) and Milstein, Rubenstein, and Cyr (1991).

publicly and privately owned housing for the elderly and the "handicapped."[5] This policy is no accident. In many respects, people with disabilities and elders share the same social isolation, poverty, and marginalization on which they stake equivalent claims to housing resources. By 1992, hundreds of thousands of units of affordable, federally assisted housing were designated as being available to elderly and handicapped people on a first-come, first-served basis.

These housing opportunities for elderly people and people with disabilities could have fulfilled much of the promise of the civil rights advances of the 1970s and 1980s. With no mandatory connection between housing and treatment, assisted housing imposed restrictions on personal freedom only that a lease arrangement would impose on any tenant. There was no programmatic or staff coercion to force residents to accept unwanted or unneeded treatment in order to avoid homelessness. To be sure, such housing was far from ideal. The practice of housing younger people with disabilities with people in their 60s, 70s, and 80s was itself isolating and an incomplete fulfillment of the promise of integration. Nonetheless, it was greatly preferable to homelessness or institutionalization.

Unfortunately, many people with mental disabilities were not able to take advantage of the availability of even these federally assisted housing opportunities. Reports of discrimination were legion. Adding to the common, stereotypical view of people with mental disabilities as dangerous and unreliable was the U.S. Department of Housing and Urban Development's own mandate to managers that they determine—in some undefined way—whether applicants with disabilities were "capable of independent living," before they could be admitted.

Thus, people with mental disabilities were more likely to continue living with parents or relatives or to be directed toward housing programs developed by state and local mental health or social service systems. These housing programs were usually highly structured, constantly supervised by professional staff, and based on the notion

---

[5]Public Law 86-372 (September 23, 1959) redefined the term "elderly family" from one that conferred eligibility in public housing on people 65 years of age or older to one that included people 62 or more and people with disabilities that met the Social Security Disability Insurance definition of "disability." Since 1959, Congress has expanded both the definition of disability and the number of housing programs that serve both elders and people with disabilities. By 1992, until the enactment of the Housing and Community Development Act of 1992, virtually every housing program serving elders was, in fact, designed as a program serving elders and people with disabilities.

that continued occupancy depended on treatment compliance rather than lease compliance.

During the late 1980s, as more people with psychiatric disabilities and those who had recovered from drug or alcohol abuse started to enforce their own housing and civil rights, they began to be accepted as tenants in federally assisted housing units. Then, after 30 years of maintaining a public policy of housing people with disabilities and elders together, Congress abruptly changed course in 1992. Some policy makers blamed an increase in early deinstitutionalization and the increasing numbers of mentally disabled who are not entering hospitals for disruption at "mixed population" properties. Others pointed to waiting lists at assisted housing projects that were increasingly filled by young people with disabilities, leading some people to fear that projects would eventually become "Disability ghettos." The resulting policy shift permitted exclusion of people with disabilities from assisted housing and promoted segregation of people with disabilities in service-based housing.

FORESHADOWING EXCLUSION: SECTION 202 HOUSING FOR THE ELDERLY AND HANDICAPPED

If any one housing program epitomizes the shift to a policy of exclusion, segregation, and service-based housing, it is the history of HUD's Section 202 program. The Housing Act of 1959 created the program as community-based housing for elders, and the Housing Act of 1964 added "physically handicapped" people to the category of individuals eligible for Section 202 housing. In 1974, Congress deleted the limiting word "physically" from the categories of individuals with disabilities eligible for occupancy [Housing Act of 1974, §210(b)]. By 1988, people with developmental disabilities were added to the list of those eligible for the housing. Despite the ever-expanding categories of people with disabilities eligible for Section 202 housing, HUD administered the program for elders and only a few people with mobility-related disabilities.

In 1988, in an action to develop more housing for people with severe disabilities within serious federal budget constraints, Congress carved out a special component of the Section 202 program for people with disabilities only (Housing and Community Development Act of 1987). By 1990, Congress authorized the splitting of the Section 202 program into two components: a Section 202 supportive housing program for the elderly and a new Section 811 program of housing and supportive services for people with disabilities (Cranston-Gonzales National Affordable Housing Act, 1990).

These actions represented a dramatic shift away from providing general occupancy housing to people who were elderly or disabled in favor of segregated programs in which continued occupancy could be linked to treatment compliance rather than lease compliance. Of the approximate 275,000 units of housing previously developed under the Section 202 program, only 28,000 remained available to people with disabilities. Of those, only 7000 units were anything more than group homes, a mere 2.5% of the total Section 202 apartments in the program (HUD Group Homes Notice 93-36, 1993).

EXCLUSION AND SEGREGATION AS NATIONAL POLICY: THE HOUSING AND COMMUNITY DEVELOPMENT ACT OF 1992

The effort to shift away from general occupancy housing for elders and people with disabilities was completed by 1992. In response to enormous pressure from private owners of assisted housing, public housing authorities, local politicians, and others, Congress amended federal law to permit both the exclusion of people with disabilities from federally supported housing and the segregation of people with disabilities in other types of service-based federal housing (Title VI of the Housing and Community Development Act of 1992).

Thus, Congress and HUD reversed the expectation that the civil rights laws would assure access to federally assisted, general-occupancy, affordable housing for people with disabilities. The extent to which Congress abandoned the promise of civil rights laws for people with disabilities in 1992 can be measured by the view it took in 1988 of the manner in which the Rehabilitation Act guaranteed access to federal housing:

> There exists an acute shortage of housing for handicapped persons. Handicapped persons capable of living independently in housing primarily for the well elderly should be permitted to do so. Such integrated living arrangements encourage handicapped persons to obtain employment, become self-supportive and avoid isolation from general society.
>
> These goals are intended to be furthered through Sec. 504 of the Rehabilitation Act as well. Like the Housing Act, Sec. 504

seeks the integration of persons with disabilities in every type of
housing financed in whole or in part by federal funds [H. R. Rep.
No. 122(I), 1987].

The original ethic is now being replaced by the exclusion of people with disabilities from tens of thousands of units of non-service-
based housing, segregating them in service-based housing.[6] While the
rest of the nation is held to a standard that forbids discrimination
against people with disabilities, the federal government operates bla-
tantly discriminatory housing.

LIFE ON THE GROUND:
COERCION IN SERVICE-BASED HOUSING

Tenants of "regular" housing typically cannot be forcibly removed
without advance notice and an opportunity for a court hearing before
a judge. However, the laws allow courts to treat federally assisted
housing programs for people with special needs differently by resorting to outdated legal concepts that divest residents of the usual rights
of tenancy.

This difference in legal status also extends to people with mental
disabilities who live in housing that is not federally assisted. At the
same time that federal policy resulted in fewer affordable housing options for everyone, including people with disabilities, a variety of
community groups attempted to respond to the growing problem of
homelessness and the increase in demand for housing for people with
special needs. These groups included civic groups, the religious community, nonprofit organizations, and local governments. At first, the
response was to institute a variety of stop-gap measures to provide
what was thought to be "emergency" shelter. Some churches, for instance, opened up their premises to shelter homeless people during
the night and required them to leave prior to the start of normal
church business in the morning.

As the number of people who were becoming homeless continued to grow, community groups realized that more than emergency

---

[6]In addition to the Section 811 and designated public housing programs, HUD's other
initiatives for people with disabilities all anticipate the provision of housing together
with services. These programs are almost all aimed at homeless people with disabilities. See, for example, the Supportive Housing Program, 42 U.S.C. §11381; Safe Havens
Demonstration Program, 42 U.S.C. §11391; and Shelter Plus Care Program, 42 U.S.C.
§11403.

shelters were needed. They developed programs that were more structured and viewed as a "transition" from homelessness to permanent housing. A variety of programs were established to provide housing and treatment including such components as social services, vocational programs, and budgeting classes. For people with psychiatric disabilities, these residential options became known as the community "continuum of care" that would help clients solve their individual problems so that they could eventually find and maintain their own permanent housing. These facilities were known as transitional group homes, transitional shelters, crisis care facilities, respite care homes, board and care homes, supervised apartments, adult care homes, and semi-independent living arrangements. Later, some permanent residences for people with psychiatric disabilities were developed, such as group homes and supported apartments.

Programs varied in terms of limits on length of stay, size, the amount of on-site assistance and supervision by staff, whether or not rent or a fee must be paid, and whether services were provided on the premises or in the community. Groups that developed and managed these programs considered them to be "residential treatment" rather than housing. The primary purpose was to teach clients the requisite skills that they presumably lacked or to change undesirable behavior so that clients could master living in the community "independently." Of course, rules were also developed to maintain order in the residential programs themselves.

Because of their smaller size and their location "in the community," these programs were intended to provide an atmosphere that was less harsh and impersonal for people with mental disabilities than that of large, regimented institutions in remote rural locations and that was less isolating than that found in run-down boarding homes in the city. The goal of providing an affordable permanent home for residents was subordinate to correcting the problems that program managers assumed had caused the residents to be homeless in the first place. The belief that clients of these residential programs had any legal rights in the context of a landlord–tenant relationship was virtually nonexistent.

As safe, affordable non-service-based housing diminishes, and service-enriched housing programs become the main source of housing for people with disabilities, the potential for coercion increases. Coercive actions in federally assisted housing programs can take place at application, where admission to housing is conditioned on the need for and acceptance of particular services. HUD's Shelter Plus Care Program (1992) imposes precisely such a requirement on people with disabilities [see 24 C.F.R. §582.315(b)]. Forced acquiescence to treatment also can occur during occupancy, when a tenant may be faced with a perilous choice either of conceding to intrusive treatment or social services or of immediate eviction.

Almost all these residential programs developed rules and requirements over and above the usual lease provisions associated with rental housing. The groups and organizations that developed and managed such programs viewed themselves as treatment or service providers rather than landlords. They had little knowledge of housing law and did not believe that there was a landlord–tenant relationship between themselves and their clients. Providers believed that their professional expertise enabled them to make treatment decisions on behalf of their clients. These decisions included immediate termination of both housing and treatment with a minimum of due process and certainly not with the usual legal protections associated with landlord–tenant law.

State courts have ruled only recently on the status of residents in these types of programs. To determine whether the usual rights of tenancy exist, judges first look to the provisions of state landlord–tenant laws, which did not develop with the rights of people in residential treatment programs in mind. Nonetheless, some states have dramatically departed from the more traditional concepts by following the 1972 Uniform Residential Landlord and Tenant Act, which affords protection against self-help evictions to occupants living in situations that do not legally rise to the status of tenancy. A New York court, for instance, ruled that an occupant who had been living in a hotel for more than 30 consecutive days should not be evicted without a special proceeding.

In Massachusetts, a court found in the *Serreze v. YWCA of Western Massachusetts* (1991) case that residents of a YWCA residential treatment program for battered women were entitled to judicial process prior to their eviction from the residential program for failing to attend counseling sessions. The women in the program did not share their apartments, they paid security and key deposits, and they signed occupancy agreements that gave them an expectation of privacy in their units. The court looked at the fact that the program provided each of the women with an apartment for which she paid state-subsidized rent. Most important was the fact that the women had exclusive possession and control of their apartments. The court decided that it wasn't necessary for a traditional landlord–tenant relationship to exist in order for the women to receive the protection against self-help eviction under the Massachusetts statute.

In another Massachusetts case, *Carr v. Friends of the Homeless* (1990), the court went further by finding that a landlord–tenant relationship existed between a resident and a nonprofit agency, Friends of the Homeless, Inc., which provided shelter and human services to homeless people. The resident, Mr. Carr, participated in the program by renting a room in a single room occupancy (SRO) building administered by the agency. After another private agency ended Mr. Carr's participation in its vocational training program, Friends of the Homeless relied on that fact to determine that Mr. Carr was not ready for an SRO program and locked him out of his room. Mr. Carr was able to obtain a court order to regain his housing because Friends had failed to give him the 7-day notice required for any occupant in possession of his room for more than 30 consecutive days.

Mr. Carr had signed a written agreement giving him possession of the unit for 1 year. He had exclusive use of his room and was responsible for its care and maintenance. He had no housekeeper service. He paid a "monthly occupancy charge" that, along with a subsidy, was his monthly rent. The agreement stipulated that he would participate in services offered by Friends or its affiliates, but none had been offered to him prior to his termination from the program. The court held that the agreement signed by Mr. Carr created a tenancy and that a landlord–tenant relationship existed between Mr. Carr and Friends of the Homeless, Inc. The court added that even when the primary purpose of a program was to provide service, a tenancy could be created by the agreement of the parties in regard to the housing portion of the program.

Other courts have come to different conclusions, especially when they determine that a program is primarily a treatment facility. For instance, a New York court found in *Fischer v. Taub* (1984) that an adult care facility should be considered an "institutional facility" rather than a "residential property" if the facility includes space for "the care or treatment of persons with physical limitations because of health or age." Residential properties are those that are "primarily occupied for shelter and sleeping accommodations of individuals on a day-to-day or week-to-week basis." An occupant of a residential property, of course, would be more likely to be afforded the legal protections of tenancy by the court. Fortunately for New Yorkers, a later case required a similar treatment center to follow the due process eviction procedures required for "tenants-at-will." The court reached its conclusion by finding that the defendant's provision of long-term supervised shelter obligated it to follow the eviction procedures required of similar landlords (*Metalsky v. Mercy Haven*, 1993).

MITIGATING COERCION: FAIR PROCESS, GOOD PROCESS

The claim asserted by people with mental disabilities to non-service-based housing is one that seeks to avoid coercion with a promise of unconditional access. Unconditional access does not, in this context, mean the right to occupy housing without *any* condition. Indeed, the promise of integration originally extended by Congress in the Rehabilitation Act, and reinforced by the Fair Housing Act and the Americans with Disabilities Act, depends on equal treatment; that is, access to housing should be, in the first instance, a function of an individual's ability to comply with the same rules of tenancy that apply to all tenants, for example, paying the rent, keeping an apartment in clean condition, avoiding disruption of other tenants' lives. The government-sponsored policy of exclusion and segregation of people with disabilities and the diminished rights of occupancy they are permitted in service-based housing substantially alters this hope of unconditional access.

Nevertheless, there are mechanisms for mitigating, if not eliminating, the coercive effect of service-based housing. A fair process of dispute resolution lessens the possibility that denials of admission, evictions, or forced treatment will occur even for people with the most severe or acute illness. Moreover, "fair process" can have more than procedural aspects. It can include dispute resolution that is attentive to the relative needs of the participant, the program, and the housing.

One example of housing that affords nearly unconditional access is HUD's Safe Havens Demonstration Program. Created by Congress in 1992, in the same law that authorized the segregation and exclusion of people with disabilities from general occupancy housing, the Safe Havens program serves "homeless persons who, at the time, are unwilling or unable to participate in mental health treatment programs or to receive other supportive services" (Housing and Community Development Act, 1992).[7] Safe Havens funded under the program provide "low demand services," that is, "health care, mental health, substance abuse, and other supportive services . . . in a noncoercive manner" [Housing and Community Development Act, 1992,

---

[7]The Safe Havens Demonstration Program was enacted by Congress as Title IV-D of the Act. Title VI of the same law authorized the designation of federal public housing as elderly only and disabled only, as well as the exclusion of people with disabilities from privately owned, federally assisted housing.

§11392(4)]. There is no limit on the time an individual may live in a Safe Haven, nor are residents required to participate in services [Housing and Community Development Act, 1992, §11394(d)(6) and (7)]. Occupancy charges may be waived for those who refuse to pay or who are unable to pay (Housing and Community Development Act, 1992, §11395). An occupant can be removed from a Safe Haven only by a formal process "that may include a hearing" and only for conduct presenting a danger to others or constituting repeated, serious violations of program rules (Housing and Community Development Act, 1992, §11396).

The Safe Havens Program is one model for providing housing that is not conditioned on acceptance of treatment. It also provides a model for resolving problems when housing *is* conditioned on acceptance of services. As the Safe Havens statute mandates, basic rules of fairness require a formal process for termination of housing rights. Fairness means that a participant know what program rule she violated and what acts or events led to the program violation. Fairness also demands that there be a forum for the participant to tell her side of the story to an unbiased decision-maker who can at the least determine whether the offensive conduct actually took place and, if it did, whether it truly constitutes a sanctionable offense.

This model for fair or "due" process is replicated in other settings. The federal Shelter Plus Care program, for example, allows for "termination of assistance" for violations of "program requirements or conditions of occupancy." In such circumstances, due process, by law, must include a "formal process that recognizes the rights of the individual to due process of law." "Due process" must include "written notice to the participant containing a clear statement of the reasons for termination," a review of the termination decision before an unbiased hearing examiner, and written notice of decision (see HUD Shelter plus care regulations, 1992, §582.320). HUD's Supportive Housing Program rules impose much the same requirements [see HUD Supportive housing program regulations, 1992, §583.300(j)]. In Massachusetts, recent amendments to state law require managers of community-based housing to offer advance notice and an opportunity for a hearing before removing an individual from a treatment facility, while at the same time limiting the access to the courts that is the right of tenants of non-service-related housing. In contrast, in the federal programs, it appears that HUD and Congress contemplate both an informal hearing at the facility and judicial process [See HUD Supportive housing program regulations, 1992, §583.300(a) (Supportive Housing Program must comply with state law standards for housing operation); see also H. R. Rep. No. 760 (1992) (hearing procedures in Safe Havens Demonstration program legislation are not intended to "pre-empt state and local laws regarding the removal of tenants from an assisted project")].

Of course, the extent to which a fair review process actually mitigates the potential for coercion in treatment-based housing is heavily dependent on the nature of the process and whether it is attentive to the coercive nature of the housing in the first place. In its most formal sense, fair process is merely about the application of preexisting rules to particular situations. Thus, if a program has a rule that imposes total acquiescence to the treatment whims of the staff as a condition of continued occupancy, no amount of fair process will save the home of an individual who seeks to exercise his right to choose or reject treatment. The expectation that a process can be "fair" can therefore be undermined when the only question involves the harsh application of a rule that itself infringes on individual choice.

In some respects, the federal homelessness programs again offer some hope of an alternative approach. The Safe Havens Program, for example, looks primarily to conduct that presents a danger to others as the point at which housing will be withdrawn (Housing and Community Development Act, 1992, §11936). HUD's Shelter Plus Care rules require that grantees "exercise judgment and examine all extenuating circumstances in determining when violations are serious enough to warrant termination, so that a participant's assistance is terminated only in the most severe cases" [HUD Shelter Plus Care Program regulations, 1992, §582.320(a)]. In Massachusetts, the law allows removal from community-based mental health facilities only if "the occupant has substantially violated an essential provision of a written agreement containing the conditions of occupancy or if the occupant is likely, in spite of reasonable accommodation, to impair the emotional or physical well-being of other occupants, program staff or neighbors."

THE CIVIL RIGHTS BUFFER: REASONABLE ACCOMMODATION FOR PEOPLE WITH DISABILITIES

It is Massachusetts's legislative resort to the concept of "reasonable accommodation" that offers one final mechanism for mitigating the impact of coercive influences in service-based housing. The concept of reasonable accommodation grew out of judicial interpretations of §504 of the Rehabilitation Act (*Southeastern Community College v. Davis,* 1979; *Alexander v. Choate,* 1985). The courts understood that individual characteristics related to disability are often real barriers to participation for people who are otherwise qualified for particular programs. The law therefore commands that landlords make reasonable modifications not only in physical structures but also in rules, policies, and procedures in order to permit a person with a disability the opportunity for full program participation. The obligation to accommodate a disability is limited only by the requirement that an accommodation be "reasonable." A "reasonable" accommodation is one that does not impose an undue financial burden and does not result in a fundamental alteration in the underlying program. These principles are codified in every civil rights law affecting people with disabilities [e.g., Fair Housing Act Amendments of 1988, §3604(f) (3)(A)(B)].

The requirement of "reasonable accommodation" holds incredible power for people with disabilities. Because it is a rule about bending rules, it extends beyond the simple "fairness" of a procedural due process hearing in which a service provider merely applies a program regulation to particular circumstances. Reasonable accommodations are of necessity individualized inquiries. Because these inquiries must focus on promoting continued participation, they are tools by which a housing relationship may be maintained even in the face of disruptive behavior. The "reasonableness" requirement describes the outer bounds of the doctrine. A waiver or modification of a rule, and a concomitant suspension of an eviction, is not required when it would impose an undue financial burden on a program or a fundamental alteration of program goals.

The reference to program goals in achieving reasonable accommodations protects more than the integrity of a service-based housing program. Program goals also define the extent to which a modification of rules is required in individual circumstances. The law is quite explicit in this regard. It forbids the use of criteria "the purpose or effect of which would . . . [d]efeat or substantially impair the accomplishment of the objectives of the . . . program . . . for qualified individuals with a particular handicap . . . unless the [program] can demonstrate that the criteria . . . are manifestly related to the accomplishment of an objective of a program or activity" [HUD Rehabilitation Act rule, 1988, §8.4(b)(4)(ii)]; see also 28 C.F.R. §35.130(b)(3)(ii) (ADA regulations)].

These words suggest an outcome far different from eviction when a person with a disability fails to attend a training program, refuses his medications, or simply disagrees with the quality and management of a residential treatment program. Rather, the requirement that the application of rules be consistent with program goals anticipates an examination of what prompted the violation in the first place, whether individual treatment goals can still be accomplished even if the violation continues, and whether alternative treatment methods consistent with program objectives are available. By this measure, sanction is appropriate only if enforcement of an underlying rule is "manifestly related to the accomplishment of an objective of a program or activity" (HUD Rehabilitation Act rule, 1988 §8.4(b)(4)(ii)).

Thus, reasonable accommodation promotes a dialogue in which program violations and program purposes are scrutinized in a context of individual circumstances and needs. If the purpose of a program rule can be served by some arrangement other than exclusion, then the law requires continued participation. This view understands the breaking of rules not as conduct subject to sanction, but as an expression of a need or desire that may or may not conflict with the purpose of the residential program. Reasonable accommodation thus strives for a way to maintain the relationship between the rule-breaker and the rule-maker by accommodating both.[8]

CONCLUSION

Principles of fair process and reasonable accommodation are not about *eliminating* coercive influences in service-based housing; they focus on *mitigating* coercion. The only real means of ending compelled acquiescence to treatment in such facilities is to separate housing from receipt of services. This kind of rule means that service providers could never use the threat of eviction to force residents to behave in ways that are unrelated to the ability to comply with leases and other housing-related standards of behavior. Lease violations like failure to pay rent, interfering with the rights of other tenants to enjoy their homes, or maintaining hazardous conditions in one's apartment

[8]These concepts of process that is attentive to the purposes as well as the text of a rule, and to the meeting of both individual need and programmatic goals, are not new (see Tribe, 1975; Gilligan, 1982; Gilligan et al., 1988).

may all justify eviction. Disputes about medication, attending counseling or day programs, or cooperating with treatment never, on their
own, justify that result.

Civil rights law still protects, of course, the occupancy rights of
people with disabilities even when housing and services are separate.
The Fair Housing Act, for example, requires landlords, including service providers, to "make reasonable accommodations in rules, policies, practices, or services, when such accommodations may be necessary to afford [people with disabilities] equal opportunity to use
and enjoy a dwelling" [Fair Housing Act Amendments of 1988,
§3604(f)(3)(B)]. Thus, if a tenant is able to show that her lease violations are related to a disability, and that some reasonable accommodation would end the violation, the housing provider must provide it, so
long as it meets the reasonableness standard applied to all accommodations (*Roe v. Sugar River Mills Assoc.*, 1993; *City Wide Assoc. v. Penfield*, 1990).

It bears noting that even in this context, civil rights law can
be turned to potentially coercive ends. To many courts, a "reasonable" accommodation means only postponing eviction for the time
required to determine whether a proposed plan of treatment will
change a tenant's evictable behavior (*City Wide Assoc. v. Penfield*,
1990). Indeed, one court has held that principles of reasonable accommodation permit an order that a tenant obtain treatment as a condition of remaining in occupancy (*Chester Commons v. Bernasconi*, 1994).

In the end, principles of equal treatment, equal access, and the individual's right to control medical decision-making demand that people with mental disabilities hold no more than the same rights of occupancy as any other tenant. That mandate forbids intrusion into the
zone of privacy defined by the home. It conditions the occupant's
right to live without interference within that zone on the obligations
of any tenant: rent payment, nondestructive behavior, behavior that
does not harm or disturb others. Where principles of reasonable accommodation, tenant's rights, and coerced treatment intersect, they
cross at a place that people with disabilities value along with their
other civil rights. If an individual rejects treatment, as is her right, she
must find her own way toward lease compliance or face loss of housing. At that place, a tenant with a disability chooses responsibility for
her own behavior. The ability to assume that responsibility, with all
the consequences of hardship and homelessness it may entail, is
among the most valued of rights.

REFERENCES

Alexander v. Choate, 469 U.S. 287 (1985).

Carr v. Friends of the Homeless, No. 89-LE-3942-S (Hampden Div., Mass. Housing Court 1990).

Chester Commons v. Bernasconi, No. 93-SP-3021 (Hampden Div., Mass. Housing Court 1994).

City Wide Assoc. v. Penfield, 409 Mass. 140 (1990).

Cranston-Gonzales National Affordable Housing Act, 42 U.S.C. §1437 *et seq.* (1990).

Cruzan v. Dir., Missouri Dept. of Health, 110 S. Ct. 2841 (1990).

Department of Justice regulations, 28 C.F.R., Part 35 (1991).

Fair Housing Act Amendments of 1988, 42 U.S.C. §3604, *et seq.*

Fischer v. Taub, 491 N.Y.S.2d 538, 127 Misc.2d 518 (Sup. Ct., Appl. Term, 1st Dept. 1984).

Gilligan, C. (1982). *In a different voice.* Cambridge, MA: Harvard University Press.

Gilligan, C., Ward, J. V., Taylor, J. M., & Bardige, B. (Eds.) (1988). *Mapping the moral domain.* Cambridge, MA: Harvard University Press.

H. R. Rep. No. 122(I), 100th Cong., 1st Sess. (1987).

H. R. Rep. No. 711, 100th Cong., 2d Sess. (1988).

H. R. Rep. No. 485(III), 101st Cong., 2d Sess. (1990).

H. R. Rep. No. 760, 102d Cong., 2d Sess. (1992).

Hitov, S. (1992). Ending homelessness among mentally disabled people. *New England Journal of Public Policy, Special Issue* (Spring/Summer).

Housing Act of 1959, 12 U.S.C. §1701 *et seq.*

Housing Act of 1964, Pub. L. No. 88-560, 78 Stat. 769.

Housing Act of 1974, Pub. L. No. 93-383, 88 Stat. 669.

Housing and Community Development Act of 1987, Pub. L. No. 100-242, 101 Stat. 1815 (1988).

Housing and Community Development Act of 1992, 42 U.S.C. §11301, *et seq.*

Housing and Urban Development Act of 1992, 42 U.S.C. §11391 (1992).

HUD, Group homes funded under section 202 and section 811, Notice 93-36 (1993).

HUD, Rehabilitation Act rules, 24 C.F.R. Part 8. (1988).

HUD, Shelter plus care program regulations, 24 C.F.R. §582.315 *et seq.* (1992).

HUD, Supportive housing program regulations, 24 C.F.R. §583.300 *et seq.* (1992).

Mental Health Systems Act, 42 U.S.C. §9401, *et seq.* (1980).

Metalsky v. Mercy Haven, Inc., 594 N.Y.S.2d 124, 156 Misc.2d 558 (N.Y. Sup. Ct. 1993).

Milstein, B., Pepper, B., & Rubenstein, L. (1989). The Fair Housing Amendments Act of 1988: What it means for people with mental disabilities. *Clearinghouse Review, 23,* 128.

Milstein, B., Rubenstein, L., & Cyr, R. (1991). The Americans with Disabilities Act: A breathtaking promise for people with mental disabilities. *Clearinghouse Review, 24,* 1240.

Monahan v. Dorchester Counseling Center, Inc., 770 F. Supp. 43 (D. Mass. 1991).

Protection and Advocacy for Mentally Ill Individuals Act of 1991, 42 U.S.C. §10801 *et seq.*

Rehabilitation Act of 1973, §504, 29 U.S.C. §701, *et seq.*

Roe v. Sugar River Mills Assoc., 820 F. Supp. 636 (D.N.H. 1993).

Serreze v. YWCA of Western Massachusetts, 30 Mass. App. Ct. 639, 572 N.E.2d 581 (1991).

Southeastern Community College v. Davis, 442 U.S. 397 (1979).

Stone, M. (1993). *Shelter poverty: New ideas on housing affordability.* Philadelphia: Temple University Press.

Tribe, L. (1975). Structural due process. *Harvard Civil Rights and Civil Liberties Law Review, 10,* 269.

Woodbridge v. Worcester State Hospital, 384 Mass. 38 (1981).

CHAPTER 7

ENTITLEMENTS, PAYEES, AND COERCION

SUZAN HURLEY COGSWELL

The Supplemental Security Income (SSI) and Social Security Disability Insurance (SSDI) programs provide financial support to persons who meet income or other eligibility criteria.[1] If a person who qualifies for payment under either entitlement program is unable to manage funds or does not maintain a permanent mailing address, an indi-

---

[1]The SSI program provides income support to persons aged 65 or older, blind or disabled adults, and blind or disabled children. Eligibility requirements and federal payment standards are nationally uniform. The program is administered by the Social Security Administration. The 1993 federal SSI benefit rate for an individual living in his or her own household and with no other countable income was $434 monthly; for a couple (with both husband and wife eligible), the SSI benefit rate was $652 (U.S. Department of Health and Human Services, 1993b).

The SSDI program provides income benefits to physically or mentally disabled workers under age 65. The federal benefit rate is based on the disabled worker's salary prior to the onset of disability (U.S. Department of Health and Human Services, 1993b).

SUZAN HURLEY COGSWELL • Legislative Office of Education Oversight, Columbus, Ohio 43266.

Coercion and Aggressive Community Treatment: A New Frontier in Mental Health Law, edited by Deborah L. Dennis and John Monahan. Plenum Press, New York, 1996.

vidual or organization is appointed "payee" to receive monthly benefits on the person's behalf (Social Security Act, 1935).

Federal regulations specify the duties that must be performed by
the entitlement payee, also called the "representative payee," including accountability requirements and safeguards against misuse of
money. Funds can be expended "only for the use of" and "in the best
interests of the beneficiary" (U.S. Department of Health and Human
Services). Little is mentioned in federal regulation, however, regarding the nature of the relationship between payee and beneficiary. Limitations on undue influence or unchecked control over the beneficiary
are not specifically addressed.

When an individual or organization assumes the role of entitlement payee, the payee gains significant control of the beneficiary's resources. Coercion occurs when this control is used to alter the behavior or life circumstances of the beneficiary in a way that meets the
needs of the individual or organization, but does not reflect the beneficiary's stated preferences. The use of the term "coercion" in this
chapter is not meant to label or condemn those to whom it applies,
but to initiate discussion regarding the possible barriers to establishing a more effective relationship between beneficiary and payee.

Coercion, in the context of community mental health treatment,
is of equal interest to consumers and providers of mental health services. Any loss or perceived loss of control in clients' lives and decision-making abilities can lead to lack of progress toward health and
self-management (Rosenfield, 1992). Conversely, increased client satisfaction enhances treatment effectiveness, rendering coercive interventions less desirable than empowering alternatives (Mowbray,
1990; Cohen, Putnam, & Sullivan, 1984; Rappaport, 1981).

Few studies have been reported regarding mental health clients
and representative payeeship. Only one study has examined the
client and payee relationship. Findings from this study are reported
later in the chapter.

MEETING THE DEMAND FOR ENTITLEMENT PAYEES

Persons who are eligible for SSI and SSDI assistance often do not receive the benefits to which they are entitled. A report from the United
States Conference of Mayors states that the greatest difficulty applicants face is obtaining the documentation required to establish eligi-

bility. The complexity of the application process coupled with the general lack of information or misinformation about the programs are cited as barriers to participation. Homeless persons with mental illness were identified as having the greatest difficulty in accessing entitlement programs (Reyes, 1988).

Current Social Security Administration policy encourages agencies and institutions to serve as representatives payees for persons with characteristics that render them difficult to serve, such as persons with substance abuse problems or homeless persons with severe mental illness (U.S. Department of Health and Human Services, 1994). In 1992, approximately 1 million persons, or 31%, of all disabled SSI beneficiaries received monthly supplemental income through a representative payee (U.S. Department of Health and Human Services, 1993b). An estimated 11% of beneficiaries with representative payees received their benefits through institutions, agencies, or public officials acting as payees; another 85% received benefits through relatives; and 4% received benefits through friends or other community volunteers (Social Security Administration, personal communication, July 11, 1994). Fewer recipients of SSDI benefits receive monthly income through a representative payee, approximately 24%.

Yet agencies resist providing payee services because of liability for the misuse of funds (Social Security Act, 1935), practical difficulties in providing money management services (Brotman & Muller, 1990), and problems extending treatment to a population that typically has remained outside the traditional system of community mental health services (Baxter & Hopper, 1982). In addition, some agencies are subject to state-level policies that discourage or prohibit mental health service providers from serving as payees because of the potential for conflict of interest (Pham, 1990).

Case managers who are called upon to assume the role of representative payee also resist providing payee services. They perceive managing clients' financial affairs as inconsistent with their clinical role. Moreover, case managers lack training and direction on how to balance the clinical aspects of their job with meeting their clients' basic living needs.

Although models for case management with severely mentally ill persons vary, nearly all are comprehensive in scope, inviting involvement in every aspect of clients' lives. Despite widespread agreement that the needs of these clients are many and various, there is little consensus about the appropriate limit of case managers' involvement in clients' lives. Once the case assignment is made, the case manager is expected to become an integral part of the client's treatment and system of support, coordinating services and functioning as an advocate for client needs.

This level of involvement is viewed with ambivalence by some clients and with fear, anger, or frustration by others (Estroff, 1981; Brotman & Muller, 1990). Clients and mental health advocates can be hesitant to accept payee services from case managers because in many instances there are few means, other than refusal of services, for the client to limit or constrain case-management activities. Still fewer routes exist for clients to monitor and appeal the financial decisions of case managers.

Despite the legal and practical concerns of agencies, the potential conflict between the roles of clinical case manager and that of representative payee, and the lack of consensus regarding how much involvement in clients' lives is necessary, the need for representative payee services remains. Moreover, the demand for such services will likely increase, as homelessness increases approximately 10% each year (Waxman, 1993).

MAKING MONEY DECISIONS

The Ohio Department of Mental Health in conjunction with the Hamilton County Mental Health Board and the FreeStore/FoodBank conducted a 3-year study of the nature of decision-making between clients and payees. The FreeStore/FoodBank is a nonprofit agency providing emergency assistance and casework services to persons residing in Cincinnati's downtown area. The clients who received services from the case management and representative payee project were identified as severely mentally ill and homeless or at high risk for becoming homeless.

In this study, 82 clients and 21 staff were asked a series of questions in face-to-face interviews about money decisions. The purpose of the questions was to explore the relationship between how money decisions were made and the degree of control and level of satisfaction felt by clients (Piazza, Ford, & Cogswell, 1991). The following sections report client responses to questions pertaining to money management, housing choice, medication compliance, and "life in general." Staff responses to questions of control are also reported.

Money Management and Payees

Clients in the study were first asked if they managed their money themselves, if their money was managed by the representative payee only, if they and the payee managed their money together, or if some other person made most of their money management decisions. About half the clients reported that they had an interdependent system of money management, and about half reported depending on the payees to manage their money for them. Fewer than 10% of clients reported managing the money themselves.

Clients were asked to rate on a 3-point scale whether they were very satisfied (3), somewhat satisfied (2), or not at all satisfied (1) with their money management. Clients reported that they were more than "somewhat satisfied" (2.5) with the way their money was managed.

Over half the clients mentioned that what they liked most about *how* their money was managed was the security of having someone manage their money, that is, knowing that their bills were paid, that their money would last to the end of the month, and that they always had spending money.

Complaints about the way their money was managed included not receiving as much money as they thought they were entitled to receive, the amount of spending money received, the disbursement schedule for spending money, and their general lack of control over their money.

Housing Choice and Payees

To assess the perceived level of decision-making control regarding housing choice, the clients were asked whether the place where they lived was chosen by them, by them with someone else, or by someone else. Half the clients indicated that they alone had chosen their housing. Most clients indicated that if they had to move, they would want to choose where they would move.

Clients were asked to report their level of satisfaction with their living arrangements, taking into consideration what they could afford because of their income. Clients expressed they were more than "somewhat satisfied" (2.2) with their living arrangements.

When asked to list what they liked best about their living arrangements, clients most frequently stated that they liked some quality of their housing (e.g., it was attractive, warm, quiet) or the convenience of its location (e.g., it was close to bus lines, restaurants, doctors, and friends). What they disliked most about their living arrangement was often the neighborhood in which they lived (e.g., concerns for personal safety, drug dealing, street noise).

MEDICATION COMPLIANCE AND PAYEES

To determine whether clients who reported taking medication felt that other persons forced them to do so, they were asked why they took their medication as prescribed. Nearly three quarters of the clients who reported taking their medication as prescribed indicated that they took it because it helped them, not because a doctor, counselor, or their payee insisted that they do so. The most commonly stated reasons for not taking or refusing medication were the side effects and that the medication did not help.

Clients who reported that their doctor or counselor insisted that they take their medication were asked what their doctor or counselor did if they did not take their medication. Responses included that they would be hospitalized, that they would be given more education or information regarding their medication, that they would be denied program privileges, or that nothing would happen.

"LIFE IN GENERAL" AND PAYEES

In order to assess the degree of control that clients felt they had over their lives, they were asked whether they made decisions about how to run their lives most of the time, some of the time, or hardly ever. Almost three quarters of the clients reported that they made decisions about how to run their lives most of the time. In general, they were more than "somewhat satisfied" with their level of decision-making.

When clients were asked whether they would like to make decisions about how to run their lives most of the time, some of the time, or hardly ever, three fourths of the clients indicated that they would like to do so most of the time. About 20% stated, however, that they would rather make decisions some of the time. When asked why only some of the time, these clients indicated that they did not always make the best decisions for themselves and would therefore like to have some assistance.

CLIENTS' ATTITUDES TOWARD PAYEES

In order to assess whether clients' attitudes toward their payees might have influenced their satisfaction with services and feelings of control, clients were asked questions about their relationship with their payees. Clients reported that they were "more than satisfied" with the relationship with their payees.

Clients reported that what they most liked about their payees was personal characteristics, such as kindness, honesty, attractiveness, sense of humor, age, gender, or ethnic group, and professional characteristics, such as punctuality, availability, efficiency, and responsibility.

The majority of clients disliked nothing about their payees. For those who did, their dislikes focused primarily on the lack of time the payee spent with them, payee attitudes, the payee's control over their money, and not being able to get money or information when they wanted it.

STAFF PERCEPTIONS OF CONTROL

Service providers in the FreeStore/FoodBank project were also surveyed to assess the level of decision-making authority needed to work with their clients. Most providers felt that they worked collaboratively with their clients and therefore had a good balance of decision-making authority. The level of authority needed and the level actually exercised were rated as low, 2.95 and 2.7 respectively, on a scale of 1 (little or no authority) to 7 (almost total authority).

The main areas in which providers felt that they had too little authority were substance use/abuse behaviors, personal hygiene, housekeeping practices, personal spending habits, and medication compliance. None of the providers felt that they had too much decision-making authority.

MINIMIZING COERCION IN THE
CLIENT–PAYEE RELATIONSHIP

The mental health agency and the case manager-payee share the responsibility for preventing the use of coercion in the payee relationship. Because the case manager-payee is more directly involved in keeping the client engaged, meeting the client's basic needs, and developing a cooperative relationship, resisting the use of coercion is the primary responsibility of the case manager-payee. The mental health agency, however, can play an important role in preventing coercion by communicating clear expectations for professional conduct, by developing processes to monitor and regulate the level of decision-making authority used by case manager-payees, and by dealing with common payee issues on an administrative level.

COMMUNICATING CLEAR EXPECTATIONS FOR CONDUCT

Agency expectations for professional conduct can be communicated through job descriptions and personal services contracts, employee orientation and in-service training, structured supervision, and peer review processes. The policy and procedure manual for the Representative Payee Program of Baltimore Mental Health Systems includes in its mission the statement that "we are committed to acknowledging the right of consumers to make choices and to be included in all clinical decisions" (Baltimore Mental Health Systems, 1992).

Staff development activities can assist case manager-payees to identify situations in which coercion is likely to occur and to more effectively develop cooperative, less coercive relationships with payee clients.

Administrative policies and funding practices that unknowingly promote coercion in payee and client relationships can blur agency expectations for professional conduct. Large caseloads, which do not permit ample time to negotiate money decisions, can result in payees' making choices *for* the clients and not *with* the clients. Service quotas, differential reimbursement schedules for indirect and direct client contacts, and the allocation of future inpatient services based on current use are examples of policies and practices that can adversely affect the amount and intensity of direct intervention used in case manager-payee and client interactions.

DEVELOPING PROCESSES TO MONITOR AND REGULATE AUTHORITY

While agencies must empower case manager-payees to make decisions that affect individual clients, they must also provide processes to monitor and regulate the level of decision-making authority exercised by case manager-payees. Client grievance procedures and agency ombudspersons can encourage clients to report concerns about their case manager-payees. These concerns can be appropriately addressed through supervisory channels and agency policy.

DEALING WITH PAYEE ISSUES ON AN ADMINISTRATIVE LEVEL

Client grievance procedures and staff development activities can help to identify common payee issues. Agency-level policies and administrative decisions can address potentially coercive situations and promote the development of effective relationships between clients and case manager-payees.

Disagreements over the clients' money frequently occur in mental health agencies. One possible response is to assign the role of case manager and the role of payee to different staff members within the mental health agency or other agency. At Skid Row Mental Health Service, Inc., of Los Angeles, financial services are clearly distinguished from social and psychiatric services. The Mental Health Center handles all client contact and provides all case management services, while the county's Office of the Public Administrator–Public Guardian provides all accounting and financial services (Stoner, 1989).

The evaluation of the FreeStore/FoodBank payee project was unable to determine whether combining the roles of case manager and payee or separating the roles was more effective in terms of the specific community outcomes measured. Staff who were surveyed during the evaluation of the project identified advantages with each model.

Advantages of combining the roles of case manager and payee included that doing so offered a more comprehensive service package and allowed more consistency and continuity of care for clients. Advantages of separating the two roles included that doing so allowed case managers to focus on clinical issues and minimized conflicts over money. While staff expressed that a significant disadvantage to separating the roles was that many clients would not choose to receive case management services, most staff believed that clients should be able to choose whether or not their entitlement benefits were to be managed by their case manager.

CONCLUSION

Entitlements such as SSI and SSDI are essential to maintaining severely mentally ill and homeless persons in the community. For some, case managers are their only means of receiving entitlements—the payee of last resort. While there are few federal restrictions on who may qualify as a representative payee, agencies have resisted providing payee services primarily because of liability issues.

Case managers assuming the role of payee take on the responsibility of managing their clients' personal financial affairs, in addition to more traditional therapeutic and advocacy roles. Such intimate knowledge of the life and circumstances of their clients can lead to the misuse of authority and to decisions marked by coercion and forced choices. Many clients are hesitant to accept needed payee services from the mental health agency because there are few means, other than refusal of services, to limit or appeal decisions made by case manager-payees.

But as the research reported in this chapter indicates, coercion does not always occur in the relationship between case manager-payee and client. The key to an effective relationship is knowing which decisions are to be made *for* the client, which are to be made *with* the client, and which are to be made *by* the client alone. The loss or perceived loss of control and decision-making abilities can impede clients' progress toward health and self-management.

The mental health agency and the case manager-payee share the responsibility for preventing the use of coercion in the payee relationship. Coercive practices can be consciously minimized or unknowingly promoted at the agency level. The case manager-payee must recognize negative agency influences and avoid the use of coercion in the decision-making process with clients. Though clients may require assistance in meeting basic needs, in a community-based system of care, they should be able to choose whether their entitlement benefits are managed by their case manager or not.

Agencies can minimize coercion by identifying situations in which it is likely to occur and monitoring these situations carefully. Agency-level policies, client grievance procedures, peer review mechanisms, and staff development strategies that address these potentially coercive situations can promote the development of an effective relationship between the client beneficiary and the case manager-payee—a relationship of increased cooperation and increased possibilities for success in a community setting.

ACKNOWLEDGMENT. Funding for the study described in this chapter was provided by the National Institute of Mental Health (Grant H84-MH42358). The opinions expressed in this chapter are those of the author and do not represent the official position of any aforementioned agency.

REFERENCES

Baltimore Mental Health Systems, Inc. (1992). *Representative payee project policy and procedures manual.* Baltimore: Baltimore Mental Health Systems, Inc.

Baxter, E., & Hopper, K. (1982). The new mendicancy: Homeless in New York City. *American Journal of Orthopsychiatry, 52,* 393–408.

Brotman, A. W., & Muller, J. J. (1990). The therapist as representative payee. *Hospital and Community Psychiatry, 41,* 167–172.

Cohen, N. L., Putnam,. J. E., & Sullivan, A. M. (1984). The mentally ill homeless: Isolation and adaptation. *Hospital and Community Psychiatry, 35,* 922–924.

Estroff, S. (1981). *Making it crazy.* Berkeley: University of California Press.

Mowbray, C. T. (1990). Community treatment of the seriously mentally ill: Is this community psychology? *Journal of Community Psychology, 18,* 893–902.

Pham, V. (1990). *Study No. 90-655.* Alexandria, VA: National Association of State Mental Health Program Directors.

Piazza, S. E., Ford, J., & Cogswell, S. H. (1991). *Case management and representative payeeship as problems for homeless severely mentally disabled persons: Final report.* Columbus: Ohio Department of Mental Health.

Rappaport, J. (1981). In praise of paradox: A social policy of empowerment over prevention. *American Journal of Community Psychology, 9,* 1–25.

Reyes, L. M. (1988). *Barriers to participation in benefit programs.* Washington, DC: U.S. Conference of Mayors.

Rosenfield, S. (1992). Factors contributing to the subjective quality of life of the chronic mentally ill. *Journal of Health and Social Behavior, 33,* 299–315.

Social Security Act of 1935, 205(a), (j), and (k), 1102, and 1631(a)(2) and (d)(1), 42 U.S.C. 405(a), (j), and (k), 1302, and 1383(a)(2) and (d)(1).

Stoner, M. R. (1989). Money management services for the homeless mentally ill. *Hospital and Community Psychiatry, 40,* 751–753.

U.S. Department of Health and Human Services, Social Security Administration (1993a). *Social security handbook.* Washington, DC: U.S. Government Printing Office.

U.S. Department of Health and Human Services, Social Security Administration (1993b). *Social security bulletin: Annual statistical supplement.* Washington, DC: U.S. Government Printing Office.

U.S. Department of Health and Human Services, Social Security Administration (1994). *Social security courier* (February). Washington, DC: U.S. Government Printing Office.

Waxman, L. D. (1993). *Status report on hunger and homelessness in America's cities.* Washington, DC: U.S. Conference of Mayors.

PART IV

RESEARCH AGENDA ON COERCION IN THE COMMUNITY

CHAPTER 8

RESEARCH ON THE COERCION OF PERSONS WITH SEVERE MENTAL ILLNESS

Phyllis Solomon

SIGNIFICANCE OF RESEARCHING COERCION IN THE COMMUNITY

Issues of concern regarding coercion of psychiatric patients, which were once relevant only to psychiatric hospitalization, are now applicable to the community arena as well. The need to understand coercive treatment strategies used in community settings for handling those with severe mental disorders is pressing, as the consequences of the competing values between preserving individual autonomy and protecting vulnerable individuals are far more visible in a growing population of mentally ill people living in the community. For example, homeless mentally ill persons on the streets of virtually every large urban area raise the issue of whether these individuals have an

PHYLLIS SOLOMON • School of Social Work, University of Pennsylvania, Philadelphia, Pennsylvania 19104.

Coercion and Aggressive Community Treatment: A New Frontier in Mental Health Law, edited by Deborah L. Dennis and John Monahan. Plenum Press, New York, 1996.

inherent right to remain in this situation or whether they should be forced into hospitals, homeless shelters, or other structured housing arrangements. These types of dilemmas that are being confronted today make the use of coercive strategies to force compliance with outpatient treatment quite attractive to some (Mulvey, Geller, & Roth, 1987). Coerced treatment includes mandated attendance at day programs, counseling, and acceptance of neuroleptic medication enforced by a threat of institutional controls. The situations that necessitate coercing patients into receiving needed treatment are not going to go away; therefore, coercive strategies will persist and "can no longer be ignored" (Steinwachs et al., 1992, p. 649).

Historically, the justification for coercive interventions for those needing psychiatric treatment was grounded in the police power of the government to protect the community's health and safety and in the state's paternalistic or *parens patriae* power. But since the 1960s, there has been increased emphasis on mentally disordered persons' civil rights and on procedural due process (Monahan & Shah, 1989). More recently, with the growing mental health consumer movement, there has been increasing value placed on an individual's right to self-determination for persons with psychiatric disorders. With the emergence of these competing value-based positions, policymakers are concerned with achieving an appropriate balance between these positions (Hoge et al., 1993).

Although there is limited research on coercion within psychiatric hospitals (Hoge et al., 1993; Monahan et al., 1995), there is virtually none on coercion of mentally ill individuals in community settings. Without valid and reliable information related to coercive practices in community settings, however, it is not possible to adjust policies effectively toward accomplishing this balance. Information is needed on how coercion is employed both formally and informally in community settings and treatment programs, the frequency of coercive acts and behaviors in a range of community settings, the circumstances under which coercive strategies are used and by whom (i.e., clinicians and family members), the determinants of the perceptions of coercion, and the efficacy of the employment of coercive strategies and treatments in order to formulate policies that will balance these competing perspectives (adapted from Hoge et al., 1993).

This chapter will discuss the conceptualization and operationalization of coercion, related methodological issues, and suggested topics of research on coercion of severely mentally ill adults within a range of community settings and programs. It is expected that this research agenda will elicit the needed data to facilitate the adjustment and development of policies and practices that will strike a balance between the competing values. It needs to be recognized that coercion is not necessarily injurious, and in some situations it is essential to protect the safety of the mentally ill person and others. Behaviors that may objectively be coercive may not be experienced as coercive. The issues of subjective and objective perceptions of coercion will be discussed under the definition of coercion.

DEFINING COERCION

Before research topics regarding coercion in the community can be discussed, there needs to be some understanding of the conceptualization of coercion. Carroll (1991) defines coercion "as a process by which an "agent" exercises certain types of control or power over a "target" (p. 130). He further elaborates on this definition by explaining that the agent uses coercive means to get the target to do something that the target would not otherwise do.

Force, manipulation, and persuasion are three types of power that may be coercive depending on the manner in which they are used, as not all forms of power are coercive. Threats of force are included within the context of coercion provided that the agent has the ability to actually follow through on the threat. For example, a threat of a return to jail on a technical violation of parole can be coercive, if the agent utilizing such a threat can and will implement it. Similarly, a spouse who threatens divorce if the target does not sign a voluntary admission is engaging in coercive behavior. Manipulation includes the use of lies, tricks, and misuse of a relationship. An example of a coercive type of manipulation is when service providers lead clients to believe that they have the legal authority to hospitalize them if they do not comply with outpatient commitment, even when the law does not allow for this, as in the state of Pennsylvania (Geller, 1987). This veiled threat may be enough to induce a mentally ill individual to comply with treatment requirements. A common technique of persuasion is the use of inducements to get the target to engage in the desired behavior. For example, an individual in a psychotic state may be convinced of the attractiveness of signing a voluntary admission as opposed to being involuntarily committed by being informed that it will convey such advantages as having grounds privileges or having the ability to initiate release at any time (Carroll, 1991).

Carroll (1991) also discusses how coercion reduces that target's freedom of choice through "removing one or more alternative courses of action" and by "making some of them less desirable" and reduces the target's control over situations through limiting the target's "ability to choose and act" (p.134). If a client is presented with only two structured residential options of where to live, then the client's opportunities or freedom to choose are reduced. The target's own control is the potential influence the client has over his or her own behavior, or what Bandura (1977) has termed "self-efficacy," which is the subjective belief that one can effectively carry out a particular course of action. Carroll (1991) expands on this by explaining that "if an agent reduced the target's control by undermining his or her self-efficacy, creating confusion or distraction, or sedating the target, then the target's opportunities have been reduced" (p. 136). Another way of viewing a lack of control is the cost that is obtained when selecting a particular opportunity has increased to the point at which it may be impossible to make certain choices and to take certain actions.

Hoge et al. (1993) have noted that two aspects of coercion have to be considered when obtaining empirical data to be used in the policy debate. First, given that coercion is extremely sensitive to the context in which it employed, the coercion process must be fully described to all parties involved in the data collection effort. Subsequently, the various aspects of a potentially coercive act require operationalization of the process in the given context, and then the appropriate methodology can be selected. The operationalization needs to take into consideration the nature of the coercive behaviors, such as physical force, manipulation, and deception, and possibly the degree to which these behaviors occur. Second, coercion is a subjective experience of an objective observable act. Both the subjective perceptions and the objective act or process of coercion need to be measured. The triangulation of various perspectives of those involved in the coercive process as well as an independent assessment from a "disinterested party", that is, research investigator or data collector, need to be measured. Thus, separate scales reflecting the views of the various "interested" and "disinterested" parties have to be developed.

MEASUREMENT DEVELOPMENT IN COMMUNITY COERCION

Before research can be undertaken in the area of coercion of mentally ill individuals in the community, work must be conducted on the development of the conceptualization and measurement of coercion. Recently, the MacArthur Research Network of Mental Health and Law developed two scales for measuring patients' perceptions of coercion at mental hospital admission (Gardner et al., 1993). These instruments may provide some direction for the construction of a coercion instrument to be employed in community settings. The development of an instrument to measure coercion in community settings will entail conducting exploratory research to assess the process in which coercion is practiced in a variety of community settings, which will be discussed below. This will include the construction of psychometrically sound scales of both objective and subjective views of coercive behaviors and the employment of formalized mechanisms of coercion, that is, outpatient commitment. Since the practice of coercive behaviors is affected by the environmental context, these scales need to take into consideration the variety of settings. Recognizing that there are a diversity of settings in the community, it may not be feasible to develop a single subjective and a single objective measure of coercion to be employed in a range of community settings for the diversity of individuals involved in the coercive processes, that is, family members, consumers, service providers, and an objective party. However, the greater the applicability of the scales, the greater their potential benefit, as the scales would allow for comparisons across community settings. In addition to scales measuring the perceptions of the coercive process and coercive behaviors, measures are needed to access the various parties' attitudes toward the acceptability of the employment of various types of coercive behaviors and legal mechanisms.

FORMALIZED MECHANISMS OF COERCION

Outpatient commitment is a court-ordered stipulation requiring compliance with community treatment enforced by a threat of psychiatric hospitalization. Similarly, arrests can lead to jail detention and subsequent probation or parole with court-stipulated compliance with treatment enforced by a threat of a return to jail. Conditional-release programs for persons found not guilty by reason of insanity combine aspects of both of these. These are all formalized legal coercive mechanisms.

OUTPATIENT COMMITMENT

The term *outpatient commitment* is a generic one that is used to encompass three approaches: (1) conditional release, (2) substitute for confinement to a psychiatric hospital, and (3) preventive commitment.

Conditional release is when the hospital releases a patient on the condition that the patient comply with specific treatment requirements. This is also known as *trial release* and is analogous to parole in the criminal justice system. The substitute for confinement in a hospital allows a patient to undergo treatment in the community instead of in a hospital. This alternative is arrived at through a civil commitment hearing and is based on the principle of the least restrictive alternative. It is analogous to probation in the criminal justice system. Preventive commitment is similar to a substitute for confinement, but employs "looser legal standards and relaxed criteria." The use of preventive commitment is "to forestall anticipated deterioration, which could result in a person's meeting the stricter standards for commitment to a hospital" (Wilk, 1988, p. 133). Preventive commitment is analogous to diversion in the criminal justice system.

Although outpatient commitment has been discussed as a potentially promising means of treating severely mentally ill individuals in the community, there is a paucity of research on this subject (Mulvey et al., 1987; Wilk, 1988). Mulvey et al. (1987) have noted that "there is neither sufficient empirical guidance for its implementation nor a great amount of evidence that it can be effective on a broad scale" (p. 575). Furthermore, Miller (1988) indicated that there are insufficient data available to develop statutes for outpatient commitment. Surveys of professionals involved in the civil commitment process found that there was a lack of knowledge of whether outpatient commitment was permitted in their state, and clinicians questioned the efficacy of its use (Miller, 1985; Miller and Fiddleman, 1984). Miller and Fiddleman (1984) discuss possible reasons for the reluctance of clinicians to utilize this option and are of the opinion that local attitudes prohibited the use of this alternative. For example, some legal personnel were reluctant to use outpatient commitment and others used it inappropriately and indiscriminately. Also, community mental health center staff were opposed to employing outpatient commitment with unwilling patients. These staff were also reluctant to use outpatient commitment due to their belief that committed patients were more dangerous than voluntary patients and due to their lack of understanding of the procedures involved in outpatient commitment. Some critics who oppose outpatient commitment are concerned that "it could be used to extend judicial and psychiatric control over a broader range of persons" (Hiday & Scheid-Cook, 1989, p. 57). McFarland, Faulkner, Bloom, Hallaux, and Bray (1989), in their survey of civil commitment in Oregon, found that a majority of judges and commitment investigators favored outpatient commitment, but were concerned that the current law did not enable enforcement of the conditions of outpatient commitment.

It seems that further research is needed to assess clinicians', families', consumers', and the general public's knowledge and views regarding the use of outpatient commitment, if such commitment is to become a viable alternative. Information from such research can suggest appropriate training to shift attitudes and alleviate fears resulting from a lack of knowledge. This information may assist in modifying outpatient commitment statutes to make them more amenable to implementation by clinicians and in the allocation of necessary funds for implementation.

Several investigators have conducted quasi-experimental studies of outpatient commitment and have found it to be effective in terms of reduction in lengths of hospitalization, continuance in treatment, and reduction in the number of hospitalizations (Hiday and Scheid-Cook, 1989; Zanni & deVeau, 1986; Van Putten, Santiago, & Berren, 1988), although the results of one study did not support the efficacy of outpatient commitment regarding reduction of readmission (Bursten, 1986). Investigators, however, acknowledged weaknesses in these studies, such as small sample sizes, use of retrospective data, and lack of control groups. Further research is needed to determine the efficacy of outpatient commitment with more rigorous designs that can feasibly be conducted and the determination of the characteristics of the population for whom outpatient commitment can be effective. These studies need to be conducted in a number of states to determine the efficacy as well as the cost-effectiveness of outpatient commitment under various conditions and statutory criteria. The usefulness of these studies would be increased with the addition of such other outcomes as patient functioning, clinical outcomes, and patient and family satisfaction (Zanni & deVeau, 1986). Future studies should also focus on the "interactions between patient characteristics, treatment intervention, treatment setting, and staff characteristics," as treatment efficacy is dependent on these interactions (Zanni & deVeau, 1986, p. 942). For example, factors related to the coercion involved in outpatient commitment and its relationship to the therapeutic alliance need to be researched (Miller, 1988).

In addition to evaluation of patient outcomes, it would be important to examine the implementation processes of these outpatient commitment efforts and of the system level changes that occur while these programs are still in their formative stages (Steinwachs et al.,

1992). The implementation process assessment needs to obtain data regarding the coercive strategies and behaviors that the service providers employ and to compare these with strategies and behaviors utilized by these same providers when working with comparable patients not on outpatient commitment. Thus, researchers need to investigate the extent to which this legal sanction influences the behavior of service providers as well as the behavior of clients.

TECHNICAL VIOLATIONS OF PROBATION OR PAROLE

With the increased stringency of criteria for involuntary hospitalization, there has been growing concern that increasing numbers of severely mentally ill individuals are entering the criminal justice system (Solomon, Rogers, Draine, & Meiserson, 1995a). Once these persons have contact with the criminal justice system through jail detention or arrest, they are often placed on criminal sanctions such as probation or parole. Offenders on probation or parole are released on the condition that they agree to the conditions of release and are aware that they are subject to incarceration should they violate these conditions. For persons with mental illness, the conditions of criminal sanctions while residing in the community can, and frequently do, include stipulations for treatment and for specific housing arrangements. These stipulations are enforced by threat of incarceration. Failure to comply with these conditions of probation or parole is referred to as a violation. Noncompliance with the conditions of parole or probation results in technical violations, while committing a new offense results in a criminal violation (Carroll & Lurigio, 1984 Solomon et al., 1995).

Also, these individuals are under extensive supervision involving multiple service systems that results in increased monitoring of their behaviors and actions, which heightens awareness of socially unacceptable behavior or noncompliance with stipulated treatment (Gottfredson, Mitchell-Herzfeld, & Flanagan, 1982; Martin & Scarpitti, 1990, Tonry, 1990). Given that these individuals are stipulated to specific treatment requirements, mental health service providers as well as substance abuse providers may augment the surveillance of the probation and parole officers and may use the stipulations of release to coerce compliance with treatment. These conditions are not unlike outpatient commitment. The enforcer, however, is the probation or parole officer, and the consequence of noncompliance is jail detention as opposed to psychiatric hospitalization. Coercive strategies are implemented by both the probation or parole officer, who may be a trained mental health professional, and the mental health service provider.

There has been virtually no research in this area, with the exception of some limited research conducted by the author and her colleague. The one study that did assess the use of coercive strategies by case managers who were serving severely mentally ill persons who were released from a large urban jail found that clients whose case managers actively sought legal stipulations to case management as a condition of probation and parole were more likely to return to jail. Case managers often went to court with their clients prior to release to request that clients be stipulated to cooperate with them, for example, take medication as prescribed, and stay in the prescribed housing arrangement, as a condition of their probation or parole (Solomon & Draine, 1995a). Case managers frequently worked very closely with probation and parole officers to coerce clients to comply with prescribed medication by threatening a return to jail. If clients continued to refuse to comply, they would prevail upon the probation and parole officers to file a technical violation of the client's condition of release. Clients would then be reincarcerated. In some instances, clients would be decompensating, but unwilling to sign a voluntary admission to the hospital. The team psychiatrist who worked with the case managers was aware that these clients could not meet the standards for involuntary hospitalization, but felt that the clients were in need of treatment. Since the jail had a comprehensive mental health program, a 49-bed inpatient psychiatric unit, stepdown units, and a psychiatric ambulatory program, reincarceration assured the receipt of needed treatment. Thus, coercive tactics of threatening and following through on reincarceration were employed to force severely mentally ill individuals involved in the criminal justice system to comply with prescribed treatment or be reincarcerated (Solomon & Draine, 1995b).

This is an area that requires further research on the nature of coercive strategies employed by service providers working with this subpopulation of seriously mentally ill individuals and on whether these strategies differ from those used with a seriously mentally ill population who do not have such legal stipulations. The question arises as to whether the coercive strategies employed with this forensic population vary from ones utilized with severely mentally ill individuals under outpatient commitment. There is also the question as to what factors, including client characteristics, case managers, and the system in which the service is delivered, influence the use of such coercive strategies. Research on the process of these coercive tactics is important in order to begin to understand the factors that influence these behaviors in order to provide direction for developing less coercive alternatives.

The efficacy of these types of benevolent coercive strategies has been questioned (Mulvey et al., 1987). Investigators need to assess the efficacy of such strategies and the questions as to which clients they are and are not effective for and whether there are less coercive strategies that can be employed more effectively. Research also needs to assess the extent to which incarceration for technical violations is being used for the management of psychiatric disorders more than for the conventional use of punishment of criminal behavior. Currently, the author is in the process of conducting such a study funded by the National Institute of Mental Health. Results from such studies are needed to begin to direct policies and programs to ensure that criminalization of seriously mentally ill individuals does not occur. The perspectives of consumers need to be assessed as some consumers prefer jail or prison over psychiatric hospitalization.

CONDITIONAL-RELEASE PROGRAMS FOR PERSONS FOUND NOT GUILTY BY REASON OF INSANITY

There are specialized programs for persons found not guilty by reason of insanity that are comparable to outpatient commitment and to conditions of probation and parole. Defendants who are found not guilty by reason of insanity frequently suffer from a severe mental disorder. The Conditional Release Program in California (Lamb, Weinberger, & Gross, 1988) is "inclined to place patients in court-mandated community outpatient treatment programs rather than simply keeping them in the hospital until their term of commitment has expired or their sanity has been restored and then having to release them unconditionally. Patients who decompensate, refuse to cooperate with their treatment plan, or become dangerous to others may have their outpatient status revoked and be returned to the forensic hospital to continue serving their term of commitment" (p. 451). Oregon's Psychiatric Security Review Board is a similar program. The board is composed of five part-time members who function independent of the court. The board members determine whether someone should be committed to the state hospital, conditionally released to the community with treatment stipulations, or discharged (Bloom, Williams, & Bigelow, 1991).

The research that has been conducted on these programs indicates that they are cost-effective when compared to hospitalization (Bloom et al., 1991), although the data from Lamb's study in California seemed somewhat less impressive in relation to its efficacy. As other states develop similar programs, there is a need for further research on the cost-effectiveness of these programs. With increased emphasis on accountability and cost of programs today, there is a need for research on cost-effectiveness of programs. Also, it would be important to conduct process evaluations in order to understand how these programs operate and, if they are effective, what elements make them effective. This information would be helpful for the development of programs for other severely mentally ill clients who are not persons found "not guilty by reason of insanity."

INFORMAL MECHANISMS OF COERCION

There are also less formalized means of coercing severely mentally ill individuals to comply with needed treatment. These means are interpersonal behaviors such as the use of deception, manipulation, and lying. These behaviors may occur in a variety of community settings, such as residential facilities, treatment programs, or the homes of families of severely mentally ill persons.

FAMILY MECHANISMS OF COERCION

As a consequence of deinstitutionalization, large numbers of mentally ill individuals reside with their families (Goldman, 1982; Carpentier, Lesage, Goulet, Lalonde, & Renaud, 1992). Families utilize an array of coping strategies in managing their mentally ill relatives, regardless of whether the relatives reside with them or not. Some such strategies are more formalized mechanisms of coercion and others are informal coercive strategies. Some families unfortunately seek to distance themselves from their ill relatives to relieve some of their burden that is untenable or for concerns of their own safety. In Philadelphia, for example, it is not unusual for a family to obtain a judicial restraining order that bars their ill relative from their home. If the relative violates this order, he or she is subject to arrest and possible subsequent jail detention. Given that the Philadelphia jails have a comprehensive mental health program, a violation of a restraining order provides a degree of assurance to the family that their relative will probably receive needed treatment, as restraining orders are often initiated due to the relative's psychiatric decompensation. However, the extent to which families employ this strategy for treatment purposes is unknown. There is no literature on the use of restraining orders by relatives of seriously mentally ill persons other than that of the author (Solomon, Draine & Delaney, 1995b), and therefore it is not known whether this is only a local phenomenon. There needs to be research on families' use of this formalized coercive mechanism. In addition, there is a need for process assessment of the conditions under which this mechanism is employed. For instance, more needs to be known about the characteristics of the ill relatives and the families, as well as the family dynamics prior to instituting this mechanism. Possibly, mediation programs could be developed that may prevent the use of this coercive mechanism. This process may lend itself to a research demonstration investigation to determine the efficacy and cost-effectiveness of a mediation program intervening or preventing this coercive mechanism from being utilized.

Families do engage in a variety of coercive behaviors and strategies to force their ill relatives to comply with necessary treatment. In some instances, this behavior may include threats of involuntary hospitalization. Greenley (1986) has reconceptualized expressed emotion (EE) as "interpersonal social control" that is a form of coercion. Greenley's explanation of social control is quite consistent with the conceptualization of formal and informal coercion: "Social control varies from formal to informal: 1) formal social control is more impersonal and has more universalistically applied controls such as those embodied in law and implemented by police, courts, and other institutional representatives; 2) informal social control is more personal and has more particularistic controls, such as those used in interpersonal discourse to try to get friends and relatives to try to change their behaviors" (p. 25). It is not uncommon for people to "try to shape each other's behavior by suggesting, nagging, threatening, arguing, criticizing, playing on feelings of obligation and guilt" (Greenley, 1986, p.25), these tactics being very similar to the major components of expressed emotion (EE), which are critical comments, hostility, and emotional overinvolvement (Brown, Birley, & Wing, 1972; Vaughn & Leff, 1976; Vaughn, Snyder, Jones, Freeman & Falloon, 1984). Critical comments are the most important component of high-scoring EE families. Greenley (1986) found that an examination of the content validity of the coded EE items supports the contention that it measures interpersonal social control.

The research in the area of EE has found that high EE is related to psychotic relapse of recently discharged relatives who reside with or have high levels of contact with their families (Brown et al., 1972; Vaughn & Leff, 1976; Vaughn et al., 1984). The findings, however, cannot specify causality; therefore, the direction of the effect is unclear (Bellack & Mueser, 1993). Research into understanding the EE phenomenon will offer some insight into the use of coercive behaviors by families. For example, to what extent are highly critical comments related to psychotic behaviors or negative behaviors of schizophrenia or to the characteristics of family members themselves? Under what circumstances are these critical comments effective in getting the relative to comply with prescribed treatment regimens? In addition, what is the relationship between these coercive behaviors and client outcomes; for example, what is the consequent symptomatology or social function? In addition, research on other possible coercive behaviors of families needs to be conducted, including the use of threats of hospitalization and the circumstances and factors that influence the use of this coercive strategy. This research needs to be both process and outcome. In addition, research needs to assess the extent to which consumers perceive various behaviors as coercive.

COERCIVE BEHAVIORS BY SERVICE PROVIDERS

Frequently, mental health service providers share common goals with the families of severely mentally ill individuals in wanting these individuals to comply with needed treatment. It is unclear to what extent service providers engage in similar types of coercive behavior to encourage clients to comply with prescribed treatment, be it medications or psychosocial treatments. Bachrach (1994) notes in a recent article that housing assignments have been used to coerce clients to comply with treatment. The most obvious use of coercion is the threat of admission to a psychiatric hospital. A scientific examination of various community residential settings is needed to assess the nature and extent to which staff of these facilities and settings engage in coercive strategies and with what consequences. Some of these residential facilities and program settings appear to utilize more controlling mechanisms to get clients to comply with rules and regulations than do others. Some staff will engage in threats of hospitalization if clients do not comply with treatment. Do settings in which staff engage in highly critical comments also have high rates of psychotic relapse? What is the efficacy of coercive strategies in these settings in terms of a variety of client outcomes, for example, symptomatology, social function, quality of life, and treatment satisfaction?

Intensive case management may function as an intensive monitoring of clients with the use of coercive methods to engage clients in what is viewed as appropriate treatment with the justification that participation in the treatment is in the client's best interest. An examination of different case management models and the nature and use of coercive techniques would seem to be important preliminary research to determine the efficacy of various coercive techniques with regard to client outcomes. Currently, little is known of the coercive strategies employed by case managers or other mental health service providers, how clients respond to these strategies, and how effective they are. It is known that intensive case managers can be highly aggressive in attempting to engage clients in case management services, as a few clients have filed for restraining orders against their case managers to get the case managers to leave them alone. In addition, it would be important to have information on the efficacy of differing strategies for a variety of subpopulations of severely mentally ill clients. Also unknown is the extent to which coercive behaviors may be detrimental to the development of a therapeutic alliance with a severely mentally ill client.

COUNTERBALANCE: CLIENT CONTROL AND CHOICE

A relatively new strategy being employed to return some control to severely mentally ill persons, a countervailing approach to coercion, is the use of advance directives. An advance directive in mental health is a signed legal document that allows patients to give instructions to mental health care providers and institutions regarding future psychiatric care when they decompensate. Thus, when severely mentally ill persons are in remission or stabilized and have the capability to make informed choices and to recognize the potential for decompensation, they provide instructions regarding their care in the event that a crisis occurs and they do not have the capacity to choose appropriate treatment. This process is generally a collaborative one involving the consumer, family, and service provider. This prior consent agreement has been termed the *Ulysses contract* (Rosenson & Kasten, 1991). Rogers and Centifanti (1991), two consumer advocates, have proposed the *Mill's will,* which enables consumers to both consent to and refuse treatment in advance of the crisis. These options give choice and freedom to the consumers. Currently, there is no published research in this area, although the Community Support Program of the Center for Mental Health Services is funding some research on this topic. There is a need to assess both the process and the outcomes of the implementation of these advance directives. If these approaches are effective, they may provide for a means to counterbalance some of the coercive strategies that are currently being employed.

There is also a need for research regarding self-efficacy of severely mentally ill clients. With increasing emphasis on consumer choice and participation in treatment decisions, little is known concerning the extent to which the degree of involvement by a consumer is related to the consumer's belief in his or her capability to successfully carry out the proposed treatment plan. Client outcomes of treatment may be related to the degree of a client's self-efficacy. The self-efficacy of seriously mentally ill individuals is an understudied area.

CONCLUSION

The area of coercion in community settings is fertile ground for research. The importance of understanding and determining the efficacy of coercive behaviors and strategies is more pressing than in the past, and yet limited research has been conducted on this topic. There is much preliminary work that needs to be conducted on the conceptualization, operationalization, and development of psychometrically sound instruments of coercion in the community, on both subjective and objective perceptions. Furthermore, there is a need for documentation of the extent and nature of coercive behaviors and strategies that are undertaken in a range of community settings by individuals in various roles and capacities, i.e., families, case managers, and other providers. The efficacy of these coercive strategies and approaches in terms of a variety of client outcomes, for example, symptomatology, social function, satisfaction with quality of life and treatment, and community settings, is imperative. Similarly, research is needed on client control and choice. This research agenda will provide direction for changes in policies and programs to better balance the competing values of client autonomy and protection of client rights in opposition to forced treatment in the best interest of the client or *parens patriae* approach.

REFERENCES

Bachrach, L. (1994). Residential planning: Concepts and themes. *Hospital and Community Psychiatry, 45,* 202–203.
Bandura, A. (1977). Self-efficacy: Toward a unifying theory of behavior change. *Psychological Review, 84,* 191–215.
Bellack, A., & Mueser, K. (1993). Psychosocial treatment for schizophrenia. *Schizophrenia Bulletin, 19,* 317–326.
Bloom, J. D., Williams, M. A., & Bigelow, D. A. (1991). Monitored conditional release of persons found not guilty by reason of insanity. *American Journal of Psychiatry, 148,* 444–448.
Brown, G. W., Birley, J. L. T., & Wing, J. K. (1972). Influence of family life on the course of schizophrenic disorders: A replication. *British Journal of Psychiatry, 121,* 241–258.
Bursten, B. (1986). Post hospital mandatory outpatient treatment. *American Journal of Psychiatry, 143,* 1255–1258.
Carpentier, N., Lesage, A., Goulet, A., Lalonde, P., & Renaud, M. (1992). Burden of care of families not living with young schizophrenic relatives. *Hospital and Community Psychiatry, 43,* 38–43.
Carroll, J. (1991). Consent to mental health treatment: A theoretical analysis of coercion, freedom, and control. *Behavioral Sciences and the Law, 9,* 129–142.
Carroll, J., & Lurigio (1984). Conditional release on probation and parole: Implications for provision of mental health services. In L. Teplin (Ed.), *Mental health and criminal justice* (pp. 297–315). Beverly Hills, CA:
Gardner, W., Hoge, S., Bennett, N., Roth, L., Lidz, C., Monahan, J., & Mulvey, E. (1993). Two scales for measuring patients' perceptions for coercion during mental hospital admission. *Behavioral Sciences and the Law, 11,* 307–321.
Geller, J. (1987). The quandaries of enforced community treatment and unenforced outpatient commitment statutes. *Journal of Psychiatry and Law, 15,* 151–158.
Goldman, H. H. (1982). Mental illness and family burden: A public health perspective. *Hospial and Community Psychiatry, 33,* 557–560.
Gottfredson, M., Mitchell-Herzfeld, S., & Flanagan, T. (1982). Another look at the effectiveness of parole supervision. *Journal of Research in Crime and Delinquency, 19,* 277–298.
Greenley, J. (1986). Social control and expressed emotion. *Journal of Nervous and Mental Disease, 174,* 24–30.
Hiday, V., & Scheid-Cook, T. (1989). A follow-up of chronic patients committed to outpatient treatment. *Hospital and Community Psychiatry, 40,* 52–59.
Hoge, S., Lidz, C., Mulvey, E., Roth, L., Bennett, N., Siminoff, L., Arnold, R., & Monahan, J. (1993). Patient, family, and staff perceptions of coercion in mental hospital admission: An exploratory study. *Behavioral Sciences and the Law, 11,* 281–293.
Lamb, H. R., Weinberger, L. E., & Gross, B. H. (1988). Court-mandated community outpatient treatment for persons not guilty by reason of insanity: A five-year follow-up. *American Journal of Psychiatry, 145,* 450–456.

Martin, S. S., & Scarpitti, F. R. (1990). An intensive case management approach for paroled IV drug users. *Journal of Drug Issues, 23,* 43–59.

McFarland, B., Faulkner, L., Bloom, J., Hallaux, R., & Bray, J. D. (1989). Investigators' and judges' opinions about civil commitment. *Bulletin of the American Academy of Psychiatry and Law, 17,* 15–25.

Miller, R. (1985). Commitment to outpatient treatment: A national survey. *Hospital and Community Psychiatry, 36,* 265–267.

Miller, R. (1988). Outpatient civil commitment of the mentally ill: An overview and an update. *Behavioral Sciences and the Law, 6,* 99–118.

Miller, R., & Fiddleman, P. (1984). Outpatient commitment: Treatment in the least restrictive environment? *Hospital and Community Psychiatry, 35,* 147–151.

Monahan, J., Hoge, S., Lidz, C., Roth, L., Bennett, N., Gardner, W., & Mulvey, E. (1995). Coercion and commitment: Understanding involuntary mental hospital admission. *International Journal of Law and Psychiatry, 18,* 249–263.

Monahan, J., & Shah, S. (1989). Dangerousness and commitment of the mentally disordered in the United States. *Schizophrenia Bulletin, 15,* 541–553.

Mulvey, E., Geller, J., & Roth, L. (1987). The promise and peril of involuntary outpatient commitment. *American Psychologist, 42,* 571–584.

Rogers, J., & Centifanti, J. B. (1991). Beyond "self-paternalism": Response to Rosenson and Kasten. *Schizophrenia Bulletin, 17,* 9–14.

Rosenson, M. K., & Kasten, A. M. (1991). Another view of autonomy: Arranging for consent in advance. *Schizophrenia Bulletin, 17,* 1–7.

Solomon, P., & Draine, J. (1995a). Jail recidivism in a forensic case management program. *Health and Social Work, 20,* 168–173.

Solomon, P., & Draine J. (1995b). One-year outcomes of a randomized trial of case management with seriously mentally ill clients leaving jail. *Evaluation Review, 19,* 256–273.

Solomon, P., Draine J., & Delaney, M. A. (1995). The use of restraining orders by families of severely mentally ill adults. *Administration and Policy in Mental Health, 23,* 157–161.

Solomon, P., Rogers, R., Draine, J., & Meyerson, A. (1995b). Interaction of the criminal justice system and psychiatric professionals where civil commitment standards are prohibitive. *Bulletin of the American Academy of Psychiatry and Law, 23,* 117–128.

Steinwachs, D., Cullum, H., Dorwart, R., Flynn, L., Frank, R., Friedman, M., Herz, M., Mulvey, E., Snowden, L., Test, M. A., Tremaine, L., & Windle, C. (1992). Service systems research. *Schizophrenia Bulletin, 18,* 627–668.

Tonry, M. (1990). Stated and latent functions of ISP. *Crime and Delinquency, 36,* 174–191.

Van Putten, R., Santiago, J., & Berren, M. (1988). Involuntary outpatient commitment in Arizona: A retrospective study. *Hospital and Community Psychiatry, 39,* 953–958.

Vaughn, C., & Leff, J. (1976). The influence of family and social factors on the course of psychiatric illness. *British Journal of Psychiatry, 129,* 125–137.

Vaughn, C., Snyder, K., Jones, S., Freeman, W., & Falloon, I. (1984). Family factors in schizophrenic relapse. *Archives of General Psychiatry, 41,* 1169–1177.

Wilk, R. (1988). Involuntary outpatient commitment of the mentally ill. *Social Work, 33,* 133–137.

Zanni, G., & deVeau, L. (1986). Inpatient stays before and after outpatient commitment. *Hospital and Community Psychiatry, 37,* 941–942.

Chapter 9

COERCION AND SOCIAL CONTROL
A FRAMEWORK FOR RESEARCH ON AGGRESSIVE STRATEGIES IN COMMUNITY MENTAL HEALTH

Anne M. Lovell

. . . the notion of an ethical–topological opposition between asylum and "community"—between, respectively, a closed space of repression and internment and an open space of liberty and solidarity—is, in some respects, both paradoxical and unreal.

—Gordon (1986)

According to the philosopher Charles Taylor (1989), the moral origins of our viewpoints remain largely implicit until some challenge pushes

Anne M. Lovell • Department of Sociology, University of Toulouse, Le Mirail, 31058 Toulouse, Cedex, France.

Coercion and Aggressive Community Treatment: A New Frontier in Mental Health Law, edited by Deborah L. Dennis and John Monahan. Plenum Press, New York, 1996.

them into the foreground. Coercion in involuntary hospitalization has been treated as a moral construct (Wertheimer, 1993), and preliminary research suggests that patients experience it as such (Bennett et al., 1993). Today, converging notions of person-centered care, individual rights, and the centrality of agency and personhood are shifting public debate in the United States from a focus on coercion in traditional, inpatient settings to evaluating its presence in community care. Opponents of coercive practices propose empowering alternatives, while proponents question whether psychiatric treatment is even possible without a sanctioned system of coercion (Gellner, cited in Group for the Advancement of Psychiatry, 1994). Research on the imposition of mental health interventions in community settings will not provide answers to the ethical questions raised. However, it can problematize coercion as a moral construct while examining its effect as a treatment strategy.

Drawing on anthropology, sociology, and social psychology, this chapter suggests a framework for thinking about research concerning the use of coercion in community mental health. After a brief review of how coercion is treated in studies of outpatient mental health, a broader conceptualization is presented. Although this alternative way of thinking about coercion runs through much of the current discussion on post-deinstitutionalization strategies in mental health, it remains latent. Following from this framework, two ways of examining coercion—in relation to its contextual determinants and in relation to its alternatives—are suggested. Finally, some measurement and design issues, pertinent to more traditional mental health services research on coercion and aggressive treatment, are raised.

VISIBLE AND INVISIBLE: COERCION IN OUTPATIENT MENTAL HEALTH

The category of "aggressive" or "assertive" treatment covers a broad range of approaches. Some, like assertive community treatment (ACT) and intensive case management (ICM), have by now been highly elaborated, codified, and replicated in different parts of the United States. Others, such as psychiatric mobile crisis teams and outreach programs, may vary more in their components, structures, and philosophies. Some proponents and opponents of ACT, ICM, and similar programs critique them for the control they exert over clients. They also warn against reproducing the negative aspects of the total institutions these community alternatives are supposed to supplant (Mowbray, 1990; Witheridge, 1991).

To date, however, coercive practices in these programs have not constituted objects of formal research. Instead, studies of aggressive and assertive treatment tend to focus on the effectiveness of extra hospital services, broadly defined, in preventing relapse, lengthening community tenure, ameliorating psychiatric symptomatology, heightening social functioning, and improving the quality of life in a multiplicity of life domains (e.g. Stein & Test, 1980; Bond, Witheridge, & Dincin, 1990).

Other research has investigated the effectiveness of aggressive treatment in meeting unmet needs, as defined by mental health providers. While not explicitly modeled as such, aggressive treatment seems to function in these studies as a mediating variable that contributes to engagement of individuals in a process, such as ongoing case management or psychosocial rehabilitation. These outcomes may themselves constitute treatment interventions, while acting as pathways to further treatment, rehabilitation, or more highly valued living situations, such as stable housing or employment (Rog, 1988; Barrow, Hellman, Lovell, Plapinger, & Struening, 1991). This needs-oriented research is concerned primarily with heavy users of psychiatric services, as well as with those homeless persons labeled mentally ill who are considered "hard to reach," if not "service-resistant." Such latter characterizations of the target group often imply, to service providers and family members, the justification of coercive mechanisms to assure that a potential patient will enter into treatment. Hence, coercion remains an unarticulated theme in these studies.

On the other hand, coercion is explicitly addressed in a quite different area of research on outpatient care. Here, coercion in community-based treatment is identified with some form of involuntary outpatient commitment (IOC). This procedure involves a judicial (court-ordered) requirement that a patient adhere to a medication regime, comply with monitoring, or actively participate in treatment, educational, or vocational programs, or some combination thereof, in lieu of hospitalization (American Psychiatric Association, 1987). Some form of IOC is permitted by most states, but the statutory provisions governing it vary (McCafferty & Dooley, 1990), as do administrators' understanding of the process (Miller, 1985, 1992), the frequency of its use, the characteristics of prototypical IOC patients, and the nature of IOC programs (Keilitz, 1990). Much of the literature on IOC is concerned with its applicability as a least restrictive alternative to involuntary hospitalization. With few exceptions,[1] empirical studies of the relative effectiveness of IOC programs focus on narrow outcomes, either rehospitalization or compliance with court-approved treatment regimens in community-based settings. This focus is understandable, given that the stated purpose of outpatient commitment is usually to avoid rehospitalization and inpatient commitment by assuring treatment that reduces the need for these measures.

From a current mental health services research perspective, however, using compliance with medication or services as outcome measures is limiting. Furthermore, compliance with treatment is itself another form of coercion, historically and currently linked to medical dominance; in fact, in earlier periods, compliance was known as "physician control" (Donovan & Blake, 1992). To comply means to defer to or act in accordance with demands, rules, requests, orders. The framing of research primarily around the issue of compliance therefore encloses it in a tautology: One coercive mechanism is examined to determine whether it leads to another.

Finally, a body of literature on self-help, originating from such diverse sources as the psychiatric survivor/consumer movement and the field of community psychology, assumes that coercive interventions, including "assertive treatment," "assertive case management," IOC, and others, are less desirable than empowering alternatives (e.g., Mowbray, 1990; Rappaport, 1981). The question of whether programs that are consumer-run or client-oriented or both work as alternatives to coercive (usual) services underlies much of this work but remains untested. Consumer/survivor groups go further in suggesting that self-help (particularly its function of validating experience), choice, and participation render many coercive forms of treatment unnecessary (e.g., Knight, Lovell, & Stastny, 1992; Fisher, 1992). Thus, they explicitly treat coercion as a moral construct.

---

[1]The North Carolina studies (Hiday and Scheid-Cook, 1987, 1989) examine behavioral outcomes. Other studies use exacerbation of symptoms as an outcome (reviewed in Keilitz, 1990). Although the question of whether outpatient commitment prevents clinical deterioration has yet to be answered with adequately designed studies, it remains a strong concern of clinicians and administrators (Miller, 1992; Group for the Advancement of psychiatry, 1994).

A SOCIAL CONTROL FRAMEWORK FOR
UNDERSTANDING COERCION

Another perspective opens the way for examining coercion within a broad conceptual framework, incorporating both legal and nonlegal, subjective and objective meanings. The sociology of mental health situates psychiatric interventions and other forms of mental health treatment within the domain of social control. Coercion in mental health practice thus emerges as an inherently *social* act, as one of the ways in which members of a society respond to forms of behavior they define as deviant or disruptive to their sense of social order.

Certainly coercion entails a psychological dimension as well. The perception of what may "objectively" appear to be a coercive practice will vary among individuals (Goffman, 1961; Rogers, 1993; Lidz, Mulvey, Arnold, Bennett, & Kirsch, 1993; Hoge et al., 1993). However, to extricate the concept of coercion from the broader framework of social control and, hence, its larger context, runs the risk of masking what actually takes place in mental health treatment. For the same reason, the rest of the chapter will use the terminology of social control and mental illness. While such language may appear to reinforce an illness paradigm, it represents social processes for what they are.

The diverse responses people make to behavior they label "mentally ill" constitute different types of social control (Horwitz, 1982). Thus, outreach techniques, therapy, arrest, and "talking down" a friend are all variations of social control. Some are based on the consent of all parties involved in the interaction, others are forced on one party by the others. The nature of the relationship between parties can be conceptualized as a series of ideal types, ranging from sheer force to persuasive techniques. Thus, the ways of obtaining desired behavior or action from a party perceived as "mentally disordered" can be pictured as lying on a continuum with "pure" coercion at one end and bilateral control or voluntarism, at the other (see Figure 1). Involuntary outpatient commitment is an example of the former, counseling voluntarily entered into illustrates the latter.

Coercion →   Coerced   → Utilitarian   → Persuasion
            Voluntarism   Compliance

FIGURE 1. Typology of social control of mental illness in outpatient settings.

Definitions and other examples of these types of social control in mental health occur in descriptions of aggressive treatment.[2] At least four main types can be identified. In *coercion,* force is used to compel the person labeled mentally ill to act or refrain from acting in a certain way. Coercion may be legally sanctioned or not. Involuntary removal of a homeless person from a public space by a mobile psychiatric team that is legally authorized to transport her to a hospital for psychiatric evaluation, as is the case in New York City, constitutes one example. The physical ejection from a drop-in center of someone who attacks a fellow client illustrates an extralegal sanction.

Both physical and emotional coercion are possible. High expressed emotion (EE) directed by family members to a relative who suffers from schizophrenia can constitute emotional coercion. Greenley (1986) has hypothesized that family members use high EE as an interpersonal form of social control over their relative when behavior arouses fears and anxiety. This hypothesis has been further refined, suggesting that emotional social control may be more likely when the locus of control of symptoms is perceived as internal (Lefley, 1992). Emotional coercion can be postulated for treatment settings as well. Pepper and Ryglewicz (1987) propose a program analogue to EE, interactional intensity (II),[3] which encompasses attitudes, behavioral patterns, individuals, and group responses to clients. Like those of EE, the attitudes expressed through II are critical, hostile, or emotionally overwhelming. Other forms of emotional coercion can be postulated. For example, indoctrination has often accompanied the political uses of psychiatry. Closer to the topic at hand would be the creation of total emotional dependency on a service provider, sometimes an explicit strategy of service providers working with clients they view as service-resistant.

A more complex, mixed type of social control applied to behavior perceived as mentally ill is *coerced voluntarism* (Peyrot, 1985). Here, one party uses the threat of a negative sanction to compel the other to accept a treatment or service intervention. The most common example in mental health is the "you sign or I sign" technique for voluntary hospitalization. An example observed in aggressive treatment settings pertains to a policeman, not part of a mental health program, who informs a homeless person that he must either accompany an

[2]The examples in the remainder of this chapter are taken from the author's fieldwork in programs for homeless persons labeled mentally ill.
[3]I thank Harriet Lefley for bringing II to my attention.

outreach worker to a residential treatment center or be arrested for trespassing and urinating in public. In another case, a client whose loud, ongoing delusional commentary keeps others in a transitional residence awake at night is told to take his medication with the tacit understanding that his refusal will result in involuntary hospitalization.

Utilitarian compliance (Lipsky, 1980) comprises an even less direct form of coercion. This type of sanction is present when practitioners demand certain behaviors or actions (e.g., medication compliance, money management, abstention from drugs or alcohol) from clients or potential clients in return for desired resources (e.g., housing, assistance with entitlements, a "clean" referral to another program). It is a commonly used coercive intervention when goods and services are scarce. Many persons targeted by urban mental health programs are poor and multiply discriminated against (as ethnic minorities, as mentally ill, and as homeless). They lack the symbolic capital (Bourdieu, 1977) of a nonstigmatized status, as well as access to needed resources. Community-based mental health programs, like other types of street-level organizations, wield wide discretion over the allocation of desired goods and services (e.g., emergency funds, shelter, and even housing) and the conferral of status (e.g., compliant patient, treatment-resistant client). Utilitarian compliance becomes an effective means of managing their client populations.[4]

In *persuasion*, both the practitioner and the client retain some control over the intervention; that is, both can enter into the relationship or terminate it at will. Persuasion entails trust and acceptance by the party subjected to the intervention. Thus, for this voluntary form of treatment to work, both parties must share somewhat the same meanings, beliefs, or symbolic system (Horwitz, 1982). Thus, it is a normative or value-driven form of control. As an example, a person engaged through outreach may agree to attend a day program because she believes, as does her worker, that it will help her in some way.

These four types of social control applied to mental health are simply ideal types, implying that many mechanisms lie somewhere in between. In reality, they can be further differentiated according to the degree to which they are invisible, or covert. It is partly this dimension of transparency that blurs the dividing lines between the various types. For example, a client may appear to engage in a voluntary rela-

[4]Utilitarian compliance in programs for homeless persons labeled mentally ill is described in Lovell (1992).

tionship when he accepts an injection of a long-acting neuroleptic that he thinks is a flu shot. In some cases, homeless persons labeled mentally ill accept anything from a sandwich to shelter without knowledge that they are engaging in a mental health program (Lovell, 1992; Lovell, Richmond, & Shern, 1995). On the other hand, the coercion may be imposed by the client. For example, some perfunctorily go through the motions of a therapeutic relationship, or accept a label of mental illness they do not really believe, in order to obtain a needed resource, be it a meal, a bed for the night, or a sympathetic ear (Lovell, 1992).

In reality, these various degrees of control exist contemporaneously in a given context of mental health and social services. By now, it is apparent that the opening up of hospitals in the United States not only gave way to more flexible, less coercive mental health interventions in the community but also perpetuated the confinement of patients in a whole range of other total and quasi-total institutions (Goffman, 1961), from prisons to nursing homes to highly restrictive residences (Castel, Castel, & Lovell, 1982; Brown, 1984). Similarly, in the absence of adequate informal ways of responding to persons labeled mentally ill, once persons labeled as such appeared in communities, the use of legal coercion to exclude and contain them multiplied (Horwitz, 1982, 108).

At another level, stricter forms of social control are deemed necessary to the effectiveness of less coercive treatment mechanisms. Hence, a Group for the Advancement of Psychiatry (1994) working group on outpatient commitment, echoing earlier literature, states that for this less coercive method to be effective, rapid police and judicial action must be available and involuntary rehospitalization must remain an option. In conclusion, the range of therapeutic interventions might be most fruitfully examined as a functioning whole, rather than as individual modalities in isolation from one another.

Having set out a framework for understanding coercion in aggressive treatment, we can now turn to specific areas of research to which it can be applied. Both the determinants and the effectiveness of social control in mental health can be examined. As the studies reviewed above present a mental health services research paradigm within which coercion can be studied, here two unexamined themes are presented: the contextual determinants of coercion and the determinants and effectiveness of noncoercive alternatives.

GETTING AT THE BIG PICTURE: CONTEXTUAL DETERMINANTS OF COERCION

Programs such as the "assertive community treatment" models and intensive case management use at least some forms of coercion, often acknowledged as "social control." These practices may be related to the client's characteristics and behavior, to the practitioner's orientation, or to similarities and differences between the two parties (see below). Can it be assumed, though, that the determinants of coercion are reducible to the relationship between practitioner and client? Several alternative hypotheses might serve as guides to a better understanding of what transpires in aggressive treatment in the community. These possibilities are presented not as givens, but as empirical questions.

First, the work of practitioners is bound to some extent by organizational constraints, reimbursement mechanisms being an obvious example. Utilitarian compliance and coerced voluntarism take place when agencies cannot afford to turn clients away, because they are funded according to a *per capita* logic. At first glance, such a possibility appears ludicrous because of the enormous number of homeless persons with psychiatric disabilities whose needs go unmet. However, many are reluctant to use services, and even more so when those services are known to employ legally sanctioned coercion, such as involuntary transportation to a hospital. Programs for homeless mentally ill do in fact work to obtain and maintain a necessary monthly quota of clients (Lovell, 1992). As is true for other types of social services, accountability within a larger funding structure may therefore coerce staff to increase the demand for their services (Lipsky, 1980; Peyrot, 1985) and thereby set in motion the different control mechanisms for getting clients.

Second, many programs, particularly for homeless persons labeled mentally ill, respond to numerous constituencies beyond the services world. In many urban areas, staff's motivations cannot easily be separated out from the interests of other parties, outside the program. In New York City, Outreach and other street-level programs have been sponsored by business groups, the parks department, and transportation authorities. Many such services developed initially in reponse to residents' fears about how "mentally ill" or "homeless" would affect property values or the appearance and safety of the neighborhood. Public and private groups, such as transportation agencies, merchant organizations, and block organizations, have funded services for the purpose of removing "undesirables" from public space (Dutton and Dukerich, 1991; Lovell, Richmond, and Shern, in preparation; Whyte, 1988). Put another way, public reactions to the Larry Hogues and Joyce Browns—individuals who take on great symbolic value as threats to public safety or comfort—exert important effects on coercive techniques for all persons labeled mentally ill. Coercive practices at a program or microlevel may in fact be determined by macro- or mesolevel demands.

Third, the relationship between scarcity of resources and coercive practices demands investigation, at several levels. Historically, during periods of "great confinement," asylums served to enclose persons without family or community resources (Horwitz 1982, p. 110). Currently, the failure of less restrictive forms of social control is thought to be associated with the paucity of mental health resources, implying that scarcity leads to more coercion. For example, mental health administrators in the United States perceive this lack as a reason for the unsuccessful application of outpatient commitment as an alternative to more coercive methods (Miller, 1992). Noncompliance with court-ordered medication, has been interpreted as related both to symptoms and to the scarcity of mental health services (Hiday & Scheid-Cook, 1991). Hence, some observers hold that coercive practices are *more* likely to be applied in environments with inadequate resources (Schwartz & Costanzo, 1987). Yet, scattered anecdotal evidence provides examples of the use of less coercive techniques despite impoverished mental health resources.

Clearly, then, the connection between coercion and resources remains an open empirical question, worthy of investigation. It could generate information necessary to understanding the potential inequities in mental health policy. Utilitarian compliance signifies an inequitable situation, in which burdens and benefits are unfairly distributed among persons labeled mentally ill. If impoverished groups are more likely to be subjugated to utilitarian compliance simply because they meet the conditions necessary for this form of social control to work, then an ethical problem is raised.[5] The analysis must shift to considerations of domination of groups or classes of persons.

---

[5]A similar logic can be applied to research projects. To what extent are patients, clients, or others persuaded to become "research subjects"? In a context of scarce resources, the potential for utilitarian compliance increases when participation in a study is tied to certain resources, such as monetary reward or access to a desired service.

Sociological and anthropological theories suggest another way in which resources will be linked to the degree of coercion used in a particular environment (Horwitz, 1982). In the postinstitutionalization era, many Western countries have responded to behavior labeled as mentally ill through a combination of neglect and coercive practices. The development of noncoercive, humane responses goes hand in hand with the creation of nondeviant roles or the reinterpretation of labels connected to psychiatric disabilities. Corin (1990) has suggested how behaviors that are currently perceived as signs of illness might be reinterpreted as positive ways of being in the world. To be able to tolerate and accept "different" ways of being and acting, however, social actors must be willing to make room for those they stigmatized in the past. Structural modifications to accomplish this might include the development of socially inclusive work roles, such as jobs with "reasonable accommodations" because of disabilities. However, such symbolic and material resources remain problematic. Some former patients fiercely reject any identification with their former status. Paradoxically, empowerment or advocacy projects may reinforce stigma by offering new roles (patient advocate, consumer-provider, etc.) meant to validate personhood over patienthood (Barham, 1994). Some ex-patients judge their mental treatment by the personal and social characteristics of the case manager, and in fact are less satisfied when that individual is a consumer (Solomon and Draine, 1994). Thus, researchers must not only be aware of coercive dimensions, but also of the unintended effects of newly deployed resources.

DETERMINANTS AND EFFECTIVENESS OF NONCOERCIVE PRACTICES

Rather than focusing exclusively on coercion in aggressive treatment, research can also concentrate on the very interventions that are hypothesized to be empowering, such as programs organized around the client's or subject's participation and choice. Several types of mental health programs based on techniques of empowerment or client-oriented practices now exist in the United States. Manuals and program descriptions of consumer-initiated and consumer-controlled initiatives have been developed by consumer groups and mental health agencies (Fisher, 1992; Zinman, Harp, & Budd, 1987). A few anthropological studies examine how mental health clients/consumers/survivors express or actualize their choice in various treatment and life domains (Lovell, 1991; Ware et al., 1992; McLean, 1995; Lovell & Cohn, 1995). While not specifically focusing on coercion, these papers, taken collectively, raise questions about the extent to which clients (as opposed to staff and administration, whether or not they are also consumers) actually exercise choices or participate in decisions affecting their lives. To date, however, outcome studies on client-oriented alternatives remain rare and focus on empowerment projects or client-oriented programs developed by nonconsumer practitioners or administrators.

A few studies are currently examining the integration of "peers" or "consumers" into mainstream outpatient mental health services (Solomon & Draine, 1994). To my knowledge, however, coercion has not been their focus. Researchers might address several questions by comparing consumer participation with professionally defined and given treatment and interventions. Two hypotheses appear relevant.

Using historical arguments and studies in the sociology of mental health, Horwitz (1982) postulated that the degree of social control utilized in mental health treatment will vary as a function of the similarity in characteristics of patients/clients and practitioners. Because they are based on shared cultural symbols, as well as trust and understanding, persuasive techniques are more likely to be used when the cultural distance between practitioner and patient is narrow. Inversely, when that distance is wide, coercive techniques will be invoked.

Cultural distance is expressed through differences in class status, ethnic identity, and even gender of practitioner versus client. Perceptions and behavior that practitioners view as incomprehensible (anomalous cognitive experiences or delusional responses) also widen this gap. It might be assumed, on the contrary, that some similarities are shared by persons who have been forced into psychiatric treatment, spent periods of time homeless, or experienced certain cognitive anomalies or events that psychiatry labels as symptoms of mental illness. Given the shorter cultural distance between such persons, are consumer staff less likely to invoke coercive techniques in outpatient settings than nonconsumer staff? Do they allow for more participation or "voice" by the client in the process of engagement in treatment, the treatment itself, or other interventions? The ideal setting for testing such a hypothesis would be outreach programs that, unlike assertive community treatment or intensive case management, do not have an a priori highly specified model. Such a study would require careful descriptions of the services rendered by both consumer and nonconsumer staff and a validated measure of coercion.

An alternative to the cultural distance hypothesis could be tested in the same type of study. Some self-help models suggest that consumer involvement need not *necessarily* result in less coercion being imposed on patients or clients. For example, self-help and substance abuse treatment programs often use peer pressure to enforce compliance with medication or abstinence from substances, in the name of an external authority or ideology. Whether or not peers' actions or the program culture would be *perceived* by the clients as coercive remains an open question.

A second type of consumer-oriented alternative provides fertile ground for examining coercion as an independent variable. Coercive practices can be compared to noncoercive or less coercive ones, such as those based on legally established prior directives for mental health treatment. Still controversial, these contracts are premised on the idea of the individual's right to autonomy and self-determination in directing his or her own treatment, even while legally considered incompetent. Contracts involve either a written advance directive or the prior naming of a proxy with decision-making power over an individual who becomes acutely ill (Sales, 1993). Examples of such prior arrangements include the Ulysses contract, whereby the individual instructs his or her psychiatrist to hospitalize and treat him or her in the event of an exacerbation of mental illness. On the other hand, directives such as the "Mills will," "living will," or psychiatric will allow the individual to refuse or request specific treatments in the case of exacerbation. The "Mills will" also permits the individual in an acute episode to revoke a previously established treatment decision (Rogers & Centifanti, 1991).[6]

The legal ramifications of these less coercive alternatives are not fully understood. In states where they are allowed, however, proactive noncoercive practices could be used to test hypotheses concerning the effects of coercion. What might these effects be? Drawing on reactance theory, Monahan et al. (1995) suggest that coercion can result in active outcomes, such as anger and attempts to restore the lost freedom, or in passive results, such as helplessness. Turning this relationship around, one could hypothesize less anger, violence, withdrawal, and other forms of passivity where noncoercive alternatives

---

[6]Still other procedures have been proposed in the case of dangerous behavior that threatens public safety. For example, Fisher (1993) emphasizes the priority of humane, supportive, voluntary crisis intervention. Should this fail, peer advocacy, legal representation and protection, and clear legal guidelines should be built into the nonvoluntary procedures.

come into play. Greater participation by the subject in the way the signs of his or her illness are handled might increase a sense of well-being, mastery, self-esteem, and subjective quality of life—outcomes currently being examined in relation to empowerment[7] (Rosenfield, 1992).

Finally, a more descriptive and richly contextual study might examine the feasibility of noncoercive alternatives within an essentially normative mental health and social service system. Can mental health consumers/survivors truly participate and express choice in a coercive environment? Community psychologists theorize that empowerment "takes on a different form in different people and contexts" (Rappaport, cited in Zimmerman, 1990; p. 169). We can hypothesize that coercive v. noncoercive practices will also vary according to the nexus in which they are embedded. When individual, organizational, and system levels of analysis are integrated, coercion and its determinants and effects become clearer, as has been shown for the construct of "choice" (Lovell & Cohn, 1995) and empowerment (McLean, 1995).

One of the reasons self-help and consumer-oriented alternatives have not been examined much concerns the nature of research techniques and designs considered to be scientifically valid and hence worthy of financial support. Experimental research based on random assignment, for example, contradicts the very process of self-determination and choice involved in self-help. Instrumentation often imposes a burden on participants that discourages their involvement or competes with other goals (Knight, et al. 1992). The normative research process hence inadvertently eliminates knowledge about potentially powerful alternatives to usual mental health practices. Less intrusive research designs, including quasi-experimental and qualitative, should be encouraged.

RECONSTRUCTING THE PICTURE: SOME RESEARCH STRATEGIES

Thus far, I have suggested hypotheses that might guide the examination of coercion within a social control framework. Two neglected ar-

[7]Clinicians and psychiatric researchers would consider most of these hypothesized reactions to be symptoms. They need not, however, be treated within an illness paradigm.

eas, the contextual determinants of coercion and the determinants and effects of deliberately noncoercive practices, have been proposed as worthy of investigation.

Coercion can also be examined within the more traditional mental health services research paradigms, which have already generated a rich body of findings on assertive community treatment, aggressive treatment, and the other community-based innovations of the last decades. Studies might examine the relative effects of different degrees of coercion by categorizing interventions according to the framework presented earlier. Preliminary to this type of research, numerous measurement and design issues remain to be worked out.

The social control framework is simply an attempt to clarify the construct of coercion in a nonreductionist manner. Another contribution to the clarification of the construct would be to render visible the many practices, both formal and informal, that comprise these treatment interventions. The specific components, or "active ingredients" (Witheridge, 1991), of such programs need identification and classification according to their degree of social control. Here, process descriptions of the different models and approaches might prove useful. Good qualitative research could help identify informal processes not officially recognized in these program descriptions. For example, informal agreements with local police or outside service providers or the identification of certain workers as important to maintaining security at a program are rarely mentioned in such program descriptions, yet they may in fact prove to be crucial to the outcomes of the formal interventions.

The recent research on coercion in inpatient hospitalization points to the need for both objective and subjective measures of coercion (Monahan et al., 1995). Thus, in addition to "objective" descriptions of program components and ingredients, the perception of the various parties must also be considered. This can be done through at least two methods.

First, a symbolic interactionist approach might be used to understand how social control practices are constructed. Here the actions and viewpoints of everyone involved in the intervention—client, peers, service providers, family members, and so forth—are taken into consideration. Different types of social control might be used at different points during the intervention.

Second, an instrument similar to what has been developed for inpatient settings (Gardner et al., 1993) would be needed to measure perceptions of coercion. Community-based settings, however, call for a different set of items,[8] including the substitution of various locales (e.g., shelter, mental health center) for "hospital." Whereas inpatient studies rely on the hospital admission as the point at which coercion is applied (or not), an instrument for community-based use would need to reflect a range of points at which coercion takes place. This point can be illustrated with the example mentioned above of a homeless man presented the options of arrest or going to a residential treatment center. Numerous outreach contacts, each involving different types of social control, might have preceded the encounter with the policeman. The threat of arrest itself might be made only after the policeman and outreach workers attempted many persuasive techniques. As this example indicates, a scale for measuring perceptions of coercion is further complicated by the fact that coercive acts can be initiated not only by the primary service provider but also from outside the program. For this reason, the triangulation of results from both anthropological and quantitative approaches is necessary.

CONCLUSION

Coercion and social control cannot be reduced to technical questions or variables to be manipulated in a research effort. Research strategies must be capable of relating the microsociological level of interaction to larger processes of domination, racism, social exclusion, etc. At the same time, researchers need to grapple with the symbolic violence of subtler forms of coercion. But coercion is also a moral construct, evoking the very notions of respect, dignity, the common good, and the obligations the members of a society have toward one another. Reflections on the genealogy of ethics in Western societies reveal how often we attempt to pin our ethics on a "higher authority," be it religion, ideology, or science. The scientific examination of coercion cannot really untangle our moral questions of autonomy and choice vs. psychiatric dominance, police powers, and *parens patriae;* of care vs. control; of resources vs. neglect. Rather, these are issues that must be debated in an ongoing public forum in which patients/consumers/survivors, family members, clinicians, advocates, and ordinary citi-

[8]A randomized trial study of involuntary commitment in North Carolina currently underway has adapted the scale of Gardner and colleagues for a community setting (Swartz et al., 1995; Monahan, personal communication).

zens continue to struggle through the complexities of coercion in out-patient treatment. Research, however, may serve to problematize co-ercion in a most positive sense. What is it, where does it arise, what are its effects, what other means of responding to behavior society labels as mentally ill are possible? How is it related to the structural exercise of power, such as the domination of an entire "class" of persons?

ACKNOWLEDGMENTS. The author would like to acknowledge Paul Hil-lengas's assistance in locating materials for this chapter and Henry Steadman's suggestion that she examine coercion in relation to social control.

REFERENCES

American Psychiatric Association (1987). Involuntary commitment to outpatient treat-ment. Washington DC: American Psychiatric Association.

Barham, P. (1994). The psychosocial predicament of the mental patient in modern so-ciety. Paper presented at the symposium, "The understanding of mental illness and dealing with the mentally ill in Western cultures," sponsored by the Freie Univer-sität Berlin and the Zentralinstitut für Seelische Gesundheit, Berin, June 2–4, 1994.

Barrow, S., Hellman, F., Lovell, A. M., Plapinger, J., & Struening, E. L. (1991). Evaluating outreach services: Lessons from five programs. In N. L. Cohen (Ed.), *Psychiatric outreach to the mentally ill* (pp. 29–45). *New Directions in Mental Health Services, No. 52*. San Francisco: Jossey-Bass.

Bennett, N. S., Lidz, C. W., Monahan, J., Mulvey, E., Hoge, S. K., Roth, L. H., & Gardner, W. (1993). Inclusion, motivation, and good faith: The morality of coercion in men-tal hospital admission. *Behavioral Sciences and the Law, 2*, 295–306.

Bond, G. R., Witheridge, T. F., & Dincin, J. (1990). Assertive community treatment for frequent users of psychiatric hospitals in a large city: A controlled study. *American Journal of Community Psychology, 118*, 865–891.

Brown, P. (1984). *The transfer of care: Deinstitutionalization and its aftermath*. Boston: Rout-ledge & Kegan Paul.

Castel, R., Castel, F., & Lovell, A. M. (1982). *The psychiatric society*. New York: Columbia University Press.

Corin, E. (1990). Facts and meaning in psychiatry. An anthropological approach to the world of schizophrenics. *Culture, Medicine, and Psychiatry, 14*, 153–188.

Donovan, J. L., & Blake, D. R. (1992). Patient noncompliance: Deviance or reasoned de-cision-making? *Social Science and Medicine, 34*, 507–513.

Dutton, J. E., & Dukerich, J. M. (1991). Keeping an eye on the mirror: Image and identity in organizational adaptation. *Academy of Management Journal, 34*, 517–554.

Fisher, D. B. (1992). A new vision of healing: A reasonable accommodation for con-sumers/survivors working as mental health providers. *NIDRR* (September), 36–47.

Fisher, D. B. (1993). The human and legal impact of involuntary interventions in mental health. Comments made at the Third Roundtable Discussion of Involuntary Interventions, Community Support Program, Center for Mental Health Services, October 1 and 2.

Gardner, W., Hoge, S. K., Bennett, N., Roth, L. H., Lidz, C. W., Monahan, J., & Mulvey, E. P. (1993). Two scales for measuring patients' perceptions of coercion during mental hospital admission. *Behavioral Sciences and the Law, 2,* 307–321.

Goffman, E. (1961). *Asylums.* Garden City, NY: Anchor Books.

Gordon, C. (1986). Psychiatry as a problem of democracy. In P. Miller & N. Rose (Eds.), *The power of psychiatry.* Cambridge, UK: Polity Press.

Greenley, J. R. (1986). Social control and expressed emotion. *Journal of Nervous and Mental Disease, 174,* 24–30.

Group for the Advancement of Psychiatry (1994). *Forced into treatment: The role of coercion in clinical practice.* Washington DC: American Psychiatric Press.

Hiday, V. A., & Scheid-Cook, T. L. (1987). The North Carolina experience in outpatient commitment: A critical appraisal. *International Journal of Law and Psychiatry, 10,* 215–232.

Hiday, V. A., & Scheid-Cook, T. L. (1989). A follow-up of chronic patients committed to outpatient treatment. *Hospital and Community Psychiatry, 40,* 53–58.

Hiday, V. A., & Scheid-Cook, T. L. (1991). Outpatient commitment for "revolving door" patients: Compliance and treatment. *Journal of Nervous and Mental Disease, 179,* 83–88.

Hoge, S. K., Lidz, C., Mulvey, E., Roth, L., Bennett, N., Siminoff, L., Arnold, R., & Monahan, J. (1993). Patient, family and staff perceptions of coercion in mental hospital admission: An exploratory study. *Behavioral Sciences and the Law, 2,* 281–294.

Horwitz, A. V. (1982). *The social control of mental illness.* New York: Academic Press.

Keilitz, I. (1990). Empirical studies of involuntary outpatient civil commitment: Is it working? *Mental and Physical Disability Law Reporter, 14,* 368–379.

Knight, E., Lovell, A. M., & Stastny, P. (1992). Report on meeting of consumer-run programs. Rockville, MD: Center for Mental Health Services, Community Support Program.

Lefley, H. P. (1992). Expressed emotion: Conceptual, clinical, and social policy issues. *Hospital and Community Psychiatry, 43,* 591–598.

Lidz, C. W., Mulvey, E. P., Arnold, R. P., Bennett, N. S., & Kirsch, B. L. (1993). Coercive interactions in a psychiatric emergency room. *Behavioral Sciences and the Law, 2,* 269–280.

Lipsky, M. (1980). *Street-level bureaucracy: Dilemmas of individuals in public services.* New York: Russell Sage Foundation.

Lovell, A. M. (1991). Meaning, de-meaning, and empowerment: Evolution of a consumer-run organization. 90th Annual Meeting of the American Anthropological Association. Chicago, November 23, 1991.

Lovell, A. M. (1992). Marginal arrangements: Homelessness, mental illness, and social relations. Unpublished PhD dissertation. New York: Columbia University.

Lovell, A. M., & Cohn. S. (1995). The elaboration of choice in a program for persons labelled psychiatrically disabled (under review).

Lovell, A. M., Richmond, L. R., & Shern, D. L. (1995). Measuring standard treatment in a complex environment. Albany: New York State Office of Mental Health (in prep.).

McCafferty, G., & Dooley, J. (1990). Involuntary outpatient commitment: An update. *Mental and Physical Disability Law Reporter, 14,* 277–287.

McLean, A. (1995). Empowerment and the psychiatric consumer/ex-patient's movement in the United States: Contradictions, crisis, and change. *Social Science and Mediane, 40,* 1053–1071.

Miller, R. D. (1985). Commitment to outpatient treatment: A national survey. *Hospital and Community Psychiatry, 36,* 265–267.

Miller, R. D. (1992). An update on involuntary civil commitment to outpatient treatment. *Hospital and Community Psychiatry, 43,* 79–81.

Monahan, J., Hoge, S. K., Lidz, C., Roth, L. H., Bennett, N. (in press). Coercion and commitment: Understanding involuntary mental hospital admission. *International Journal of Law and Psychiatry.*

Mowbray, C. T. (1990). Community treatment of the seriously mentally ill: Is this community psychology? *Journal of Community Psychology, 18,* 893–902.

Pepper, B., & Ryglewicz, H. (1987). Is there expressed emotion away from home?: "Interactional intensity" ("II") in the treatment program. *Tie-Lines, 4,* 1–3.

Peyrot, M. (1985). Coerced voluntarism: The micropolitics of drug treatment. *Urban Life, 13,* 343–365.

Rappaport, J. (1981). In praise of paradox: A social policy of empowerment over prevention. *American Journal of Community Psychology, 9,* 1–25.

Rog, D. J. (1988). *Engaging homeless persons with mental illness into treatment.* Alexandria, VA: National Mental Health Association.

Rogers, A. (1993). Coercion and "voluntary" admission: An examination of psychiatric patient views. *Behavioral Sciences and the Law, 2,* 259–267.

Rogers, J. A., & Centifanti, J. B. (1991). Beyond "self-paternalism": Response to Rosenson and Kaster. *Schizophrenia Bulletin, 17,* 9–14.

Rosenfield, S. (1992). Factors contributing to the subjective quality of life of the mentally ill. *Journal of Health and Social Behavior, 33,* 299–315.

Sales, G. N. (1993). The health care proxy for mental illness: Can it work and should we want it to? *Bulletin of the American Academy of Psychiatry and the Law, 21,* 161–178.

Schwartz, S. J., & Costanzo, C. E. (1987). Compelling treatment in the community: Distorted doctrines and violated values. *Loyola of Los Angeles Law Review, 20,* 1329–1429.

Solomon, P., & Draine, J. (1994). Satisfaction with mental health treatment in a randomized trial of consumer case management. *Journal of Nervous and Mental Disease, 182,* 179–184.

Stein, L. I., & Test, M. A. (Eds.) (1980). *The training in community living model: A decade of experience. New Directions in Mental Health Services,* No. 26. San Francisco: Jossey-Bass.

Swartz, M. S., Burns, B. J., Hiday, V. A., George, L. K., Swanson, J., & Wagner, H. R. (in press). New directions in research on involuntary outpatient commitment. *Hospital and Community Psychiatry.*

Taylor, C. (1989). *Sources of the self.* Cambridge: Cambridge University Press.

Ware, N. C., Desjarlais, R. S., AvRuskin, T. L., Breslau, J., Good, B. J., & Goldfinger, S. M. (1992). Empowerment and the transition to housing for homeless mentally ill people: An anthropological perspective. *New England Journal of Public Policy, 8,* 297–314.

Wertheimer, A. (1993). A philosophical examination of coercion for mental health issues. *Behavioral Sciences and the Law, 2,* 239–258.

Whyte, W. H. (1988). *City: Discovering the center.* New York: Doubleday.

Witheridge, T. F. (1991). The "active ingredients" of assertive outreach. In N. L. Cohen (Ed.), *Psychiatric outreach to the mentally ill* (pp. 47–64). *New Directions in Mental Health Services*, No. 52. San Francisco: Jossey-Bass.

Zimmerman, M. A. (1990). Taking aim on empowerment research: On the distinction between individual and psychological conceptions. *American Journal of Community Psychology, 18*, 169–178.

Zinman, S., Harp, H., & Budd, S. (1987). *Reaching across: Mental health clients helping each other.* Sacramento: California Network of Mental Health Clients.

Part V

COERCION IN THE COMMUNITY
THE OPEN QUESTIONS

CHAPTER 10

WHEN PUSH COMES TO SHOVE
AGGRESSIVE COMMUNITY
TREATMENT AND THE LAW

JESSICA WILEN BERG AND RICHARD J. BONNIE

Previous chapters have identified some interventionist features of mental health practice in the community that lead practitioners or observers to describe them as "aggressive" or "assertive" or "tenacious." The purpose of this chapter is to consider the legal implications of these practices. This is unexplored terrain, so our goal is a modest one: We aim to sketch a framework, and offer a conceptual vocabulary, for thinking about these practices and for connecting them to established legal ideas. By identifying possible concerns, we do not aim to raise objections to aggressive community treatment. To the contrary, we recognize the benevolent aims of most interventions as well as their value in a community treatment model. Our purpose in identifying possible legal or ethical concerns is to heighten practi-

JESSICA WILEN BERG • Department of Psychiatry, University of Massachusetts Medical Center, Worcester, Massachusetts 01655.   RICHARD J. BONNIE • School of Law, University of Virginia, Charlottesville, Virginia 22903.

Coercion and Aggressive Community Treatment: A New Frontier in Mental Health Law, edited by Deborah L. Dennis and John Monahan. Plenum Press, New York, 1996.

tioners' awareness of potential conflicts and, in this way, to help them shape appropriate guidelines.

Two aspects of "aggressive" community care require separate examination. First, aggressive outreach and monitoring implicate fundamental notions of privacy. The clinical objective of these practices is to reach out toward (or "into the living space of") targeted individuals in order to assess whether mental health services are needed and to monitor the well-being of clients believed to be at risk of deterioration. Identification, monitoring, and surveillance are classic public health tools[1] that have only recently been utilized in mental health care. The second feature of aggressive community practice that requires systematic examination is its "coerciveness." The critical clinical challenge is to get the target population to "accept" needed services or to comply with prescribed treatment. The underlying legal concern, of course, is the degree to which these practices implicate the right of the targeted individuals to make their own decisions regarding mental health treatment and, specifically, to refuse such treatment.

Coercion is a conceptually difficult and highly moralized subject (see Chapters 8 and 9). For this reason, it is important to draw a clear distinction between descriptive and normative vocabularies. Descriptively, we refer to a spectrum of pressures or influences that are brought to bear on mental health clients to get them to comply with treatment recommendations, typically to take prescribed medication. In analogous contexts, it has been useful to categorize these influences in terms of persuasion, inducements, threats, and force (see Chapter 1). Whether and under what circumstances an influence should be characterized as "coercive" is a highly contextual determination with potentially preclusive legal implications (Wertheimer, 1993). Although we do not aim to present a definitive legal analysis, the "coerciveness" of these influences will be connected to applicable legal concepts.

Issues relating to intrusiveness (privacy) and coerciveness (liberty or autonomy) will be explored in four clinical or programmatic contexts. We will begin with an analysis of the relevant features of outpatient civil commitment (see Chapter 2). We do this for two rea-

---

[1]For example, a New York City Health Department regulation permits health workers to visit homes of tuberculosis patients who have a history of not following their treatment plans, to assure that pills are taken. (Navarro, 1993).

sons: First, because outpatient commitment represents the most extreme form of legal intervention, an analysis of its limitations will provide a useful baseline, or point of departure, for subsequent discussion of less formal, nonjudicial interventions. Second, even on its own terms, outpatient commitment raises concerns about intrusiveness and coercion that have not yet been fully explored.

The next section addresses conditional access to benefits. Many targets of aggressive mental health intervention are poor people who receive or qualify for various forms of public support and assistance. In the effort to identify and monitor patient well-being, and to promote treatment compliance, the government (or its private surrogates) may condition access to the benefits on the clients' surrender of their privacy and decision-making autonomy. This conditioning can be done by formal agreements or by legal prescription. The legal framework governing these arrangements is unclear, but the underlying issue is easy to understand: Should these techniques be characterized as noncoercive inducements (offering clients a benefit or carrot to which they are not otherwise entitled) or as coercive practices (waivers of privacy and decisional freedom induced by threats to withhold a needed benefit to which clients are otherwise entitled)?

A less formal method of inducing clients to comply with prescribed treatment is for the mental health provider to have control over the client's income. This can be accomplished by designating the provider as the client's representative payee under the Supplemental Security Income/Social Security Disability Insurance (SSI/SSDI) system.[2] This practice raises puzzling ethical and legal problems that have not yet been adequately explored.

The final section of the chapter addresses informal techniques of aggressive mental health practice, especially in relation to homeless people. To what extent are outreach workers constrained by legal norms in their efforts to identify, target, and monitor mentally ill persons? When these practitioners induce a form of clinical dependency, and then use this relationship as leverage to facilitate treatment, have they overstepped ethical or legal boundaries? In general, we believe that these practices raise ethical issues rather than legal ones.

[2]SSI is basically a government welfare program; eligibility is determined in part by income level. SSDI, on the other hand, is a federal disability insurance program. Workers contribute to the fund during their working years and receive benefits when they retire or become disabled.

OUTPATIENT COMMITMENT[3]

SURVEILLANCE AND MONITORING

In the hospital setting, a committed patient surrenders almost all of his or her "privacy" and is subject to extensive inspection and monitoring. Human rights regulations and patient bills of rights (P. Allen, 1976) may carve out a little private space, but not much. Although outpatient commitment may impose fewer constraints upon a person's physical liberty, in many ways it may be more intrusive with regard to a person's privacy interests. Yet there appear to be few formalized protections of patient privacy beyond the general protections of the Fourth Amendment, which bars "unreasonable searches and seizures."

In its continuing effort to interpret and apply the open-textured language of the Fourth Amendment, the Supreme Court has grounded its analysis in whether a person has a "reasonable expectation of privacy." Thus, a patient committed to an inpatient facility who is subject to daily room inspections and other monitoring practices has a reduced expectation of privacy, and the government has correspondingly broad authority to search the patient's belongings and living area without a warrant. By contrast, it is not unreasonable for an outpatient to expect a level of privacy in his or her own home equivalent to that which people not subject to commitment orders have come to expect. As a result, surveillance and monitoring of outpatients should be subject to greater constitutional scrutiny and concern.

The critical issue is whether, and in what way, the state's therapeutic purposes in civil commitment shape the Fourth Amendment

[3]The term *outpatient commitment* is used to cover three different procedures: commitment to outpatient instead of inpatient treatment as a least restrictive alternative, conditional release from inpatient commitment, and preventative commitment. The first of these mechanisms uses a commitment standard identical to that used in inpatient commitment—mental illness combined with dangerousness. The second is analogous to parole—an individual is released from the hospital with the stipulation that if he fails continue to treatment he can be rehospitalized. The final category is the most controversial, since it apparently allows outpatient commitment upon a showing of predicted dangerousness based on deterioration. Since it is unclear whether a state is justified in restricting a person's liberty when he or she is not at present a danger to either self or others, this third category of outpatient commitment is most often challenged as unconstitutional (see generally Slobogin, 1994, Hinds, 1990; Stefan, 1987; Schwartz & Costanzo, 1987).

norms. Consider, as a starting point, the application of the warrant requirement to "searches and seizures" carried out by the police to implement orders for emergency psychiatric hospitalization of a person who is not already subject to a judicial commitment order. Ordinarily, warrantless entry into the home and "seizure" of the person from the home are prohibited in the absence of exigent circumstances such as fear of imminent destruction of evidence, "hot pursuit" of a fleeing suspect, or immediate danger to public safety. This general proposition would seem to imply that the state has no authority to enter a person's home to effectuate the civil commitment process in the absence of a prior judicial authorization, based on probable cause to believe the commitment criteria are met, unless the person is thought by the police to present an imminent danger to himself or others. In some states, however, the police are empowered to enter a person's home and take the person into custody based on an order issued by a mental health professional, not a judge. In many instances, the circumstances are not so emergent as to preclude any opportunity to obtain a search warrant. So the question is whether the benevolent aims of the civil commitment process justify a practice of warrantless entry into the home that would not otherwise by justified.

In *Wyman v. James* (1971), the United States Supreme Court upheld a New York statute that made receipt of welfare benefits contingent upon the beneficiary's assent to a home visit by a state social worker. The court stated that New York's home visitation requirement is a "reasonable administrative tool" serving "a valid and proper administrative purpose for the dispensation of the AFDC program." Noting that the purpose of the home visit requirement is "both investigative and rehabilitative," the court concluded that it is not the functional equivalent of a search in the traditional criminal law context.

Does the "noncriminal," therapeutic purpose of the civil commitment process justify warrantless, nonexigent, invasion of the home? A federal district court in Massachusetts recently rejected this proposed analogy to *Wyman v. James*. In *McCabe v. City of Lynn* (1995), the judge granted summary judgment in a federal civil rights action on behalf of a 64-year-old woman who had a fatal heart attack when the Lynn police broke into her home to execute a civil commitment order under what the court found to be nonexigent circumstances. The court rejected the idea that "a physician's blessing somehow strips a putative mental patient of the safeguards of the Fourth Amendment." Against this backdrop, we should consider the bearing of the Fourth Amendment on an outpatient commitment order.

A number of outpatient commitment orders serve as a continuing authorization to search for and "pick up" a noncompliant patient (McCafferty & Dooley, 1990). This authority is generally conferred upon law enforcement officers (typically sheriffs) and allows them to take someone to a mental health center either for observation or to enable a treatment provider to attempt to obtain compliance. In this context, does the sheriff need to obtain a warrant, based on probable cause, in order to enter a person's home to look for him or her? An analogy can be drawn between outpatient commitment and a probation order imposed on a person convicted of crime. The Supreme Court has upheld warrantless searches of a probationer's home, noting that the special needs of the probation system require the ability to quickly "intervene before a probationer does damage to himself or society" (*Griffen v. Wisconsin*, 1987, p. 879). Yet even these searches must meet reasonableness requirements (*Griffen*). In deciding whether a particular search is reasonable, one factor to consider is the extent to which a person's absolute liberty is constrained. The greater the restrictions on liberty, for example, hospitalization or incarceration, the more diminished is the expectation of privacy.

Although both probationers and outpatient committees may have fewer privacy protections than people who are not subject to any type of judicial order, the two situations are not fungible—the committed patient has committed no crime—and this fact should affect the reasonableness of the intrusion. A second factor affecting reasonableness relates to whether a person has prior notice. Since the outpatient commitment order itself may explicitly authorize the sheriff to bring in a noncompliant person, the patient is theoretically on notice. It may be unclear, however, what actions will prompt a search—failing to show up for a meeting, reports from family members, or simply disagreements with the treatment provider. As a result, the "discretion to invade private property" is left to "the official in the field," suggesting that states should impose careful safeguards to protect patients' privacy interests (*Camara v. Municipal Court*, 1966, p. 532).

The effect of an outpatient commitment order, if it is construed to provide continuing authorization to bring someone in, is to avoid the requirement of additional judicial approval for a search. This does not mean that the outpatient is without any legal protection or that a sheriff may initiate a search at will. On the contrary, there is a spectrum of possibilities in this context. At the least protective end, the initial judicial order could allow a search upon no more cause than the provider's assertion that the patient missed an appointment. Like the probationer who missed a meeting with his or her probation officer, the outpatient would technically be in "violation" of a judicial order. However, to the extent that the outpatient situation is more akin to the administrative context, rather than the criminal one, more substantial justification may be required to justify a search.

The most stringent safeguard against illegal searches is the "probable cause" requirement, which would require reliable evidence of an outpatient's noncompliance before a search would be permitted. Probable cause is evaluated on a case-by-case basis; thus, what constitutes probable cause in one situation (the provider's assertion both that an appointment was missed and that every time an appointment was missed it was due to noncompliance) may not be sufficient in another (this is the first time an appointment was missed, or other times appointments were missed the outpatient had a good reason). Because judicial interpretation of "cause" for executing outpatient commitment orders has not been studied, it is not possible to assess current practice. For the present, it is enough to recognize that varying degrees of protection can be provided even if continuing judicial oversight is not required.

The authority of a treatment provider to enter a person's home is also uncertain. Most statutes confer authority on law enforcement officers, rather than mental health professionals, although the clinicians can institute proceedings to have a noncompliant patient taken into custody. Searches by a caseworker instead of a law enforcement officer are thought to be less intrusive from a Fourth Amendment perspective, since they are primarily rehabilitative rather than investigative (*Wyman v. James*, 1971). Unlike health or safety inspectors, however, mental health treatment providers do not generally have the authorization to enter a person's home without that individual's consent. In the outpatient commitment setting, such consent is hardly voluntary when a patient may be unaware of his or her ability to bar the therapist from entering or when the alternative involves police action. The California Supreme Court noted with respect to searches by social workers that a "request for entry by persons whom the beneficiaries knew to possess virtually unlimited power over their very livelihood posed a threat" (*Parrish v. Civil Service Commission*, 1967, p. 229). Furthermore, the therapist may be going to the person's home without even a suspicion of a violation, but rather seeking to "checkup" on a patient to prevent relapse.

In the absence of clear-cut constitutional limitations on the authority of community service providers to enter a person's home, local agencies should prescribe their own procedural safeguards. For example, they might require "searches" to be conducted only during business hours and with notice to the patient. Furthermore, outpatients could be informed of their right to refuse entry to a caseworker and the consequences, if any, of such a refusal. Moreover, agencies could set up a process through which complaints about abuses can be lodged.

An additional concern in this area is the appropriateness of therapists taking an active role in checking for noncompliance. Such actions bring to light the possible antitherapeutic aspects of mental health professionals' use of intrusive or coercive measures (McCafferty & Dooley, 1990) (see also Chapter 3). The lack of separation between the roles of treatment provider and law enforcer may undermine an attempt to create a collaborative treatment plan and instead place the mental health provider in the undesirable role of "policing" patients (Geller, 1986a). On the other hand, having a caseworker show up at one's door is surely less disconcerting than having the sheriff appear. Furthermore, active involvement by mental health professionals in the field may reduce the likelihood of deterioration, thereby reducing the likelihood of emergency intervention—a result far more intrusive than a preventative home visit. Thus, it becomes extremely important for the mental health professional's role to be clearly defined, with specified limits on unwarranted intrusions.

Another issue is the use of routine physical testing to monitor medication compliance or, in some cases, to monitor the use of alcohol or illicit drugs. The Fourth Amendment protections cover both searches of premises and searches of the person, including blood and urine samples (*Schmerber v. California*, 1966; *Skinner v. Railway Labor Executives' Association*, 1989). One author writing about the use of urine testing for evidence of drug use on probation noted that such methods could be used "to monitor mentally ill or retarded offenders who have been released from custody to detect non-compliance with drug therapy regimens" (Rosen, 1990). Other authors, referring to the use of such mechanisms in outpatient commitment, have stated that it is "the most efficient and valid way to monitor compliance with a chemically based treatment program" (Mulvey, Geller, & Roth, 1987). This is exactly what is being done in some conditional release programs involving mentally ill criminal offenders or insanity acquittees (e.g., McDonald & Teitelbaum, 1994). Moreover, commentators who have evaluated the criminal programs have suggested that these methods are "well suited to serving mentally ill persons who have not yet come into the criminal justice system" (McDonald & Teitelbaum, 1994, p. 2; see also Torrey, 1994; Jaffe, 1994). Geller (1986b), described an outpatient commitment plan in which patients were required to have blood drawn to determine drug levels. He stated that involuntary inpatient commitment of individuals whose drug levels "showed inadequate intake was arguably in compliance with the [state commitment] statute," since "discontinuance of medications . . . led to conditions which fell within the [statutory] definition of 'serious harm'" warranting hospitalization (p. 1261). He recognized, however, that his criteria required a stretching of the statutory language and thus began to resemble a type of impermissible "preventative commitment" (Geller, 1986b; see also Slobogin, 1994).

SECURING TREATMENT COMPLIANCE

In addition to the privacy issues raised by surveillance and monitoring, liberty or autonomy issues arise from the use of coercive measures to secure treatment compliance. The lack of explicit sanctions for noncompliance in some statutes has prompted mental health professionals and courts to question the efficacy of outpatient commitment orders. One author noted that such orders function "merely as a form of judicial intimidation," and thus "[c]ompliance is achieved only if the person fears rehospitalization or mistakenly believes that the court's order must be obeyed" (Wisor, 1993). The debate about enforcement of outpatient commitment orders raises two important issues: first, whether an outpatient commitment order authorizes forcible administration of medication; second, whether noncompliance with the court order provides a sufficient predicate for commitment to an inpatient setting.

It has been argued that forcible administration of medication may be unconstitutional because the need for treatment does not outweigh a competent patient's right to refuse antipsychotic medication (Slobogin, 1994; Hinds, 1990). The Supreme Court has held that involuntary medication of prisoners is permissible only where the individuals in question were in need of treatment *and* posed a risk of serious harm (*Washington v. Harper*, 1990). An individual who is mentally ill and dangerous would meet the criteria for inpatient hospitalization. Thus, states with outpatient commitment statutes that require a judicial determination that the person meets general commitment criteria

(Keilitz and Hall, 1985) could presumably permit forcible medication to the same extent as in the inpatient setting. However, a few states impose different requirements for outpatient and inpatient commitment, allowing the former in cases where the individual is not presently dangerous (Stefan, 1987). Under these circumstances, forcible treatment of competent mentally ill persons is less likely to be permissible (Stefan, 1987; Schwartz & Costanzo, 1987). It must be emphasized that legal authority is not the sole consideration in deciding whether to permit involuntary medication of committed outpatients. Even if doing so would be constitutionally permissible, it may not be desirable to do so, for both clinical and ethical reasons. This conflict explains why clinicians seem to be less comfortable with forcing treatment in an outpatient setting (Schwartz & Costanzo, 1987).

It has been argued that using hospitalization as an enforcement mechanism is inappropriate, since the person is unlikely to meet the statutory requirements at the time of noncompliance (Slobogin, 1994; see also Hinds, 1990). Even in those states that have adopted a preventative commitment model, noncompliance alone, without further review, is not a basis for hospitalization (Stefan, 1987). Without effective means to ensure compliance, however, outpatient commitment may be a legal illusion—a court order that does not have to be obeyed. Geller acknowledges that while unenforceable outpatient commitment may be effective, the result is that treatment providers are left in the ethical quandary of having either to lie or to mislead patients with regard to sanctions for noncompliance (Geller, 1986a).

There are a number of possible solutions to Geller's quandary. First, the court that issues the initial order could inform the patient about the possible sanctions for noncompliance. However, because doing so may undermine the perceived authority of the commitment order and render it useless, courts may be tempted to remain silent on the subject. Silence may be an acceptable compromise—although courts should not lie, they may not be obligated to inform patients of all their rights. Another likely candidate to educate the patient would be the attorney. This too is problematic, though, since the attorney is unlikely to be present every time medication is taken. One author noted that "[o]utpatient commitment, even more than inpatient commitment, isolates an individual both legally and practically from those who might advocate for his rights" (Stefan, 1987). As a result, it may well fall to the clinician to deal with queries about sanctions. In such cases, the therapist, like the court, is under no legal duty to inform the outpatient about the limits of his or her authority. Outright deception, however, would be unethical. If asked directly about the consequences of noncompliance, the therapist may point out that the sheriff will pick up and bring in a recalcitrant patient, and in addition, inpatient commitment proceedings will be instituted if the patient's condition deteriorates.

Thus, in one sense, the coercive nature of an outpatient commitment order is dependent upon a patient's conception, or misconception, of the available enforcement mechanisms. When a person is merely informed of the availability of inpatient commitment, but not threatened with commitment in inappropriate circumstances, such information cannot be properly categorized as coercive. This situation is analogous to the inpatient commitment context, where a patient who meets all the criteria for involuntary hospitalization is told she will be involuntarily committed if she refuses to admit herself voluntarily. The decision in such a case is more appropriately categorized as either a statement of fact or persuasion by inducement (i.e., greater freedom associated with voluntary admission and perhaps also reduced stigma), rather than coercion (Carroll, 1991; Wertheimer, 1993). The coercive aspect arises when the threat of involuntary commitment is illegitimate. Similarly, a person who meets the criteria for inpatient commitment and is given the choice between complying with an outpatient commitment order or being committed to a hospital is asked to make a difficult choice, but not a coercive one. The more problematic situation is when the person clearly does not meet the criteria for inpatient commitment (although he or she may become committable at a later date due to deterioration) and is similarly "threatened" with immediate hospitalization under circumstances in which the law would not allow it.[4] Like the classic "your money or your life" proposal, the alternatives limit rather than expand the patient's options and are therefore properly characterized as coercive (Wertheimer, 1993).

If the patient knows the limitations of the enforcement mechanisms, what is the actual coercive effect of outpatient commitment? In our view, the essential operational effect of an outpatient commitment order is that it subjects the patient to a coercive effort to persuade him to comply (Hiday & Scheid-Cook, 1990; Stefan, 1987). Thus, even if

[4]It has been suggested that states should amend their statutes to allow rehospitalization upon noncompliance with an outpatient commitment order. Whether such changes are constitutional is questionable.

forcible treatment or rehospitalization is not an option, an outpatient can be picked up and brought into a clinic in order to allow a therapist to try to convince him to take his medication. It would be unethical for the therapist in this situation to make coercive threats that could not be carried out or to deceive the patient about the therapist's authority. As pointed out earlier, however, it would be permissible for the clinician to emphasize the need for treatment and the possibility of inpatient commitment at some later date. Without other enforcement mechanisms, outpatient commitment thus functions "as more a method for encouragement than coercion" (Stefan, 1987). Ultimately, then, the efficacy of outpatient commitment may be linked more to surveillance and monitoring than to the sanctions for noncompliance. Further study of outpatient commitment may show that "service factors, such as transportation and intensive case management . . . [account] for positive outcomes rather than the legal coercion, since many mental health centers respond to court orders by aggressively reaching out with services to capture the treatment resistant chronic patients" (Hiday, 1992, p. 373). At least one study has shown that monitoring and clinical interaction can facilitate compliance when no enforcement mechanism is available (Hiday & Scheid-Cook, 1990) (see Chapter 2).[5]

Of course, the "outreach" may be more intrusive in certain respects. Privacy is sacrificed even while the patient's "right to refuse treatment" is preserved. In this sense, the corrosion of privacy may be more of a concern from a human rights perspective than the possibility of constraints upon liberty. Perhaps intrusions into privacy are less troubling than constraints upon liberty, and this possibility may reinforce the idea that warrantless intrusions are "reasonable." But one must be on guard against the trivialization of the committed patient's expectations of privacy. In the absence of specified limitations, a sweeping outpatient commitment order could be regarded as a serious affront to human rights—"a daily continuous intrusion that could lead to a lifetime of constraint and diminution of the individual's privacy rights" (Stefan, 1987, p. 292).

[5]The study found that mildly intrusive measures such as telephoning or sending a letter were effective in reducing the percentage of "no shows." Only as a last resort were such measures as calling the sheriff or instituting a new petition for civil commitment undertaken. Thus, it seems apparent that outpatient privacy rights can be maintained to a large degree without undermining the efficacy of the commitment order (Hiday & Scheid-Cook 1990).

CONDITIONAL ACCESS TO BENEFITS

Persons who suffer from mental illness may be unable to support themselves and may be unable to work. Depending on whether they meet other eligibility criteria, they may be entitled to welfare benefits or SSI benefits, together with Medicaid. The question to be addressed here is whether and to what extent the government may condition these benefits on compliance with treatment or on surveillance designed to monitor compliance: May an otherwise eligible mentally ill recipient of these benefits be required to surrender constitutional rights as a condition of eligibility? Are such conditions fair? Should they be regarded as unduly "coercive"?

An analogous problem arises in the context of housing. Here, the condition is more likely to be specified in an agreement with the housing agency or landlord: The individual agrees to comply with treatment and to permit entry by the landlord or the treatment provider. Thus, a benefit is conditioned upon a waiver of privacy rights or compliance with treatment or both. The tenant has a "choice," of course—he or she could always say "no"—but whether the choice is a meaningful one depends on whether the prospective tenant has genuine options. Should such an "agreement" be enforceable? Or has the tenant's acceptance of these conditions been unfairly "coerced"?

This is a hard problem. It is made harder by the fact that there is no consensus on whether the government is obligated to provide either the benefits or the housing. On one hand, one could view these benefits as the open hand of a generous society that can be offered on whatever conditions the society finds convenient. On the other hand, welfare, disability benefits, and subsidized housing provide necessities of life to poor people who feel that they have little choice but to comply with any conditions that may be prescribed. It seems intuitively acceptable to condition a benefit upon conduct closely linked either to administration of the program or to the need to prevent abuses (e.g., conditioning welfare upon home searches that are designed to ensure that the funding is being properly utilized). However, it seems less acceptable to condition a benefit on conduct unrelated to the purpose of the program (e.g., conditioning SSI upon compliance with mental health treatment).

Alan Wertheimer (1993) notes the distinction between a threat that is coercive and an offer that is not. At the heart of this distinction is the recognition of a relevant baseline from which all proposals are evaluated; thus, a proposal that makes a person worse off is a threat, whereas one that does not make a person worse off is an offer. There are two problems: first, setting the initial baseline; second, recognizing that the baseline is sensitive to small changes in the person's situation. Beyond recognizing the baseline and its sensitivity to various changes, which Wertheimer labels as analytical questions, there are also justification questions, for example, "[w]hether we are morally permitted to coercively impose therapy on mentally disordered persons" (Wertheimer, 1993, p. 239). This chapter explores the analytical problem, without aiming to present definitive answers regarding whether coercion is justified.

Surveillance and Monitoring

Privacy concerns are implicated in situations in which the government conditions receipt of benefits upon a "waiver" of Fourth Amendment protections. As noted earlier, in *Wyman v. James* (1971), the Supreme Court held that termination of an AFDC recipient's benefits after she refused to allow a caseworker entry to her home was not unconstitutional. The New York program used home visits to determine that the funds provided were being properly used for the benefit of children. The Supreme Court justified these intrusions on the ground that the petitioner could choose to refuse entry to the caseworker—resulting only in the termination of benefits, not in criminal prosecution—and thus there was no element of force or compulsion. Moreover, the court held that the intrusion was not a "search," since the caseworker served a welfare function rather than an investigative role, and even if such action could be categorized as a "search," it was not an "unreasonable" one in light of the government's interest in ensuring proper distribution of benefits. Although there is no evidence that the government has sought to link the welfare benefits of mentally ill persons to waivers of Fourth Amendment rights, the possibility of doing so tests the limits of *Wyman* and calls attention to the outer limits of a practice of conditioning benefits on waivers of constitutional rights.

As pointed out in Chapter 6, residents of housing linked to the community mental health services system are typically confronted with extensive conditions. There is little "expectation" of privacy in most group homes. Even in individual living arrangements, leases may include clauses that allow either the landlord or a caseworker to enter without obtaining further consent or without any prior notice. For example, one relatively pro-privacy community housing agreement states that a "[r]esident will be notified that staff will have keys and access to all apartments. This is for cases of emergency; clients' rights to privacy will not be violated beyond what is indicated as a requirement of treatment." By contrast, another program's house rules state that "[a]n inspection of rooms is made regularly. Counselors will inspect." For may mentally ill persons who have no other housing alternatives, privacy must be sacrificed to obtain shelter. In addition, Korman and colleagues (Chapter 6) recognize that the civil rights statutes that require reasonable accommodation can be interpreted to authorize landlords to insist on adherence to various conditions.

In some respects, the problems that face the homeless mentally ill are shared by all poor persons. One article noted that "[p]resent case law and social policy . . . treat the privacy interests of poor people as commodities which are protected only to the extent that the person claiming privacy has the money to pay for the material goods and benefits that are required to exercise privacy" (Collin & Collin, 1991). Poor people, since they are unable to pay for housing, are thus treated as second class citizens with regard to privacy rights (A. Allen, 1988). Commentators on this subject have argued that the rationale behind such treatment is the lack of an affirmative duty in the Constitution forcing the government to provide for basic human needs (Collin & Collin, 1991). Instead of reasoning that housing might be necessary to protect a person's constitutional right to privacy, the government has taken the position that since there is no constitutional right to housing, privacy may be diminished. The result is that poor people are subject to "mandatory, periodic, and occasionally unannounced intrusions by government caseworkers" (Collin & Collin, 1991, p. 193).

Part of the problem in this context is whether the housing plans constitute an agreement between the parties or simply the provision of a benefit subject to conditions. This distinction may be important in determining whether to apply contract law or landlord–tenant law, as one would in the context of an agreement, or instead to focus on the "welfare state" issue of conditioning benefits. Clearly, one of the purposes of these agreements is to provide housing for individuals who need a stable environment as part of a treatment plan. Furthermore, the offer of housing provides a strong incentive for persons who would otherwise be homeless to remain in treatment. At least one court has held that "even where the primary purpose of a program is services rather than housing, a tenancy may be created by the agreement of the parties relative to the housing portion of the program" (*Carr v. Friends of the Homeless*, 1990, p. 7). Thus, it may be necessary to separate the housing component from the treatment plan to some degree to ensure compatibility with applicable tenant protections in landlord–tenant codes.

SECURING TREATMENT COMPLIANCE

In *Wiggens v. State Department of Health and Rehabilitative Services* (1993), a Florida court considered the appeal of a woman whose parental rights were terminated in part because she failed to comply with conditions of psychiatric care. After her children were removed from her care, Ms. Wiggens agreed to undergo psychiatric treatment in order to regain custody. The performance agreement included a requirement that she follow her psychiatrist's recommendations and that she continue to take prescribed medication. Ms. Wiggens failed to comply with these conditions, and the trial court terminated her parental rights, holding that there was evidence that the children were neglected and that the failure to comply with psychiatric treatment constituted additional proof of unfitness. Upholding the trial court's decision, the appellate court distinguished an earlier Florida case, *In the Interest of T.D.*, (1989), which held that mental illness per se, without other evidence of neglect, was insufficient to warrant termination of parental rights. In that case, the mother also failed to comply with a performance agreement, but the court found no additional evidence of neglect to support the termination of parental rights.

The *Wiggens* and *T.D.* cases provide a useful context for illustrating the pivotal issue of the "baseline" in analyzing the coerciveness of therapeutic conditions. If Ms. Wiggens were an otherwise fit parent who refused to comply with treatment, she could not be made to choose between her constitutional right to refuse treatment and her interest in maintaining her parental rights; a threat to remove her children would be coercive (and clearly unconstitutional). However, her children *can* be removed from her care if she is determined to be an unfit parent. Ms. Wiggens' children had already been legally removed, and the state used the prospect of regaining custody as an inducement to facilitate treatment compliance. From a normative perspective, this is not coercion. The difficult cases lie between these two polar situations. Suppose, for example, that there has not yet been any judicial intervention, but family services threatens to file for termination unless Ms. Wiggins gets treatment. Discretionary interactions in the shadow of law also arise in the context of civil commitment when a person is threatened with the possibility of inpatient commitment proceedings unless she seeks treatment voluntarily. If commitment, or removal of the children, would not be legally authorized, are these threats unfairly coercive? Are they ethically permissible? Does this depend on whether the "intervenor" knows that there is no legal basis for the threatened action?

The situation becomes more complicated when one moves beyond the custody context and into the area of government benefits. Since an individual has a fundamental constitutionally grounded interest in retaining custody of his or her children, taking a person's children away if he or she fails to comply with treatment (when there are no other grounds for termination) is clearly unconstitutional. But this is less obvious if the treatment is linked to welfare benefits or SSI. On one hand, there is no constitutional right to such benefits even for a poor person, and the government is not constitutionally obligated to create these programs. On the other hand, these benefits are not entirely a matter of grace under existing constitutional doctrine, since the government could not prescribe *any* condition, other than those that are related to administration of the program. If this were not so, the government could buy up constitutional rights of poor people through the use of conditional benefits.

Let us suppose that the government were to explicitly condition receipt of SSI[6] upon compliance with treatment. It might offer two justifications for doing so. First, society has an interest in encouraging SSI recipients to take steps to regain vocational capacity and in assuring that they do not remain disabled due solely to a failure to comply with prescribed treatment. Second, even if the recipient remains disabled and unable to work, society has an interest in minimizing the social costs of disability. The first of these theories is embodied in Department of Health and Human Services regulations precluding SSI benefits for claimants who willfully fail to comply with prescribed treatment that would remove the disability. For example, in *Brown v. Bowen* (1988), the Third Circuit held that a claimant with epilepsy was not entitled to SSI disability benefits since his "blood drug levels were lower than therapeutic levels" (p. 1214). (The regulation in question explicitly stated that epileptics qualified for benefits only if the im-

---

[6]We refer here to SSI exclusively, omitting SSDI, because SSDI is more like an insurance program than a floor of social support.

pairment persists despite anticonvulsive treatment.[7]) The same idea will probably be incorporated into the Americans with Disabilities Act (ADA) in some form. For example, in *Franklin v. U.S. Postal Service* (1988), the plaintiff, who suffered from a mental illness, was required to comply with a treatment regimen in order to maintain her job. The court held that since she could control her "handicap" and refused to do so, she was not an "otherwise qualified handicapped person" and therefore could not claim discrimination under the Rehabilitation Act of 1973 when she was discharged after discontinuing treatment and engaging in dischargeable conduct.

These two settings are not normatively identical; and receipt of SSI benefits can be distinguished from employment with respect to setting the initial baseline. These benefits are legal entitlements under the applicable statute and provide basic subsistence; in contrast, employment has never been conceptualized as an entitlement in American law. Thus, SSI benefits are more likely to be incorporated into the relevant baseline and should be accorded greater protection (O'Neil, 1966). Furthermore, the *Franklin* situation is similar to the *Wiggens* case; since Ms. Franklin could not be considered qualified for her job without treatment, the employer did not have an obligation to keep her on. The possibility of continued employment served as an added inducement to ensure compliance with treatment, as did regaining custody of her children for Ms. Wiggens.[8]

Housing is a more complicated case. As noted above, government-subsidized housing contracts may contain explicit agreements that the individual comply with a medication treatment order.[9] Failure to comply can result in expulsion from the home. These situations involve contractual agreements and thus can be said to be voluntary to some extent. In Chapter 6, Korman and colleagues address this question in much greater detail, focusing on the restrictions found in

---

[7]The Social Security Act excludes from the definition of disability those persons who willfully refuse to undertake prescribed remedial measures. For the mentally ill, this may mean that where an individual refuses to comply with treatment, the government can withhold benefits on the grounds that the person is not "disabled" under the act.

[8]Notwithstanding *Franklin*, however, employers cannot require employees to comply with treatment when "reasonable accommodations," such as minor changes in the job description, are available.

[9]Housing contracts may be either government-funded, in which case the Fourteenth Amendment protects against discrimination, or privately funded, in which case the Americans with Disabilities Act applies. Although the analyses differ slightly, the underlying concerns are the same; in both situations, an individual is forced to accept otherwise impermissible conditions in order to receive housing.

the Fair Housing Act and the ADA, and thus we will not deal with it here. It suffices to note that these cases involve using housing, a necessity, as a means of leverage. Since there is an inadequate supply of affordable housing, control of this scarce resource places an enormous amount of leverage in the hands of housing providers. Not surprisingly, patients would prefer to live in housing that is not controlled by service agencies. In a recent survey of hospitalized patients and treatment teams regarding their housing preferences and service needs after discharge, patients and staff diverged on key issues relating to independence. For example, living in housing not controlled by the service provider was rated as "very important" by 46% of the patients, but was rated as equally important by the teams in only 8% of the cases (Minsky, Riesser, & Duffy, 1995).

In many ways, the conditioning of benefits may appear more acceptable than the other outpatient interventions discussed in this chapter, since the state has an implicit right to control the allocation of scarce resources. The Constitution, however, places certain restrictions on the government's power. The "unconstitutional conditions" doctrine establishes that where the government has discretion to provide a benefit, it may not discriminate on the basis of an individual's exercise of a recognized constitutional right. For example, "the government may not condition tax exemptions or government jobs on political silence or conformity, public unemployment compensation on acceptance of work on one's Sabbath day, or public broadcasting subsidies on abstinence from editorializing" (Sullivan, 1989, p. 1416). The purpose of the doctrine is to prevent the government from indirectly burdening a constitutional right when it cannot do so directly. In the mental health context, the benefits are being conditioned on a surrender of the person's right to make treatment decisions free from unacceptable government interference or pressures (cf. Klapper, 1993).

The unconstitutional conditions doctrine has provoked a great deal of controversy. It appears that the only area of agreement is that the government cannot link benefit programs to a surrender of First Amendment rights (freedom of speech and religion). Application of the doctrine to other constitutional rights is unclear. Consider, for example, the right to make treatment choices. Although this right is constitutionally grounded (in the "liberty" of the due process clause), it probably does not rise to the same level as First Amendment rights, and conditions relating to treatment compliance are not so clearly unconstitutional. For one thing, the government need not be neutral on treatment; it is entitled to use its largesse to "induce" citizens to accept treatment rather than refuse it. For example, in *Maher v. Roe* (1977), the Supreme Court implied that a state *may* use its power over health care funding to "push" treatment decisions in a desired direction; a state may choose to pay for childbirth but not for abortion, thereby favoring one choice over the other, even though this burdens the poor woman's constitutional right to choose.

Application of the unconstitutional conditions doctrine to mental health treatment is also confounded by the perception that the government may not appear to be forcing a detrimental choice. The individuals in question may seem to be better off because of the government's offer of aid—that is, they receive welfare or SSI support *and* needed treatment. In a sense, however, this argument ignores the constitutional value at stake—the presumptive right of the person to make his or her own choices about treatment free from paternalistic interventions by the state. If the state has no authority to force treatment, perhaps it should not have the authority to induce treatment by withholding the necessities of life. In response, it can be argued that promoting treatment compliance is a legitimate governmental aim, and since the government has no duty to provide the benefits, linking the two is not unconstitutional.

A more promising line of analysis may be the nondiscrimination principle of the Equal Protection Clause and the ADA; that is, even though a person might be better off with treatment, the government must nonetheless justify the decision to link benefits with treatment for persons suffering from mental illness while not doing so for other benefit recipients. Judi Chamberlin, author of *On Our Own*, writes: "Why not authorize police to pick up anyone who misses her chemotherapy, or her insulin shot, or her AZT shot, or her high blood pressure pill? People who neglect these treatments are also endangering their health and welfare" (Chamberlin, 1978).

As always, this is a central issue in mental health law: What justifies differential legal treatment of persons with mental illness? And, as always, two possible justifications must be considered. First, a police power or public safety justification might be available if people suffering from mental illness present a greater risk of violent behavior (Torrey, 1994; Jaffe, 1994). However, the majority of people with mental illness are not dangerous, and those who are can be subjected directly to involuntary treatment with appropriate constitutional protections. Second, the validity of a *parens patriae* rationale (i.e., that treatment is in the person's best interests) turns on the issue of competence. When the law selectively conditions government benefits on treatment compliance for people with mental illness, but not for other people who are unwilling to accept needed services, the justification for doing so must lie in the greater prevalence of decisional impairment among persons with mental illness. Recent studies by Appelbaum and Grisso (1995) confirm that impairments of competence-related abilities (understanding, appreciation, and reasoning) are more prevalent among people with schizophrenia than among people with other illnesses. Their research also shows, however, that many people with schizophrenia and other severe mental disorders do *not* have significant impairments. These findings call attention to the critical importance of the principle of individualized assessment that lies at the heart of the ADA. The bottom line is that any formal linkages between treatment compliance and housing should be based on a careful individualized assessment of clinical necessity and not on overbroad generalizations about the incapacities of people with mental illness.

REPRESENTATIVE PAYEE

Leverage over persons with mental illness can also be exerted under the Social Security Program's representative payee system (see Chapter 7). Children, adults who have been adjudicated incompetent, and anyone else whom a physician or an SSA claims representative believes is incapable of managing his or her financial affairs is not entitled to receive benefits directly, but must do so through an intermediary. The representative payee has complete control over the funds, as the checks come in the payee's name, rather than the beneficiary's. Moreover, there is very little regulation of abuses, and in cases in which they do occur, civil or criminal sanctions are rare. In addition, when an appropriate payee cannot be found, SSA may suspend payments, leaving a beneficiary without any financial support (Farrell, 1992).

In order to enable persons with mental illness to receive benefits, a mental health provider is often designated as the representative payee for a number of clients; thus, the health care provider is responsible for handling both treatment services and financial services. Although there is no documented evidence that these service providers are abusing their dual roles, it is clear that the mere fact that they control a client's finances could lead to coercive pressures. The more caseworkers are involved in the daily activities of their clients, the more power they have to both monitor and control them. Like other interventions, this one is motivated by paternalistic concerns; Many mentally ill individuals are unable to manage their financial resources in a responsible manner and may welcome the security of having someone else manage their money. Although this type of intervention may be helpful and appreciated, the caseworker should be sensitive to possible abuses. Thus, it becomes important to separate the roles of treatment provider and financial manager.

A local mental health authority may utilize a range of safeguards to define the role of a representative payee. At the least coercive end, an administrator could be appointed as the representative payee for all the clients and could distribute specified amounts of money at designated intervals. Although this arrangement would prevent conflicts between treatment and financial management, it could also undermine one of the purposes behind SSI. Representative payees are required when an individual is deemed unable to manage his or her financial affairs. Thus, having the treatment provider take clinical factors into account in distributing money is arguably closer to the paternalistic role envisioned by the SSI system. At the other end of the spectrum is the possibility that coercion will be used—that is, the explicit or implicit condition that clients will not receive their money if they do not comply with everything that the therapist recommends. In one forensic conditional release program that utilizes the representative payee system, "[f]ailure to comply with a treatment plan can result in withholding a scheduled cash allowance" (McDonald & Teitelbaum, 1994, p. 7). Community mental health service organizations that are not affiliated with criminal outpatient treatment programs, but are involved in the representative payee system, need to be aware of the possible ethical conflicts. A community mental health service center should develop protocols to deal with financial management complaints that are separate from treatment concerns. Thus, clients should be able to disagree with the way that their finances are being handled without being concerned about negative repercussions on the provision of treatment, such as being labeled "uncooperative" and thus an improper candidate for a particular outpatient service.

There is an additional concern in this area. Unlike government benefit programs that explicitly condition receipt of benefits on compliance with treatment, the coercive agent here is the mental health care provider. Thus, abuses of power are less easily regulated than in contexts in which the coercive aspects are explicit and can be addressed. In this situation, coercion is largely unregulated and to some extent unrecognized. Although one study reported that clients whose caseworker served as their representative payee felt that they were not coerced into making treatment decisions (Piazza, Ford, & Cogswell, 1991), the data are far from conclusive. Even if the melding of the roles of caseworker and financial manager does not create unwarranted pressure on clients, the role of mental health care providers in this context should be more clearly defined. The Social Security regulations add a confounding variable to the discussion of coercive measures in community treatment, since the standards for determining whether someones needs a representative payee and who should be appointed are vague and applied haphazardly (Farrell, 1992). In the absence of administrative and legislative reforms, it falls to the mental health system itself to regulate the coercive power of representative payees.

INFORMAL INTERVENTIONS

In everyday clinical practice, aggressive community treatment of the chronically mentally ill highlights the conflict between respecting individual autonomy and seeking to help a patient (see Chapter 4). If privacy is defined as noninterference, freedom to be let alone means freedom "to starve, or to die for want of means of subsistence" (McCloskey, 1965). Outreach to assist individuals unable to care for themselves is a requirement of basic humanity. But in the absence of commitment, is it permissible to thrust needed services upon unwilling recipients?[10]

Two issues arise in this context: First, some aggressive outreach programs seek to identify homeless individuals who suffer from mental illness. (This targeting of homeless persons is based upon their higher risk for mental illness.) Second, outreach teams seek to persuade homeless people with mental illness (or other mentally ill individuals who may already be enrolled in mental health programs) to accept or comply with treatment. Here, the focus is on what limits should be placed on efforts to ensure compliance with a treatment regimen.

---

[10]We assume for purposes of argument that we are dealing with public programs, that is, those run by local community agencies. Therefore, the persons involved are state actors, not private ones.

SURVEILLANCE AND MONITORING

People have an interest in privacy even if they do not have a house. The Fourth Amendment's protections extend beyond the traditional home to any place where an individual has a reasonable expectation of privacy. Do homeless individuals have any expectations of privacy? They are unable to deny access to their living quarters; their home lacks a door that can be barred. They have no way of preventing "intrusions" by people wishing to help them. As a practical matter, then, people with homes have greater protection against aggressive interventions than people who are homeless. In short, the privacy interests of homeless individuals are almost ephemeral under a traditional Fourth Amendment framework. From an ethical standpoint, however, the individual's interest in being left alone is the same whether he or she is living in a house or on the street. Furthermore, from the therapist's viewpoint, it may become ridiculous to try to distinguish between the privacy interests of patients who live in a house, a shack, a cardboard box, or on a park bench (see Chapter 5). At the very least, it may be important to recognize that the most destitute are the most vulnerable to unwanted intrusions.

Therapeutic interventions may well be justified in many cases. Not only is homelessness a risk factor for serious mental illness, but also mental illness may prevent a homeless person from seeking available benefits that would facilitate improvement in his or her living conditions. The denial of illness that prevents a person from obtaining treatment may also prevent the person from seeking shelter, food, or other necessities.

Outreach is a classic public health tool. Consider, for example, a program of contact tracing, in which health officials actively seek out people who have been identified as sexual partners of people with sexually transmitted diseases (STDs). Although confidentiality is strictly protected, this form of outreach is intrusive and does present concerns about privacy. Nonetheless, contact tracing has been widely used and is viewed as an appropriate measure to control the spread of STDs including AIDS. Likewise, targeting homeless persons in order to screen for mental illness is a reasonable aim of aggressive outreach teams.

SECURING TREATMENT COMPLIANCE

The underlying purpose of aggressive community treatment is to help people who are unable to help themselves; those targeted are generally people who lack insight into their illness and are unable to take advantage of available social services. Even acknowledging the beneficial value of outreach services, however, therapists should be sensitive to the coercive features of their actions and should be conscious of the homeless mentally ill person's unusual susceptibility to such pressures. Outreach workers have a level of control over homeless mentally ill persons that they would not have over individuals who have access to basic medical care, clothing, food, and shelter. The result is that the more a person "needs" help, the more vulnerable he or she is to coercive pressures. Persons who have no source of food and are offered food on a regular basis are more susceptible to pressures to enter into counseling if they fear that the food source may be taken away.

A recent report of the American Psychiatric Association's Task Force on the Homeless Mentally Ill identified a chronology of outreach services provided to individuals who are living in shelters or public places (Susser, Valencia, & Goldfinger, 1993) (see also Chapter 4). It advocates the classic "foot-in-the-door" method of providing services, noting that mental health treatment services are rarely overtly proposed, but are usually hidden among offers for food, shelter, and basic medical care. Using such techniques, an outreach worker can encourage an individual to rely on him or her for basic needs, eventually introducing further treatment. Although outreach workers may not explicitly require compliance with additional mental health treatments as a condition to continued provision of basic necessities, the connection may be an implicit one. Homeless mentally ill persons may be fearful of losing whatever benefits they have, or of losing the outreach worker's friendship, if they do not comply with treatment suggestions. Under this model, the individual's subjective feelings may be important; whether a proposal is seen as a threat or an offer may determine whether a client feels constrained or coerced, which in turn may influence treatment efficacy.

Interventions such as these appear to lack any coercive element because they give a homeless person *more* choices and seem to make the person better off. It can be argued, however, that destitute individuals shift their baseline of expected entitlements to include food once it has been offered by a generous provider. As noted earlier, the "baseline," the reference point from which gains and losses are evaluated, is extremely sensitive to specific circumstances. Most disturbing in these situations is that the benefits that are involved can be considered necessities for living, for example, food, clothing, or shelter.

Mb Wb Wb

Thus, it may be important for an outreach worker to distinguish between "nonnecessities," such as paper or charcoal pencils (see Chapter 5), and necessities, such as food or housing. Even though a person may come to expect the nonnecessary items, their loss would not be as devastating nor would the coercive nature of their threatened removal be as strong. The issues here are similar to those in the previous section, where the government conditions a benefit upon treatment. However, the "coercive aspects" of aggressive outreach services are more appropriately considered an ethical issue, rather than a legal one, and should be monitored by community mental health boards.

CONCLUSION

The intent of this chapter was more to raise questions than to answer them. In order to do so most effectively, we have discussed some "aggressive" interventions that have not yet been attempted. Today's speculation, however, may become tomorrow's assertive strategy. Mental health treatment in the community has largely replaced inpatient services; as a result, innovative programs are being developed and new questions and issues are being raised. Outpatient commitment, conditional access to benefits, and aggressive outreach programs are designed to remedy some glaring deficiencies of the present services system, and these methods are not likely to be abandoned. Indeed, they are more likely to be strengthened and broadened in the coming years. It is therefore crucial to begin to consider some of the ethical and legal implications of these practices. The law in this area is far from settled. Community treatment providers should be aware of the relevant issues and should begin to shape their own guidelines, rather than wait for litigation and thereby surrender responsibility to the courts.

REFERENCES

Allen, A. (1988). *Uneasy access: Privacy for women in a free society.* Totowa, NJ: Rowman & Littlefield.
Allen, P. (1976). A bill of rights for citizens using outpatient mental health services. In H. Richard Lamb et al. (Eds.), *Community survival for long-term patents* (pp. 147–176). San Francisco: Jossey-Bass.

Appelbaum, P., & Grisso, T. (1995). The MacArthur treatment competence study. III. Abilities of patients to consent to psychiatric and medical treatments. *Law and Human Behavior, 19*, 149–174.

Brown v. Bowen, 845 F.2d 1211 (1988).

Camara v. Municipal Court of the City and County of San Francisco, 387 U.S. 523 (1966).

Carr v. Friends of the Homeless, Inc., No. 89-LE-3492-S Mass. Housing Court, Hampden Division (1990).

Carroll, J. (1991). Consent to mental health treatment: A theoretical analysis of coercion, freedom, and control. *Behavioral Sciences and the Law, 9*, 129–142.

Chamberlain, J. (1978). *On our own: Patient-controlled alternatives to the mental health system.* New York: McGraw-Hill.

Collin, R. M., & Collin, R. W. (1991). Are the poor entitled to privacy? *Harvard Blackletter Journal, 8*, 181–219.

Farrell, M. (1992). Administrative paternalism: Social Security's representative payment and two models of justice. *Cardozo Law Review, 14*, 283–349.

Franklin v. U.S. Postal Service, 48 Emp. Prac. Dec. ¶38,482 (S.D. Ohio 1988).

Geller, J. (1986a). The quandaries of enforced community treatment and unenforceable outpatient commitment statutes. *Journal of Psychiatry & Law, 14*, 149–158.

Geller, J. (1986b). Rights, wrongs, and the dilemma of coerced community treatment. *American Journal of Psychiatry, 143*, 1259–1264.

Griffen v. Wisconsin, 483 U.S. 868 (1987).

Hiday, V. (1992). Coercion in civil commitment. *International Journal of Law and Psychiatry, 15*, 359–377.

Hiday, V., & Scheid-Cook, T. L. (1990). Outpatient commitment for "revolving door" patients: Treatment and compliance. *Journal of Nervous and Mental Disease, 179*, 85–90.

Hinds, J. (1990). Involuntary outpatient commitment for the chronically mentally ill. *Nebraska Law Review, 69*, 346–412.

In the Interest of T.D., A Child, 537 So.2d 173 (Fla.App. 1 Dist. 1989).

Jaffe, D. J. (1994). How to reduce both violence and stigma. *Innovations and Research, 3*, 1–2.

Keilitz, I., & Hall, T. (1985). State statutes governing involuntary outpatient civil commitment. *Mental and Physical Disability Law Reporter, 9*, 378–397.

Klapper, A. (1993). Finding a right in state constitutions for the community treatment of the mentally ill. *University of Pennsylvania Law Review, 142*, 739–835.

Maher v. Roe, 432 U.S. 453 (1977).

McCabe v. The City of Lynn, 875 F. Supp. 53 (D.Mass 1995).

McCafferty, G., & Dooley, J. (1990). Involuntary outpatient commitment: An update. *Mental and Physical Disability Law Reporter, 14*, 277–287.

McCloskey, H. J. (1965). A critique of the ideal of liberty. *Mind, 74*, 483–508.

McDonald, D., & Teitelbaum, M. (1994). *Managing mentally ill offenders in the community: Milwaukee's community support program.* Washington, DC: National Institute of Justice.

Minsky, D., Riesser, G. G., & Duffy, M. (1995). The eye of the beholder: Housing preferences of inpatients and their treatment providers. *Psychiatric Services, 46*, 173–176.

Mulvey, E., Geller, J., & Roth, L. (1987). The promise and peril of involuntary outpatient commitment. *American Psychologist, 42*, 571–584.

Navarro, M. (1993, March 10). New York City to detain patients who fail to finish TB treatments. *New York Times,* pp. A1, B3.

O'Neil, R. M. (1966). Unconstitutional conditions: Welfare benefits with strings attached. *California Law Review, 54,* 443–478.

Parrish v. Civil Service Com'n of County of Alameda, 425 P.2d 223 (1967).

Piazza, S. E., Ford, J., & Cogswell, S. H. (1991) Case management and representative payeeship as problems for homeless severely mentally disabled persons: Final report. Columbus: Ohio Department of Mental Health.

Rosen, C. (1990). The fourth amendment implications of urine testing for evidence of drug use in probation. *Brooklyn Law Review, 55,* 1159–1253.

Santos, A., Hawkins, G., Julius, B., Deci, P., Hierst, T., & Burns, B. (1993). A pilot study of assertive community treatment for patients with chronic psychotic disorders. *American Journal of Psychiatry, 150,* 501–504.

Schmerber v. California, 384 U.S. 757 (1966).

Schwartz, S., & Costanzo, C. (1987). Compelling treatment in the community: Distorted doctrines and violated values. *Loyola of Los Angeles Law Review, 20,* 1346–1405.

Skinner v. Railway Labor Executives' Association, 489 U.S. 602 (1989).

Slobogin, C. (1994). Involuntary community treatment of people who are violent and mentally ill: A legal analysis. *Hospital and Community Psychiatry, 45,* 685–689.

Stefan, S. (1987). Preventative commitment: The concept and its pitfalls. *Mental and Physical Disability Law Reporter, 11,* 288–302.

Sullivan, K. (1989). Unconstitutional conditions. *Harvard Law Review, 102,* 1413–1506.

Susser, E., Valencia, E., & Goldfinger, S. (1993). Clinical care of homeless mentally ill individuals: Strategies and adaptations. In H. Lamb, L. Bachrach, & F. Kass (Eds.), *Treating the homeless mentally ill* (pp. 127–140). Washington DC: American Psychiatric Association Press.

Torrey, E. F. (1994). Violent behavior by individuals with serious mental illness. *Hospital and Community Psychiatry, 45,* 653–662.

Washington v. Harper, 494 U.S. 210 (1990).

Wertheimer, A. (1993). A philosophical examination of coercion for mental health issues. *Behavioral Sciences and the Law, 11,* 239–258.

Wiggens v. State Department of Health and Rehabilitative Services, 616 So.2d 127 (Fla.App. 2 Dist. 1993).

Wisor, R. (1993). Community care, competition and coercion: A legal perspective on privatized mental health care. *American Journal of Law & Medicine, 19,* 145–175.

Wyman v. James, 400 U.S. 309 (1971).

CHAPTER 11

REGULATION FROM WITHOUT
THE SHADOW SIDE OF COERCION

KIM HOPPER

. . . the world will have turned into one huge hospital where everyone is everybody else's humane nurse.

—GOETHE, as cited in Rieff, 1968, p. 24n

Two preoccupations frame these remarks on the foregoing chapters: margins and managed care—specifically, the depletion of the first and the ascendancy of the second. I use the term *managed care* (a bit loosely, perhaps) to designate the growing practice of subjugating to the accountant's ledger certain "medical" decisions about what constitutes appropriate or allowable care (cf. Schreter, 1993). In particular, I want to flag the constraints it is likely to impose on deviations from set norms. By *margins,* I mean those endangered spaces on the civic landscape that supplied forgiving accommodations to misfits of all sorts, at a cost conventionally figured in disgrace rather than dollars.

KIM HOPPER • Nathan Kline Institute for Psychiatric Research, Orangeburg, New York 10962.

Coercion and Aggressive Community Treatment: A New Frontier in Mental Health Law, edited by Deborah L. Dennis and John Monahan. Plenum Press, New York, 1996.

Here, persons who failed to meet thresholds of acceptability else-where—by virtue of temperament, damage, pathology, or the rude wish to be left alone—could find a home. Precincts of "disreputable housing" (Groth, 1983), zones of discard (Schneider, 1986, p. 181), skid rows, and tenderloins—such places provided welcomed "anchors for people in a social and cultural limbo" (Groth, 1994, p. 130). Put sim-ply, they made it possible for alternative livelihoods to make do, if not thrive. I do not want to romanticize the appointments or civilities of such spaces, which were meager and few, but neither do I want to dis-count the freedom they accorded those whom difference could make difficult. Above all, I want to stress the logic of accommodation im-plicit in their operation. It was the flexibility of habitat—literally, the room to move—and not some elaborate underworld code of conduct, that made it possible to hold trouble within tolerable limits.

THE WORLD WITHOUT

These two formidable "secular" developments provide the indispens-able backdrop against which the dramas of psychiatric coercion ex-amined in this volume are played out. Doubtless, cultural factors also intrude—in particular, the increasingly fierce remoralization of poverty and demonization of the mentally ill. But changes at the level of clinical administration[1] and marginal housing matter more, it seems to me, because these changes substantially determine the field of possibles, without ever undertaking to do so as a matter of policy or professed intent. In a phrase, what I am driving at is the unobtru-sive shadow side of highlighted moments of coercion: the framing compulsions (or structural constraints) that shape what come to be seen as the ordinary, taken-for-granted bounds of everyday choice and, over time, may stunt capacity and scuttle hope in the bargain.[2]

[1]"Clinical administration" is shorthand for the entire regulatory and reimbursement apparatus that governs benefits for persons diagnosed with severe mental illness who are also dependent upon government support for their livelihood and treatment.
[2]"Framing compulsions," as I use the phrase here, refer to those limits and pressures that shape choice in the given instance. They have as much to do with questions not asked, opinions not solicited, lines of inquiry never broached, courses of actions ruled out from the start—the whole penumbra of excluded options—as they do with specific influence exerted to pick one from among a select set of choices. Critically, their very unobtrusiveness, coupled with the fact that they operate "prior" to the decision point in question, can make their influence difficult to detect, not least of all by the actor himself or herself.

My contention is that these two developments will likely revolutionize the terms and conditions under which people with severe mental illness obtain clinical services and survival goods. In a word, both government and market will have an unprecedented stake in *stability*. Here's what I mean: (1) Margins provide dirty work, rudimentary shelter, and rough tolerance. They may not be fancy, but their shrinkage over the past quarter century (e.g., Lee, 1980; Marin, 1987) has made life in urban interstices much more difficult to sustain. Their depletion would mean that it falls to government to attempt to do with deliberation and planning what the market once achieved through profiteering, waste, and frictional inefficiency, abetted by lax or absent oversight (Hopper & Baumohl, 1994). With no buffer (vacancies in the SRO down the street) to fall back upon, and social capital (kin and friends) an uncertain or unavailable recourse for many, a premium will be placed on staying put. For those whom government supports, residential mobility in an era of depleted margins promises to be unduly costly. (2) The same logic applies to community-based treatment under a regime of managed care. Current schedules of reimbursement for clinical services and survival goods may be riddled with inefficiencies and inequities, but their replacement with a system predicated on predictable illness trajectories and cost-savings could hold fresh hell in store. For those providers who have carved out a niche for themselves and their clients, may even have begun to explore the potential of genuinely collaborative practice, the danger is replacing a muddle that can be made to work for some with a machine that will strenuously resist being plied outside a narrow range of tolerances.

Granted, evidence to date is mixed and preliminary. While providers champion the gains in efficiency, flexibility, consumer-centeredness, and access that capitation makes possible, they also worry. Cost-containment drives managed care, and what is "medically necessary" may fall well short of what is socially (or, in the extended sense, clinically) appropriate. People with "complex needs" are likely to be left out (Wells, 1995). Among the identified trends that prompt such concerns: (1) As private inpatient facilities take over from the state, reliance on involuntary treatment orders increases, the better to ensure medication compliance, more rapid stabilization, and shorter stays (Fleischner, 1994); (2) "cost shifting" (from providers to consumers and their families) is likely (Wells, 1995); (3) community-based treatment is becoming increasingly segmented and episodic, limited to "identifying a chief complaint that can be addressed in a short-term intervention" (Schreter, 1993, p. 326); and (4) the precarious but undeniable legitimacy of consumers in public mental health systems will not readily find a home in a world of "private firm[s] negotiat[ing] to define medical necessity clearly in order to fix the boundary of responsibility and limit their liability" (National Association of State Mental Health Program Directors & American Behavioral Healthcare Association, 1994, p. 6).

To glimpse just how consequential such developments may prove, consider only the sometimes unruly, often arduous "work of recovery" (Davidson & Strauss, 1992) in which some recipients of mental health services are engaged. Like some long-standing self-help efforts (e.g., Powell & Knight, 1994), alternative sources of asylum (Fisher, 1994; Clay, 1994), and the new generation of ACT teams Diamond discusses in Chapter 3, the work of recovery values growth—messy, nonlinear, full of pitfalls and setbacks—over stability. "Keeping things complicated" (Estroff, 1994) will serve neatly as the watchword for these pioneering efforts. But complexity, the recognition that behind the one-dimensional "expatients" are fully fledged adults whose changing needs can prove an awkward fit for programs that fail to keep pace (Davidson, Stayner, & Haglund, 1996), may prove costly. Demands that the mental health system be reoriented to promote the work of recovery, both within and outside its own apparatus of care and support, are predicated upon assumptions of abundance and flexibility that have become increasingly difficult to credit. The enabling material and attitudinal armature may not be there.

Admittedly, such concerns bias my reading of these chapters. I tend to throw into sharp relief what are sometimes less than prominent (even passing) comments of some of the contributors to this volume—Diamond on limited resources and the default nature of coercion, Lovell (Chapter 9) on the "contextual determinants of coercion," Solomon (Chapter 8) on the imitative coupling of clinical and criminal justice systems, Berg and Bonnie (Chapter 10) on the ambiguous mandate of public health, Monahan and colleagues (Chapter 1) on practical, negotiated alternatives to the rapid transit model of psychiatric admission. Conversely, I find myself perplexed by the silence of others, too easily mistaking it for an innocence or studied disregard we can no longer afford. My argument here will revisit one made long ago with respect to the limits of symbolic interactionism. Although blessed with a finely tuned sense of the microdramas of power in everyday life, its practitioners (argued Paul Rock) turned a blind analytical eye toward those "structural arrangements which *organize the contexts* of defining encounters" (Rock, 1974, p. 144; emphasis added).[3] Something similar, I suggest, is going on in these discussions of psychiatric coercion. (Lovell's is the notable exception.)

SOME HIGH POINTS

Not that there aren't moments of real insight, studies that address genuine dilemmas, and extended riffs of hard thinking and self-reflection on display here. There are, plainly. Let me comment on a number of themes that run throughout.

VEXED NATURE OF THE DEPENDENT VARIABLE

When not simply resolved by fiat, the notion of "coercion" gave most authors trouble and prompted a number of efforts at clarification. Useful distinctions are drawn, for example, by Monahan and colleagues (operationalizing its meaning and dissecting the varieties of influence at work in the admission process), Berg and Bonnie (as against certain prized values), by Diamond (case management vs. collaboration), by Lovell (the continuum of social control), by Solomon (the substitution effect of resorting, informally, to criminal justice sanctions to "solve" mental health problems), and by Lopez (Chapter 5) (strategic accumulation of trust in the interest of equipping to choose). But most of these discussions are less concerned with conceptual clarity than with the moral rightness of whatever we choose to call coercion. All beg, it seems to me, the oldest prior question of all: compared to what? We need some working knowledge of the varieties of coercion (troublesome and otherwise) in lives as yet unencumbered by severe mental illness, the better to take the distinctive measure of the difference *that* misfortune makes. To be sure, the circumstances of constraint discussed here are often exceptional and occasionally extreme. Still, a general "theory of social influence," as

[3]More recently, Eric Wolf has drawn anthropologists' attention to that modality of "power that not only operates within settings or domains but that also *organizes and orchestrates the settings themselves,* and that specifies the distribution and direction of energy [or dollar] flows" (Wolf, 1990, p. 586; emphasis added).

Monahan et al. 1995 call it, would both inject realism and cast in sharper resolution the specific densities of influence at issue here.[4]

That said, certain ambiguities of influence still seem to me worth pondering. We need, for example, to draw distinctions in modalities of *agency* (self-initiated action, cooperation, or submission), and not simply because apparent compliance can be feigned or merely "utilitarian" (Lovell) in intent, or tricked up out of a subject's working misunderstanding (Berg and Bonnie), or extorted in exchange for housing [Korman and colleagues (Chapter 6)]. Rather, like "beliefs" in general (Jenkins, 1988), perceived *non*coercion can be essentially *strategic* in nature, motivated by an ill-appreciated concern for the implications of believing thus-and-so rather than otherwise.[5] Knowing whether one was unjustifiably coerced, and to what degree, may be a difficult sounding to take in some circumstances. Ethnographic inquiry can help. "Beliefs do a job," Luhrmann (1989, p. 353), shows us[6] and the subtle, out-of-awareness shaping of conviction by cumulative practice, the auto-rhetorical (or "persuasive") power of faithfully going through the motions with committed others who consistently interpret one's actions as accurately reflecting one's intents, is one of ethnography's signal findings (and a methodological blind spot of

[4]This theory will probably need to go beyond the convenient literature of "social control," the shortcomings of which as an analytical concept are becoming increasingly obvious (Mayer, 1985). Too easily, the term becomes a sort of magical realism device, conferring the appearance of organized influence on a wide range of formal and informal exercises of regulating power. That such exercises are incompletely documented (for either execution or effect), but are instead categorically inferred from the suspect motives of ruling elites or the dismaying passivity of subordinates or both, only compounds the reader's suspicion that sleight of hand has taken the place of analysis (cf. Rock, 1974; Lukes, 1974).

[5]Jenkins (1988), for example, was able to show that Mexican-American parents of sons and daughters diagnosed as schizophrenic opted for the folk category *nervios* rather than the seemingly more appropriate *loco*. On analysis, it became clear that the former carried with it a host of implications regarding familial culpability, stigma, and prognosis that were far preferable to the darker and more disturbing connotations of the latter.

[6]Luhrmann's splendid ethnography of present-day magicians argues convincingly that "the ideas associated with their practice become persuasive because people rationalize an imaginative, emotional involvement. Their beliefs are not fixed or consistent, for they are often presented to justify some action. . . . Ideas and beliefs *drift*, in a complex interdependency of concept and experience" (Luhrmann, 1989, p. 353; emphasis added). Clearly, confinement to a hospital is a far cry from the "serious play" of witchcraft, but one wonders about the interplay between being treated and acting "as if" one were a patient, and coming to terms with the fact of one's confinement. See following note.

survey methods).[7] The ironic upshot: Not only resistance (Monahan et al., 1995), but also protestations that one's choice was self-initiated, may, paradoxically, be the last refuge of self respect in those facing no real alternatives.[8] Such a dynamic suggests that researchers should be alert to instances of apparent initiative or consent, where unperceived but real coercion may be detected by disinterested others.[9]

AMBIGUITIES OF JUSTIFICATION

No philosopher is cited more frequently by these authors than Wertheimer (1993), who makes three points critical to my argument here: (1) Jousting over definitions (what kinds of influence should properly count as coercion?) is silly; the substantive issue is what distinctions among kinds of pressure, exerted by whom, and under what circumstances are *morally relevant* in deciding whether such pressure is permissible? (2) No "univocal" account of questionable situations will suffice, in part because multiple perspectives are needed simply to flesh out the various meanings of "what happened?". (3) Not only perspective, but *stake* in outcome—and, it turns out, process as well (see below)—matters in judging the moral consequentiality of pressure in question.

[7]It may help explain, for example, why end-of-hospital assessments of the appropriateness of care tend to be more favorable than those around time of admission (Monahan et al., 1995). Intuitively, it would seem to require a great deal of "identity work" (Snow and Anderson, 1987) to hold out against the inertial force of ward routine, like-minded others, and the endless assault of environmental cues. Alternatively, it could be the case that in the course of hospitalization they actually secured some of what they sorely missed in the admission process—being listened to and treated with respect (Monahan et al., 1995).

[8]As Bakke (1940, pp. 25–26) once noted with respect to self-blame among newly unemployed men during the Great Depression. A corollary situation is one alluded to by Diamond: that a severely constricted field of choice will be perceived not as unfair but as fittingly "appropriate" to one's differentness.

[9]In the absence of conflict, of course, conceptual and methodological complexities multiply. At the very least, it can be very difficult to demonstrate the relevant counterfactual: that *but for* the specific influence exerted by person/context/circumstance A, B would very likely have acted otherwise. As we are only recently learning to appreciate with respect to psychiatric coercion [as Lovell and Diamond note in this volume and Monahan and colleagues note both in this volume and elsewhere (1995)], accurately to infer routine but inapparent coercion requires that we "examine how people react to opportunities—or, more precisely, perceived opportunities—when these occur, to escape from subordinate positions in hierarchical systems" (Lukes, 1974, p. 48). The self-help movement is a stunning case in point.

These considerations pertain not only to judgments of the "moral force" of consent in a given instance (specifically, whether an alleged influence may be said to have "nullified" consent), but also to the "moral baseline"—what a subject in extremis may properly ("has a right to") expect of others—against which proposed threats and offers are measured. Here difficulties mount. Most of the discussions in these pages necessarily skirt the issue of what prospective patients "may properly expect" because there is neither social consensus nor moral or legal clarity on that issue at present (Chapter 10). "Least restrictive alternative" seems obscenely inapplicable to the circumstances of the street-dwelling homeless poor, for example; "reasonable accommodation," neatly enough, would seem to hold some promise. But unless the moral baseline is explicitly spelled out, other forces—bureaucratic and budgetary in particular—will "regulate" the issue by default. One way in which this is already happening is the proposal to restrict time limits on SSI benefits to recipients whose claim to disability is based on substance abuse. Another is by redefining the warrant of public health.

Traditionally, the scope of public health has been construed both widely as an affirmative obligation to maximize common weal (Beauchamp, 1985) and more narrowly as an obligation to protect the public against specific threats like contagious disease (Chapter 10). In its broadest appeal, it approaches the domain of "public works"; in its narrowest, that of the police. When applied to mental health, the argument gets famously vague. Is the warrant to protect the public against dangerousness? This question arises (only to disappear in the smoke of official dissembling) every time the press reports an unprovoked attack on a stranger by an "emotionally disturbed person." Is it to relieve the burden on families, as some have suggested in explaining the origins of the asylum in the 19th century (Scull, 1977)? Is it, as seems increasingly fashionable to claim in places like New York City, to sanitize public space against the visual contamination of "disorder" (*Walley v. New York City Transit Authority*, 1991)? [An internal NYPD memo cites "dirt, grafitti, homeless people, noise" as threats to quality of life (Kunen, 1994, p. 10).] Might it even be construed, as Diamond's concluding covert treacheries suggest, to maximize the self-determination of those whom genes, rotten luck, bad timing, and hostile environment have conspired to wound?

No doubt, sustained attention to the specifics of these and other putative interpretations of that warrant is bound to produce a host of competing claims. Certain interests have a well-organized head start. As Korman and colleagues show us, the modest expectation that persons with a psychiatric history may properly aspire to certain types of unsegregated dwellings has been successfully contested. More germane to my argument here is the prospect that the public fisc could substitute for the common weal as the referent point for "harm," such that "wasteful" or "excess" spending will be seen as the functional equivalent of assault on the body politic. "Utilization review" would then serve as a warrantless search.

Pragmatics of Everyday Dispute Resolution

A stake in the outcome (e.g., the prospect of being "better off") isn't the only interest salient here. As important is how the negotiation proceeds. This seems to me one of the more durable and useful lessons of the evidence and experience reviewed in these chapters (see especially Chapters 1, 3, and 9). In situations in which disputes are likely to arise, forced choice happens more often when suitable, agreed-upon conflict resolution procedures are unavailable. A measure of comity, mutual respect, a chance to make one's case and be heard, the participation of trusted others: these are the sorts of processual elements that—even in the absence of the substantial resources needed to significantly expand the field of choice—materially affect one's sense that the ordeal has been fair. [That the efficacy of outpatient commitment may depend to an inordinate degree upon the subject's working *mis*understanding of actually enforceable sanctions for violations of psychiatric probation (Chapter 10) strikes me as a fatal design flaw.] And while commitment to equitable process could conceivably become a fetish, leading to grotesque gambits designed to get people to "feel good about" patently unjust choices, the risk seems worth taking.

Opposition to the thoroughly workable, eminently reasonable proposals that surface in these pages is to be expected. And just as research ought to "problematize coercion as a moral construct" (Lovell, Chapter 9), so should it problematize correction as a practical one. It isn't enough to demonstrate that reform is feasible; we will also need to document and find ways of circumventing the unobtrusive "linkages that block or redirect the impetus for reform" (Weir, 1992, p. 168). "Demonstration" projects mounted by eager researchers from the outside that show up routine practice as inferior and possibly cruel,

without at the same time garnering support from within for continuing to refine and implement the needed changes, are quickly con-
signed to the journal shelves.

HOUSING AND OTHER SURVIVAL GOODS AS BAIT AND HOOK

In dealing with difference, "rights talk" isn't the only language that
applies (Minow, 1990). The craft of "outreach," as Lopez practices it
(and writes about it in Chapter 5), is premised on the imperative to
connect: to restore those tentative ties of affiliation, trust, and dependency, not merely as a modality of instrumental aid (though it can
work that way), but as the stuff (provisional to be sure) of an elemental social contract. Nobody has a "right" to be connected, but because
culture goes to the heart of what makes us human, we all have a presumptive interest in being so. In fact, as Michael Ignatieff (1984) has
argued, it is because certain features of our essential nature—he has
in mind belonging, love, fraternity, dignity, solidarity—are so difficult
to define as rights that we seek to "specify them as needs and seek,
with the blunt institutional procedures at our disposal, to make their
satisfaction a routine human practice" (p. 14).[10] So there is, or can be, a
more ambitious motive behind the arduous work of outreach than
mere harm reduction. Liberty, autonomy, and privacy, as Berg and
Bonnie remind us in Chapter 10, are prized values that need to be fac-
tored in; had we any doubts about it, the courts have ruled that even a
homeless man's outdoor camp is entitled to the same privacy protections as a conventional "home" (*New York Times*, October 16, 1991,
p. B8). The burden of Lopez's argument, it seems to me, is to force us
further into the ethics of the public health warrant. She implies not
only that the need to connect may be the root premise of outreach, but
also that its work over time should strengthen the machinery of
choosing and, as a by-product of reconnection, complicate the domain of choice. Doubtless such a rationale is subject to mischief, as the
varieties of vigilante action that can be passed off as "outreach" attest
(e.g., Lambert, 1995). Nonetheless, appeal to the logic of solidarity
serves strikingly to reframe the usual arguments about justifiable
quid pro quos.

---

[10]That the street-dwelling homeless have lost capacity for or interest in connecting is
one of the storied simplicities of our time, as even a brief sojourn there attests (e.g.,
Lardner, 1991; Hopper, 1992). This is not to deny that the exigencies of street life exact
a toll in trust or raise the stakes in risking reconnection; they do, and that is what
makes outreach more of an art than an "offer."

For one thing, it suggests that the engagement process itself (and not simply the terms of the exchange) may be an important vehicle for recognizing the humanity/agency of the other. If it is not to flirt with entrapment, engagement takes time and effort to do properly. For another, it suggests that enhancing capacity to choose is as much a matter of raising the other's stake in rejoining the collectivity, of complicating one's choices as it were, as it is one of repairing damaged equipment. Negotiated cooperation, even in stages replete with setbacks, is an obvious concern of the former; it isn't quite so compelling if the job is to get someone "into the shop" for a tune-up. On prima facie grounds, the impatient logic of efficiency under managed care seems a hostile limiting force.

At the same time, the whole point of the earlier lament over the loss of margins was that misfits need not *stay* connected as a condition of social membership. Moving from the street to housing may well propel the relative ballast of liberty and privacy ahead of the invariably intrusive solidarity of outreach. In particular, as Korman and colleagues (Chapter 6) stress, one should not be obligated to "go to program" as a condition of tenancy. Good neighbor obligations surely apply, as they do on the margins, but required therapy (no less than mandated conviviality or binding attendance of religious services) smacks more of a management tool than a gesture of either solidarity or clinical desiderata.

DECREASING THE NEED FOR (OBVIOUS) COERCION

If future discussions of these issues are not to become endless rounds of anguished debates over Hobson's choices, then the host terrain of these quandaries—as well as the scripts and players—will have to change. Hopeful signs that ground rules can be rewritten, *given* a sufficiency of "time, resources, training and attitude" (Diamond), are scattered throughout this volume. Specific, practical, and embarrassingly simple means of decompressing the admission[11] process have been identified (Monahan and colleagues); fresh forays into the uncharted waters of collaborative casework have been initiated by the

---

[11]It may be useful, too, in future research to examine the different trajectories that bring prospective patients to the psychiatric ER. The "decision to admit" may gloss a variety of threshold situations: imminent danger, exhausted nerves, impossible burden, panic, punishment, and simple convenience (see Sheehan 1994). Conceivably, not only the final deliberations on whether to admit but also the sometimes twisted process of getting there will affect perceptions of coercion.

"second generation" of ACT teams (Diamond); and a variety of inventive devices (ranging from "advance directives"[12] and other negotiated alternatives for handling prospective conflicts to use of peer specialists to reduce "cultural distance") have come out of the self-help movement (Lovell). If we move from the individual to group level of practice, issues of governance become paramount. In the case of "consumer-run" households, for example, collectively agreed-upon means (short of evicting the offender) are needed for arresting and resolving what can be the rapidly spiraling and destructive effects on the group of one tenant's therapeutic contract gone awry. (This can happen, for example, when disputes over the proper use of earmarked funds spill disruptively into household routine [see Ware, 1994].) In the absence of such mechanisms, collectively understood to have been established for the purpose, coercion by default (Diamond)—justified by "final straw" actions and "having no alternative but. . ." constraints—is inevitable.

REDRAWING THE BOUNDS OF CIVIL DISCOURSE

A depoliticized language of the public good is just another excuse for academics to keep talking. This chapter goes to the editors on the 50th anniversary of FDR's death, which makes an otherwise hopelessly ill-timed suggestion apt: Why not take the rich array of things that can no longer be dismissed as undoable, generated even in the fairly focused confines of these pages, and join what has been of late a largely one-sided debate over fundamentals, core values, and orienting ideals? Sentinel duty in the vicinity of what Katznelson (1986) once referred to as the "silences" of American social and economic policy—that vast region of preemptively banished discourse—is a lonely watch these days. Resurrecting the notion that an ethic of public health (let alone a welfare state) might be grounded in such values as equality and solidarity will be neither easy nor fashionable. But it would serve notice that, at least in some arenas of clinical practice, it is feasible to build bridges and make common cause with others not given to easy trust or facile cooperation, and to do so while playing by the rules of elemental respect. And that would be a welcome distraction from the dreary bombast about "personal responsibility" and bootstrapping that currently presides.

---

[12]See also Sherman (1994). It should be noted that mechanisms like "Ulysses contracts" have their own problems in practice (Rhoden, 1982).

CONCLUSION

Maxine didn't really want to return to the supportive-living program,
because she didn't want anyone harrying her to go to work or to do her
share of the cleaning, but it was her only option.

—SHEEHAN, 1994, p. 205

When there was a buck to be made on the margins, misrule found a ready home. Regulation stayed away, content to let "the market" do the dirty work of seeing to the needs of the indigent and unruly. What happened there was better left unseen, let alone examined. The war on poverty never gained a toehold there; reformers for the most part ignored it; good citizens knew better than to cross that turf. It may have been haphazard, but such disregard was providential: These "zones of discard" proved to be places of sanctuary or "refuge" (Cohen & Sokolovsky, 1989) as well. So long as the costs of accommodation were tallied in disrepute and buried in the ledgers of rooming houses, shabby hotels, and taverns (and, later, in the "bad debt" accounts of hospitals and the cheap soil of potter's fields), no one—least of all the budgeteers[13]—paid much mind. Not so today.

The chapters in this volume offer abundant reasons for hope, in principle. They lay out an imaginative range of alternatives already under development: other ways of handling difficult admissions, novel means of mediating disputes, advance directives, recipient-initiated research on self-help and peer support, more collaborative decision-making, and functional equivalents of asylum. They also give a skeptical reader stubborn cause for worry: the easy overlap between clinical disposition and criminal justice systems, the constant refrain of limited resources and cramped routines, and (my own candidate nemesis) the new and somewhat shady cast of "behavioral health care" specialists ("firms") at the helm of reform. Some of the dilemmas are long-standing in nature, dealing as they do with "reasoning the need" in others who reason otherwise. A few (the new federal move to resegregate those diagnosed with severe mental health problems) bear evidence of a brave reform lately betrayed. Others, one suspects, are pending as institutional inertia collects itself to do battle with the insolent yield of applied research and demonstration pro-

---

[13]There were exceptions, of course. For an early warning that the state of New York was spending far too much on clinical services to the neglect of everyday living conditions, see Jurow (1979).

jects. Still others owe their poignancy to the straitened (and largely unyielding) circumstances under which they arise (the vicissitudes of strategic dependency in outreach work). The many rhetorics of leverage that take shape in these pages properly resist being reduced to the terms of an abstract ethical calculus. But if the argument sketched here has any merit, all of them will find fresh cause for anxiety in a world where room for maneuvering is much diminished.

So Goethe may have got it half right. In some quarters, the world may be well on its way to becoming a hospital. But it is the accountant's calculator, not the nurse's chart, we spy in "everyone's" hand.

REFERENCES

Bakke, E. W. (1940). *The unemployed worker.* New Haven: Yale University Press.

Beauchamp, D. E. (1985). Community: The neglected tradition of public health. *Hastings Center Report, 15,* 28–36.

Clay, S. (1994). Presentation at the Work of Recovery Conference, October 1994. Sponsored by the Center for the Study of Issues in Public Mental Health, Croton-Harmon, NY.

Cohen, C., & Sokolovsky, J. (1989) *Old men of the Bowery.* New York: Guilford Press.

Davidson, L., Stayner, D., & Haglund, K. E. (1995). Phenomenological perspectives on the social functioning of people with schizophrenia. In K. T. Mueser & N. Tarrier (Eds.), *Handbook of social functioning in schizophrenia* (in press).

Davidson, L., & Strauss, J. S. (1992). Sense of self in recovery from severe mental illness. *British Journal of Medical Psychology, 65,* 131–145.

Estroff, S. E. (1994). Keeping things complicated: Undiscovered countries and the lives of persons with serious mental illness. *Journal of the California Alliance for the Mentally Ill, 5,* 40–46.

Fischer, D. (October 1994). Presentation at The Work of Recovery Conference, October 1994. Sponsored by the Center for the Study of Issues in Public Mental Health, Croton-Harmon, NY.

Fleischner, R. D. (1994). Managed health care: Implications for involuntary care and systemic coercion. In *Symposium proceedings: Involuntary interventions,* May 5–7, 1994. Houston: University of Texas.

Groth, P. (1983). Forbidden housing. Unpublished doctoral dissertation. Berkeley: University of California.

Groth, P. (1994). *Living downtown: The history of residential hotels in the United States.* Berkeley: University of California Press.

Hopper, K. (1992). Counting the New York homeless: An ethnographic perspective. *New England Journal of Public Policy, 8,* 771–791.

Hopper, K., & Baumohl, J. (1994). Held in abeyance: Rethinking homelessness and advocacy. *American Behavioral Scientist, 37,* 522–552.

Ignatieff, M. (1984). *The needs of strangers.* New York: Viking.

Jenkins, J. H. (1988). Ethnopsychiatric interpretations of schizophrenic illness: The problem of *nervios* within Mexican-American families. *Culture, Medicine and Psychiatry, 12*, 301–329.

Jurow, G. L. (1979). Financing long term care for the chronically mentally impaired in New York State. Paper prepared for the State Communities Aid Association Institute on Care of the Mentally Impaired in the Long Term Care System, June 4, 1979. New York.

Katznelson, I. (1986). Rethinking the silences of social and economic policy. *Political Science Quarterly, 101*, 307–325.

Kunen, J. (1994). Quality and equality. *New Yorker*, Nov. 28, 1994, pp. 9–10.

Lardner, J. (1991). Shantytown. *New Yorker*, July 1, 1991, pp. 67–76.

Lee, B. (1980). The disappearance of Skid Row: Some ecological evidence. *Urban Affairs Quarterly, 16*, 81–107.

Lipsky, M., & Smith, S. R. (1989). When social problems are treated as emergencies. *Social Service Review, 63*, 5–15.

Luhrmann, T. M. (1989). *Persuasions of the witch's craft.* Cambridge: Harvard University Press.

Lukes, S. (1974). *Power: A radical view.* London: Macmillan.

Marin, P. (1987). Helping and hating the homeless. *Harper's Magazine*, January 1987, pp. 39–49.

Mayer, J. A. (1985). Notes toward a working definition of social control in historical analysis. In S. Cohen & A. Scull (Eds.), *Social control and the state* (pp. 17–38). London: Basil Blackwell.

Minow, M. (1990). *Making all the difference.* Ithaca: Cornell University Press.

National Association of State Mental Health Program Directors & American Behavioral Healthcare Association (1994). *Public mental health systems, Medicaid restructuring and managed behavioral health care.* Draft white paper, Alexandria, VA.

Powell, I. G., & Knight, E. (1994). Empowering the disempowered. In J. P. Troxel (Ed.), *Government works* (pp. 425–445). Alexandria, VA: Miles River Press.

Rhoden, N. K. (1982). "Commentary" on "Can a subject consent to a 'Ulysses contract'?" *Hastings Center Report, 12*, 28.

Rieff, P. (1968). *The triumph of the therapeutic.* New York: Harper.

Rock, P. (1974). The sociology of deviancy and conceptions of moral order. *British Journal of Criminology, 14*, 139–149.

Schneider, J. C. (1986). Skid row as an urban neighborhood. In J. C. Erickson & C. Wilhelm (Eds.), *Housing the homeless* (pp. 167–189). New Brunswick, NJ: Center for Urban Policy Research.

Schreter, R. K. (1993). Ten trends in managed care and their impact on the biopsychosocial model. *Hospital and Community Psychiatry, 44*, 325–327.

Scull, A. (1977). *Decarceration: Community treatment and the deviant—A radical view.* Englewood Cliffs, NJ: Prentice-Hall.

Sheehan, S. (1995). The last days of Sylvia Frumkin. *New Yorker*, Feb. 20, 1995, pp. 200–211.

Sherman, P. S. (1994). Advance directives for involuntary psychiatric care. In *Symposium proceedings: Involuntary interventions*, May 5–7, 1994. Houston: University of Texas.

Snow, D. A., & Anderson, L. (1987). Identity work among the homeless. *American Journal of Sociology, 92*, 1336–1371.

212   KIM HOPPER

Ware, N. (1994). Money management: Power and the regulation of resources in community-based psychiatric care. Paper presented at the 93rd Annual Meeting of the American Anthropological Association, Atlanta.

Weir, M. (1992). *Politics and jobs.* Princeton: Princeton University Press.

Wells, S. M. (1995). Exploring the promises and pitfalls of managed care. *Access, 7.*

Wertheimer, A. (1993). A philosophical examination of coercion for mental health issues. *Behavioral Sciences and the Law, 11,* 239–258.

Wolf, E. (1990). Distinguished lecture: Facing power—old insights, new questions. *American Anthropologist, 92,* 586–596.

INDEX

213